Accounting for Cultural Heritage Management

Michela Magliacani • Valentina Toscano

Accounting for Cultural Heritage Management

Resilience, Sustainability and Accountability

palgrave
macmillan

Michela Magliacani
University of Pavia
Pavia, Italy

Valentina Toscano
University of Milano-Bicocca
Milano, Italy

ISBN 978-3-031-38256-7 ISBN 978-3-031-38257-4 (eBook)
https://doi.org/10.1007/978-3-031-38257-4

This Palgrave Macmillan imprint is published by the registered company Springer Nature Switzerland AG.
The registered company address is: Gewerbestrasse 11, 6330 Cham, Switzerland

Paper in this product is recyclable.

Declarations of Interest: none

The world will be saved by beauty.
Fëdor Dostoevsky, The idiot, *1869*

Acknowledgments

The authors wish to thank the reviewers for the recommendations they had on how to improve this manuscript. We are particularly grateful to Niloofar Jafari, an alumna of the "Castiglioni Brugnatelli" College in Pavia, for her kind and precious support in improving the level of readability of this publication. A special thanks goes to Mauro Rizza, General Secretary of Parma 2020+21, for his valuable help in data collection. In addition, we would like to thank all the curators and administrative employees of University Museums, Corporate Museums and Archives, and the other professionals of Italian cultural heritage who have favorably participated in our study.

To the dear people who have been close to us during the writing of this work, we would like to extend special thanks. To all of them—*we do not name them, but they know*—we dedicate this monograph.

Contents

List of Figures

List of Tables

CHAPTER 1

Introduction: Research Aims, Methodology, and Design

Abstract The transformative role of culture, its ability to create value for the benefit of current and future generations, is widely recognized by academics of many disciplines, professionals, and policymakers. Notwithstanding, how can culture be a driving force for economic growth, a source of welfare and a tool for social inclusion? In answering to this research aim, the relevance of accounting knowledge for managing cultural heritage by sustainable, resilient, accountable organizations will come out. In this Introduction, the manuscript outline per chapter with key questions, methods, and expected results is reported.

Keywords Transformative role • Culture • Accounting • Sustainability • COVID-19 pandemic

The debate on the challenges that cultural organizations face in carrying out activities of great value for society and the economy has been boosted by political and managerial issues related to the Sustainable Development Goals (SDGs) of Agenda 2030 as well as external shocks such as the COVID-19 pandemic.

It is widely recognized by academics and professionals in that sector that culture plays a transformative role, namely, its ability to create value

M. Magliacani, V. Toscano, *Accounting for Cultural Heritage Management*, https://doi.org/10.1007/978-3-031-38257-4_1

for current and future generations. Even so, it is still important to investigate "how" culture can serve as a driving force for economic growth, a source of welfare and a tool for social inclusion in a wide range of contexts, including those at the local, national, and international levels. In this regard, SDG#11—"Sustainable Cities and Communities"—promotes, among other targets, strengthened efforts to achieve sustainability in the field of cultural heritage. This is aligned with the Framework Convention on the Value of Cultural Heritage for Society (Council of Europe 2005), which recognizes the role of cultural heritage in the construction of a peaceful and democratic society, in the processes of sustainable development and in the promotion of cultural diversity. Moreover, the Council of Europe recommends the definition and promotion of principles for effective management through cooperation among public, institutional, and private actors (Pinz et al., 2018, p. 16). Aligning with this recommendation, Agenda 2030 encourages the implementation of sustainable accounting practices such as strategic planning, long-term impact assessment, and related data dissemination (Bergmans et al., 2014). Thus, recent studies demonstrate how accounting has been studied more in terms of its technical nature and less in terms of how it can enable and disable actions and behaviors in society and organizations. In this lens, accounting is viewed as a social practice in creating, sustaining, changing, and communicating social reality and as a moral practice in reflecting human interaction (Carnegie et al., 2021). Although the role of accounting practices in pursuing organizational changes has been widely acknowledged, sustainable accounting practices have been neglected as a subject of theoretical research and in-depth investigation (Guthrie et al., 2010).

Managerial accounting studies have focused on cultural organizations as different "places of culture," from museums to theaters and from archaeological parks to libraries/archives (Zan, 2006; Zan et al., 2016). However, the same literature calls for more studies on operational conditions, principles, and accounting practices that enable cultural organizations, both public and private, to be resilient according to the sustainable development paradigm (Guthrie et al., 2010; Osborne et al., 2014; Pinz et al., 2018; Moldavanova & Goerdel, 2018).

The main objective of this research is to develop an ontological and exploratory path of the operational conditions of cultural organizations, which are required to promote and enhance this heritage—tangible and intangible—through the application of managerial accounting skills capable of creating and measuring value as a result of socioeconomic and cultural factors (Piber, 2020). Considering their mission to contribute to the recovery from degrading the planet and people and ensure prosperity for all, how can cultural organizations ensure the cost-effectiveness of the value creation process during times of austerity? Research aims will be pursued through investigations that have, as their common denominator, the "value" created by cultural organizations, explored in their everyday lives. It is also examined how accounting can assist cultural organizations in making the value they create accountable to current and future generations. In this study, the value of cultural heritage management is examined in ordinary and extraordinary circumstances, that is, when external shocks result in emergencies.

Considering the first context (ordinary conditions), the ontological purpose of this study could be stated as follows:

In what ways does cultural heritage affect the lives of current and future generations? However, do cultural institutions recognize that they are organizations? How does accounting contribute to the management of cultural heritage? In cultural organizations, how can accounting systems be designed to facilitate rational and responsible decision-making? What are the preconditions for starting such a process of building inter- and intraorganizational accounting knowledge?

The study examines the role of cultural organizations in the pursuit of Agenda 2030 in regard to public policies aimed at achieving Sustainable Development Goals. A sustainability perspective explores the "value" they create. Hence, the research questions are formulated as follows:

What are the most efficient ways of reporting cultural performance? What accounting tools could be used to measure the degree of current achievement of sustainability goals?

Considering extraordinary conditions, such as the emergencies generated by the COVID-19 pandemic, the value created by cultural organizations in terms of resilience is investigated. Particular attention will be focused on digital technology to the creation of value by cultural organization in its relations with the stakeholders, *in primis*, the audience. Accordingly, we will investigate the following research questions:

How do cultural organizations prove to be resilient? In what ways has accounting for organizational resilience played a role?

Regarding the objectives and questions of the research, the qualitative approach has been considered suitable for social studies research (Table 1.1). According to Flyvbjerg (2006), research methods are those formulated by managerial accounting studies to answer questions based on "whether," "what," and "how."

Table 1.1 The research protocol

Aims	*Methods*	*Context of the study*
• In what ways does cultural heritage affect the lives of current and future generations? Do cultural institutions recognize that they are organizations? • How does accounting contribute to the management of cultural heritage? • In cultural organizations, how can accounting systems be designed to facilitate rational and responsible decision-making? • What are the preconditions for starting such a process of building inter- and intraorganizational accounting knowledge?	Case studies, Ethnographical observations, Interviews	Civic Museums of Pavia (Italian Smart City) Museum of Electrical Technologies of the University of Pavia Rural Cultural Network
• What are the most efficient ways of reporting cultural performance? • What accounting tools could be used to measure the degree of current achieving of sustainability goals?	Case studies, Content Analysis	Palermo, the Italian Capital of Culture (2018) Matera, the European Capital of Culture (2019) Parma, the Italian Capital of Culture (2020+21) Procida, the Italian Capital of Culture (2022) Bergamo and Brescia the Italian Capitals of Culture (2023)
• How do cultural organizations prove to be resilient? • In what ways has accounting for organizational resilience played a role?	Survey, Interviews, Content analysis	Italian University Museums Italian Corporate Museums and Archives

This study is divided into seven chapters, beginning with this introduction and concluding with final remarks. The *file rouge* of them is twofold: the value created in managing cultural heritage and the role of accounting in doing this. The value created by cultural organizations is explored to respond to the literature call about how to manage cultural heritage from a sustainable perspective. The role of accounting is investigated to fill the literature gap on how to measure the value created by cultural organizations, making them accountable to current and future generations according to the intergenerational equity principle (Throsby, 2017). Considering those literature gaps, this study also aims to understand the role of cultural heritage in the economy and in society in facing the new challenges deriving from the enactment of Agenda 2030 without neglecting the contingency arising from the COVID-19 pandemic emergency.

Chapter 2 discusses how managerial accounting can contribute to the awareness of cultural institutions as organizations. The cultural institutes that recognize themselves as organizations capable of developing a self-diagnosis with respect to the relative mission and think strategic, taking into account its strengths, weaknesses, as well as the opportunities and risks that arise from the external context. It is based on knowledge of one's own processes of creating value (cultural products and services) and spreading it among various stakeholders, most importantly users. In other words, cultural organizations must recognize the relevance of managing common goods to fulfill the needs of the actual and future generations of visitors/users.

"Value-creation ability," understood as the ability to create value and distribute it equally and harmoniously among various stakeholders, naturally must take into account not only its economic nature but also its social and cultural components. In Chap. 3, the conceptual models of reference will be proposed for each of these dimensions: from the theory of public value (Moore, 1995) to the theory of cocreation of value (Vargo & Lusch, 2004, 2008, 2016) applied to cultural organizations. These logics are supported by value measures derived from the "3E" model (effectiveness, efficiency, and cost-effectiveness) when considering the output of the cocreation process (Tommasetti et al., 2020) and by analyzing visitor satisfaction with respect to its outcome, that is, its impact on the community's well-being starting with the users (Kroll, 2013).

As a result, accounting plays a significant role in this measurement, which is a prelude to cultural organizations' accountability under a sustainable development approach. Studies focusing on the management of cultural heritage address that research to investigate the managerial logics applied to projects that enhance cultural heritage in a sustainable manner (Donato & Lohrasbi, 2017). Based on the results of these empirical studies, it is evident that organizational learning does not physiologically result from strategic planning when it is exclusively aimed at obtaining funding (Lusiani & Zan, 2013). This literature requires further analysis. As a result, building accounting capacity could be useful for continuous improvement when viewed from a sustainability perspective. Toward this end, the study provides, in Chap. 3, an in-depth analysis of the concept of planning, strategies, and the related processes and tools necessary to design a path to value creation. In addition to simulated applications, this analysis was supported by an empirical survey of rural organizations that, although not operating in the cultural sector, also contribute to the enhancement of a territory's tangible and intangible cultural heritage.

According to the UNESCO "Culture 2030 indicators" framework, Chap. 4 discusses how accounting can also be used to measure the contribution of culture to achieving the goals of the 2030 Agenda. The experiences of the Capital Cities of Culture (Dessein et al., 2015) demonstrate how the principles of intergenerational equity (Throsby, 2017) are integrated into their projects and how they are supported by economic, social, and moral accounts adopted to shed light on the impact of culture on society and the economy.

Despite the COVID-19 pandemic, cultural managers have continued to create and spread value owing to their strong motivation to work for the common good, in the awareness that culture can generate economic and social welfare for current and future communities. From the experience found in Italian University Museums as well as in those of private companies, they had to acquire or strengthen their digital skills *ex novo*. As discussed in Chap. 5, digital competences have proven to be a powerful driver of social innovation, but they have also been an important contributor to organizational resilience. In that scenario, accounting has shown its value as a social practice in the accountability of digitized activities. This demonstrates how it should be included in the resilience models crafted in relation to organizational features.

The results of the field research are critically discussed in light of theoretical frameworks related to the theory of value and its cocreation (Bozeman, 2007; Vargo & Lusch, 2016; Saunila et al., 2018). In organizations that manage common goods as cultural heritage, the discussion of practical case studies can enhance the managerial and accounting culture.

From the findings and their discussion, a conceptual model based on the role of accounting for sustainability and resilience is proposed in Chap. 6. This model is designed to manage the cultural heritage of communities under a sustainable perspective, even in times of crisis.

The limitation of this study concerns the robustness of the results attributed to the context explored (Yin, 2018), the Italian context. However, the triangulation of the sources (Jack & Raturi, 2006), of the methods (content analysis, surveys, ethnographic observations) and of the findings discussed has contributed to framing conceptual propositions that obviously require validation through further investigations.

Below are the theoretical and practical implications of this study for the management of cultural heritage. Based on a theoretical perspective, conceptual models are proposed that address the ability of cultural organizations to create value, to be resilient, and to be sustainable, as well as the relationship between these pillars of good management. Consequently, they may provide insights for future research that can be applied to other Italian contexts and countries. The purpose of this work is to provide capacity-building support to cultural managers who are required to not only carry out projects in Europe but also prepare European projects to raise funds, as well as provide useful information to evaluate the contribution to achieving sustainable development as defined by the UNESCO sustainability indicators.

The study provides food for thought for professionals who share similar concerns regarding the subjects discussed in the case studies, namely, how to collect and produce information for designing and implementing value creation paths, measuring and reporting that value not only economically but also socially and culturally. The signs and comments reported in the guestbook have been elaborated, as have the "likes" received from users who have lived the cultural experience proposed before in person and then online as a result of the COVID-19 health emergency. It is therefore expected that social implications will also emerge that will draw the attention of cultural managers to methods of restoring dialog with one's audience in the context of value cocreation (Chap. 7).

This study seeks to provide cultural practitioners, scholars, and students with an understanding of how the art of keeping accounts represents essential knowledge for the narration of our history to posterity.

According to Dostoevsky (2002), "the world will be saved by beauty." Accounting will find a way to accomplish this.

References

Bergmans, A., Vandermoere, F., & Loots, I. (2014). Coproducing sustainability indicators for the port of Antwerp: How sustainability reporting creates new discursive spaces for concern and mobilization. *Journal of Communication Studies, 7*(1), 107–123.

Bozeman, B. (2007). *Public values and public interest: Counterbalancing economic individualism*. Georgetown University Press.

Carnegie, G., Parker, L., & Tsahuridu, E. (2021). It's 2020: What is accounting today? *Australian Accounting Review, 31*(1), 65–73.

Council of Europe. (2005). Council of Europe Framework Convention on the Value of Cultural Heritage for Society, Council of Europe Treaty Series - No. 199, Faro, 27.X.2005.

Dessein, J., Soini, K., Fairclough, G., Horlings, L., Battaglini, E., Birkeland, I., et al. (2015). *Culture in, for and as sustainable development: Conclusions from the COST Action IS1007 investigating cultural sustainability*. University of Jyväskylä.

Donato, F., & Lohrasbi, A. (2017). When theory and practice clash: Participatory governance and management in Takht-e Soleyman. *Journal of Cultural Heritage Management and Sustainable Development, 7*, 129–146.

Dostoevsky, F. (2002). *L'idiota* (Vol. 2147). Feltrinelli Editore.

Flyvbjerg, B. (2006). Five misunderstandings about case-study research. *Qualitative Inquiry, 12*(2), 219–245.

Guthrie, J., Ball, A., & Farneti, F. (2010). Advancing sustainable management of public and not for profit organizations. *Public Management Review, 12*(4), 449–459.

Jack, E. P., & Raturi, A. S. (2006). Lessons learned from methodological triangulation in management research. *Management Research News, 29*(6), 345–357.

Kroll, A. (2013). The other type of performance information: Nonroutine feedback, its relevance and use. *Public Administration Review, 73*(2), 265–276.

Lusiani, M., & Zan, L. (2013). Planning and heritage. *Journal of Cultural Heritage Management and Sustainable Development, 3*(2), 108–115.

Moldavanova, A., & Goerdel, H. T. (2018). Understanding the puzzle of organizational sustainability: Toward a conceptual framework of organizational social connectedness and sustainability. *Public Management Review, 20*(1), 55–81.

Moore, M. H. (1995). *Creating public value: Strategic management in government*. Harvard University Press.

Osborne, S. P., Radnor, Z., Vidal, I., & Kinder, T. (2014). A sustainable business model for public service organizations? *Public Management Review, 16*(2), 165–172.

Piber, M. (Ed.). (2020). *Management, participation and entrepreneurship in the cultural and creative sector*. Springer.

Pinz, A., Roudyani, N., & Thaler, J. (2018). Public–private partnerships as instruments to achieve sustainability-related objectives: The state of the art and a research agenda. *Public Management Review, 20*(1), 1–22.

Saunila, M., Ukko, J., & Rantala, T. (2018). Value cocreation through digital service capabilities: The role of human factors. *Information Technology & People, 32*(3), 627–645.

Throsby, D. (2017). Culturally sustainable development: Theoretical concept or practical policy instrument? *International Journal of Cultural Policy, 23*(2), 133–147.

Tommasetti, A., Mussari, R., Maione, G., & Sorrentino, D. (2020). Sustainability accounting and reporting in the public sector: Toward public value cocreation? *Sustainability, 12*(5), 1909.

Vargo, S. L., & Lusch, R. F. (2004). Evolving to a new dominant logic for marketing. *Journal of Marketing, 68*(1), 1–17.

Vargo, S. L., & Lusch, R. F. (2008). Service-dominant logic: Continuing the evolution. *Journal of the Academy of Marketing Science, 36*, 1–10.

Vargo, S. L., & Lusch, R. F. (2016). Institutions and axioms: An extension and update of service-dominant logic. *Journal of the Academy of Marketing Science, 44*, 5–23.

Yin, R. K. (2018). *Case study research and applications.* Sage.

Zan, L. (2006). *Managerial rhetoric and arts organizations.* Springer.

Zan, L., Baraldi, S. B., Lusiani, M., Shoup, D., Ferri, P., & Onofri, F. (2016). *Managing cultural heritage: An international research perspective.*

CHAPTER 2

Cultural Heritage Under a Managerial-Accounting Perspective

Abstract A knowledge of cultural institutions from an accounting and managerial perspective is essential to preserving and enhancing a community's cultural heritage. In what ways does cultural heritage affect the lives of current and future generations? However, do cultural institutions recognize that they are organizations? This chapter provides some insights based on case studies regarding the management of cultural heritage in an Italian smart city—Pavia—located in the region of Lombardy.

Keywords Cultural heritage • Value cocreation • Cultural and creative production ecosystem • Value added statement • Measurement and reporting

2.1 Introduction

Cultural heritage has been defined by the Council of Europe in the Framework Convention on the Value of Cultural Heritage for Society—widely known as the Faro Convention (Faro, 27.x.2005) as follows:

> A cultural heritage is a group of resources inherited from the past, which people identify, independently of ownership, as a reflection and expression of their constantly evolving values, beliefs, knowledge and traditions. It

M. Magliacani, V. Toscano, *Accounting for Cultural Heritage Management*, https://doi.org/10.1007/978-3-031-38257-4_2

Fig. 2.1 The concept of *cultural heritage*. (Source: Our adaptation from http://www.unesco.org/)

> includes all aspects of the environment resulting from the interaction between people and places over time. (Art. 2—Faro Convention)

UNESCO also recognizes this intrinsic value to tangible as well as intangible assets, which are both evidence of civilization. A tangible cultural heritage consists of collections, sculptures, monuments, archaeological sites, manuscripts, paintings, etc.; an intangible heritage is composed of practices, customs, rituals, and performing arts (Fig. 2.1).

From a managerial point of view, the notion of cultural heritage refers to the tangible and intangible elements included in fixed or fixed assets. These elements are an expression of the potential for organizations to create value. In this interpretation, we gain a deeper understanding of the actors called to care for this heritage, such as museums, libraries, archives, archaeological sites, and parks. In particular, the museum, as a particularly privileged object of this study, is defined by the International Council of Museums (ICOM)[1] as follows:

[1] ICOM is a nonprofit association, established in 1946, with the mission of research, conservation, continuation, and communication to society of the cultural and natural heritage, present and future, material and immaterial (art. 2, ICOM Statute).

> A museum is a not-for-profit, permanent institution in the service of society that studies, collects, conserves, interprets and exhibits tangible and intangible heritage. Open to the public, accessible and inclusive, Museums foster diversity and sustainability. They operate and communicate ethically, professionally and with the participation of communities, offering varied experiences for education, enjoyment, reflection and knowledge sharing.[2]

Accordingly, what emerges from this definition is the notion of "institution" qualified as "nonprofit" and "permanent." These adjectives justify the managerial approach in the context of multidisciplinary research focused on cultural heritage. These concepts taken from the definition of museum are consistent with the following notion of organization (Zappa, 1956, p. 37):

> An economic institution destined to persist which, for the satisfaction of human needs, orders and carries out the production or procurement and consumption of wealth in continuous coordination [our English translation].

Permanence represents a prerogative of the organization, which must aspire to achieve an economic equilibrium that lasts over time in order not to compromise its stability.

From an epistemological point of view, the interest of managerial academics in the study of cultural heritage and its actors is clear. This is even more evident from the definition of museum revisited by the ICOM, which adds, among its functions, that of operating at the service of society and its sustainable development. From the managerial point of view, the museum is an organization, but does it recognize itself as such? Or rather, does it need to recognize itself as such? The academic and professional debate on cultural heritage management seems to answer these questions affirmatively. A theoretical and empirical explanation for this assertion will be provided in the following sections.

More specifically, after a review of the main features of cultural organizations, this chapter sheds light on their value creation processes developed to achieve the mission of preserving and enhancing the cultural heritage of a community. A particular focus on the multidimensional

[2] This comprehensive definition of museum was approved by the ICOM Extraordinary General Assembly in the framework of the 26th ICOM General Conference held in Prague. The vote is the culmination of an 18-month participatory process that involved hundreds of museum professionals from 126 National Committees from all over the world.

values created and their measurements and reporting is provided. The relevance of cultural organizations for the society and economics of a community springs up by the notion of cocreation, which addresses the cultural and creative production ecosystem. Two critical case studies, taken from Pavia, a smart city located in Lombardy (Italy), have been carried out to provide evidence on the capability of cultural organizations to create value (both economic and sociocultural) for the local community.

As a final remark, this chapter proposes, following the discussion of these case studies, a conceptual model describing the main drivers of value creation, which should stimulate cultural organizations to become more aware of the need to operate in accordance with the 3E: effectiveness, efficiency, and cost-effectiveness. Developing specific managerial and accounting skills is necessary to manage cultural heritage in accordance with these criteria.

2.2 The Managerial Features of Cultural Organizations

The managerial literature uses a broad notion of cultural organizations within the cultural and creative ecosystem (Imperiale et al., 2021), which will be addressed later in this chapter. In this paragraph, on the other hand, the entrepreneurial characteristics that concern each type of cultural organization have been highlighted, even if, as previously underlined, the attention is focused on those that manage the cultural heritage.

From the definition of museum given by the ICOM, it can be inferred that it is to be considered an organization. In fact, it refers to all those characteristics that the management accounting literature proposes as essential features for identifying it. These features represent real conditions for the existence of any organization (Catturi, 2012):

- a community of people;
- endowed with a unitary and coordinated system of resources or assets;
- legally recognized within a specific legislative framework.

A physiological characteristic of an organization, in other words, identifies its daily activities, in addition to its so-called morphological characteristics. Specifically, physiological features can be referred to in the following aspects:

- functions performed by the specific bodies that make up the organizational structure;
- decision-making and accountability to stakeholders;
- mission and goals;
- value creation processes.

The features are interrelated elements since they constitute the entire organization. They can be analyzed individually without neglecting the more or less close correlation with the others. With respect to this, an examination of both morphological and physiological features of museums, reported below, can be extended to other cultural organizations in charge of managing the cultural heritage of a community.

2.2.1 Community of People, Organization, Decision-making/Responsibility

The community of people is to be understood as a unitary coordination of individuals with specific skills, experience, and knowledge. These individuals are united by their interest in achieving the organization's objectives and mission. In this regard, Catturi (2003, p. 154) states that

> Organization is much more than a group of people; it visually and operationally represents and expresses the deep bond, the communion of relationships, which unites several people who share the same objectives because they are driven by the same values [our English translation].

The community of people is presented, technically, by an organizational chart—an organigram—which makes it possible to understand the positions of power and responsibility within the organizational perimeter. In other words, it is the organizational structure that also allows an external subject to understand which activities are performed by the organization center/office, the dedicated personnel. The organigram highlights the position of who decides at the managerial/operational level, who is responsible for these choices, and to whom. More specifically, if the organization has an articulation of bodies or centers of responsibility to which tasks included in specific functions have been assigned, then the organizational structure will be represented by a functional organization chart (Fig. 2.2).

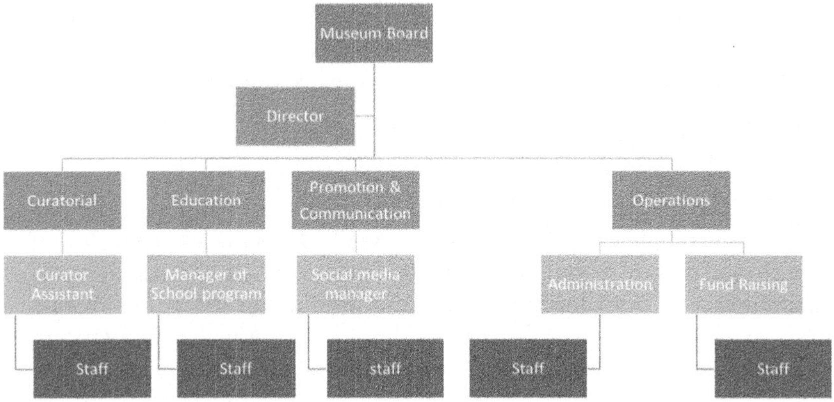

Fig. 2.2 Functional organigram

Looking at the functional organization chart from top to bottom, it is possible to determine how decision-making power is distributed within the museum; differently from the bottom to the top, the levels of responsibility are deduced according to which the subordinate is accountable for the activities undertaken and the results achieved to the superior. Managers, at the head of a function, being on the same line of the organization chart, have the same decision-making power. Each function manager leads a team that carries out individual activities included in specific positions. Personnel, occupying these positions, are accountable for their performance to the department manager, who in turn must report to the director. The latter is accountable for the results of the museum as a whole to the board.

There is also an organizational structure known as the departmental organigram that is divided into strategic areas (strategic business units or SBUs) that perform specific tasks within the organization. Managers of functions are accountable to the SBU manager, who reports its results to the museum's Chief Executive Office regularly (Fig. 2.3).

An organizational structure characterized by departments and functions in common has been acknowledged as a "hybrid organization" in relation to their strategic complexity (Lentz, 1996; Battilana et al., 2017). This organizational chart illustrates how some functions (promotion and communication and fundraising) are performed by the same manager and staff for each department without any internal operational duplication (Fig. 2.4).

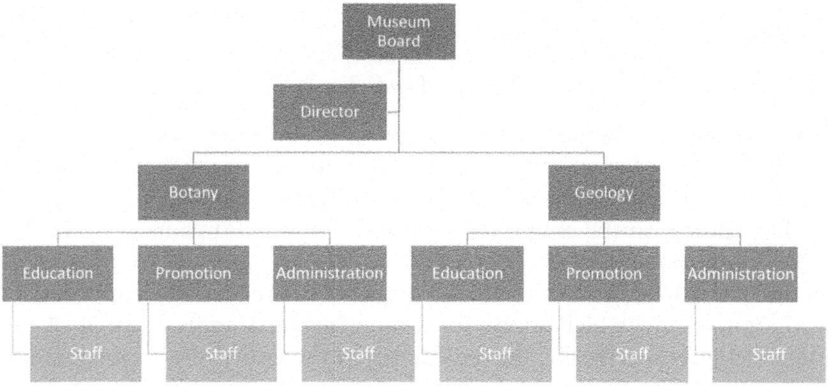

Fig. 2.3 Departmental organigram

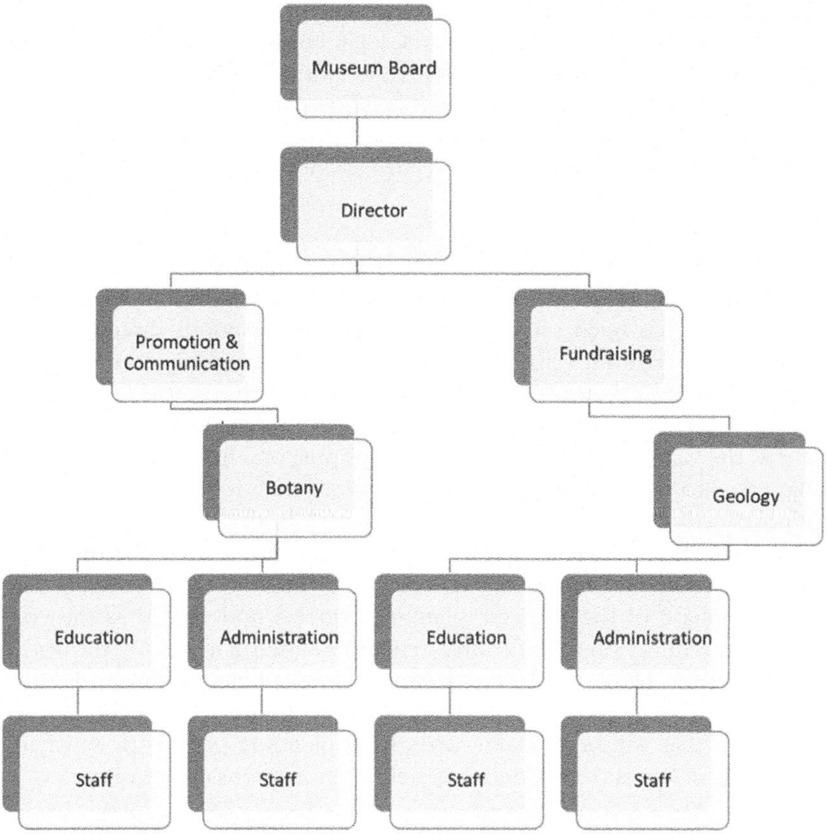

Fig. 2.4 Hybrid organigram

2.2.2 *Legal Form*

The management of cultural heritage is basically affected by the political system of reference and the administrative culture of the sector to which the cultural organization belongs (Peters, 2021).

Depending on the country's regulations, cultural organizations have a legal form. Managerial studies include judicial recognition among organizational features. In addition, it distinguishes between a legal entity and an economic entity, which allows for a more detailed understanding of the organization. Specifically, the legal entity is the entity in whose name the economic activity is exercised, owner of the rights and obligations derived from its management; otherwise, the economic entity is represented by the person or group of people who exercise the governing power within the organization.

In cultural organizational contexts, legal entities could be private, and nonprofit. The economic entity of private cultural organizations could be public if the shareholders are publicly owned entities. Nevertheless, regardless of who owns the cultural assets or the legal entity, cultural organizations provide a public service regardless of who owns the assets.

2.2.3 *Mission and Objectives*

The term "mission" refers to the institutional function of the organization for which it has been set up. In general, it corresponds directly to the rationale for creating value in any organization, according to managerial theory. However, in practice, it is formulated in such a way as to bring out the distinctive characteristics with respect to the needs it has set out to satisfy, the value it intends to create for this purpose, how it communicates that value to stakeholders, and which ethical values it bears in the context of reference.

Both within and outside the organization's boundaries, the organization states and disseminates its mission. Its formulation represents, in fact, the first phase of the strategic planning process understood as the conscious determination of the course of actions aimed at achieving the objectives (Koontz, 1958). From the mission arises the objectives to be pursued in the medium-long term and in the short term, defined on the basis of the funds that will be available within the planning period. By satisfying the needs of key stakeholders, they help organizations create value.

Mission Statement	Key questions
Mission	What needs does organization want to respond to?
	With what value?
	How to respond to stakeholders?
	What are our core values?
	What makes the organization unique and different?
Vision	What are our future perspectives? What is the image of the organization in the future?

Fig. 2.5 Mission statement

An organization's mission must be aligned with those ethical values that qualify it as a community. They should pervade goals, actions, and results to ensure a harmonious internal environment. This will ensure that this community can be increasingly efficient and stimulated by a management by objectives approach (Normann, 1977). In its website or statute, the organization discloses the same values as its mission statement and manifesto. The organization's ethics also underlies the impression it intends to give of itself, that is, the so-called *vision*, the projection of the organization into future scenarios.

The following key questions could be considered as a guideline to prepare a mission statement (Fig. 2.5).

2.2.4 *Assets*

There is no organization without assets. It represents a structural feature that qualifies any organization from a morphological point of view since that unitary and coordinated system of resources characterizes its operations.

Cultural heritage and natural heritage are both part of the Italian law governing the cultural sector. Indeed, as stated by Antonio Paolucci (1996, pp. 14–15), who, with specific regard to museums, maintains:

> It is true that in Italy, museums cannot be viewed as a closed universe, as a "spaceship of history". Here, it extends beyond its borders, spreads out into squares and streets, occupies churches and palaces, and multiplies its

masterpieces in cities and in the countryside. All of Italy is an open-air museum [our English translation].

From the previous quotation, it appears clear how the museum, as a place of culture, must interact with other organizations. This is to pursue the mission of the interpretation center of the territory. In doing so, the museum must be aware of managing a share of that environmental heritage, which is represented by its collections. This is represented by those tangible and intangible expressions of the cultural heritage of the community. This conceptualization also derives from the managerial approach to the subject of cultural heritage. In fact, the notion of environmental heritage as a unitary and coordinated system of resources is structured into three categories (Catturi, 2003):

- *Heritage of knowledge*, that is, ideas, skills, professional abilities, innovative capabilities possessed by the members of the community operating in a given territory;
- *Heritage of historical values*, which pertains to assets created by man as a subject of history;
- *Natural and cultural heritage*, made up of the natural and cultural resources of the area.

The skills and abilities of people who work within cultural organizations are to be considered qualifying components of the *heritage of knowledge*. It is precisely on the latter that it is necessary to stimulate creative and innovative processes aimed at preserving the other heritage packages. This will allow their enhancement for the quality of life of current and future generations. The conservation, promotion, and use of the collections that are part of the cultural heritage, understood in its broad meaning given by the legislation on the subject and shared by the economic-business discipline, require investments and loans that constitute the organization's assets in its accounting value. In fact, the *heritage of historical values* is made up of three other resource packages:

- *Fixed assets*, represented by the use of technical-fixed capital, which is an expression of the organization's production potential;
- *Current assets*, made up of the assets that activate that technical-fixed capital for the exercise of activities;

- *Financial assets*, including both monetary investments and sources of financing.

The three categories of assets are recorded in the Balance Sheet, an accounting document that comprises the Assets and Liabilities Statements together with the Income Statement. The drafting of this report is mandatory for every type of organization, including cultural institutes, in relation to their legal form. On the other hand, regarding the heritage of natural and cultural heritage and knowledge, there is no obligation to provide information. However, they can be reported in social or sustainability reports in accordance with the organization's communication policies (Niemann & Hoppe, 2018). These documents appear almost strategic for cultural organizations to demonstrate the results of the conservation and enhancement activities of the assets they manage.

2.2.5 The Creation Processes

The physiological feature that expresses the *modus operandi* of organization is represented by value creation processes. They employ resources acquired from economic third parties to transform them, through the activities carried out within the organization, into aggregate value that will be offered externally. It occurs in any service organization (Normann, 2001), such as cultural organizations. In more detail, a map of creation processes can be structured on the basis of this taxonomy:

- *Core processes*, represented by the "core" activities for which the cultural organization is set up;
- *Collateral processes*, consisting of initiatives that enrich the cultural offer, thus optimizing the use of available resources;
- *Auxiliary processes*, made up of activities that integrate the cultural offer through the provision of additional services;
- *Supporting processes*, identified by transversal activities that deliver value to all those included in the previous processes.

Regarding museums, the core processes can therefore be traced back to those activities identified by the same ICOM definition. Specifically, the care and conservation of the collections are ascribed to them, including the research and loan activities of assets for exhibitions and study but also the activities of display and enhancement of the collections (permanent and temporary), which include the museum project, the setup, the activities that facilitate their use for purposes of study, research, and edutainment.

Collateral processes are instead identified in the organization of special events (e.g., movie festivals, conferences, etc.), but also in publishing activity, in the provision of library and photo library services, and in the transfer of usage rights to the collections to which the museum has the copyright. In fact, failure to carry out these activities does not affect the identification of the museum as a cultural organization.

The auxiliary processes are typically represented by the services of the cafeteria, bar, restaurant, bookshop, and other profitable activities such as the cloakroom or paid parking.

The supporting processes include a vast and heterogeneous range of services attributable to reception (e.g., ticket service, info point, etc.) provided free of charge. Added to these are also those related to safety and cleaning as well as administrative, fundraising, digital communication, and promotion activities.

The map of the value creation processes in the museum is summarized in Fig. 2.6.

2.3 Value Cocreation

The study of value creation has been developing under different managerial perspectives within the service system (Vargo & Lusch, 2004) as well as public administration literature (Moore, 1995). Both strands of research have contributed to extending the understanding of this phenomenon with strategic implications for the market and the state. Their common point is the notion of value acknowledged as (Bozeman, 2007, p. 13):

> a complex and broad-based assessment of an object or set of objects [...] characterized by both cognitive and emotive elements, arrived at after some deliberation, and because a value is part of the individual's definition of self, it is not easily changed, and it has the potential to elicit action.

This notion of value is closely linked to the cognitive but also the emotional elements of those who produce and those who perceive that value (Hodgkinson et al., 2017; Ng & Vargo, 2018). The creation of value is, in fact, intimately linked to personal factors such as self-fulfillment, for having influenced the creation of that value, especially if it is provided for the benefit of the community (Bovaird, 2007; Alonso et al., 2019).

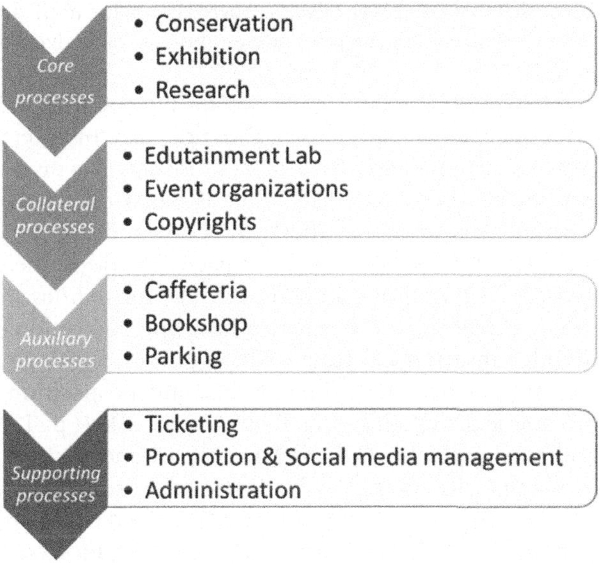

Fig. 2.6 The map of museum value creation processes

Moreover, the adjective "individual" or "public" ascribed to value concerns the same object. Alford and Hughes (2008) define private value as value consumed individually by users, while public value is received collectively by citizens based on their needs and wants (Edvardsson et al., 2011). In particular, the research focused on the relationship between consumer and provider introduces the concept of "value in use" as an alternative to "value in exchange." According to the Service-Dominant (S-D) logic, the value in exchange is created by the provider and exchanged in the marketplace for money. Conversely, the value in use is based on users' perceptions and is created throughout and from the collaboration and interaction between the user and the provider in mutual exchanges during consumption or experience (Petrescu, 2019).

According to S-D logic, providers and consumers do not have distinct roles because value is always cocreated through reciprocal and mutually beneficial relationships. Precisely, value is cocreated when resources are used (Pinho et al., 2014). Hence, the notion of value cocreation is based on this fundamental proposition (Lusch & Vargo, 2006, p. 44):

The customer is always cocreator of value: there is no value until an offering is used, and experience and perception are essential to value determination.

The conceptual framework of value cocreation recognizes the centrality of encounters, such as the processes and practices of interaction and exchange within consumer and provider relationships (Payne et al., 2008). Whether consumers' ability to create value is based on the information, skills, and operant resources that they can access and use. On the other hand, the providers' one is based on the capacity to add to the consumers pool of resources in terms of competences and capabilities for creating value. Meetings, therefore, are crucial for boosting cocreation. Those are interactions and transactions through which parties exchange resources, competences, and practices according to the value proposition that value is created by experience (Prahalad & Ramaswamy, 2004, p. 172). Recent investigations have applied S-D logic to complex and multiactor service systems (Normann & Ramirez, 1993), developing a revised version of the conceptual model (Nenonen & Storbacka, 2010; Best et al., 2019). Value networks (systems of service) are relatively self-contained, self-adjusting systems of resource-integrating actors connected by shared institutional arrangements and mutual value creation through service exchange (Vargo & Lusch, 2016, p. 161). By facilitating encounters among actors within the service system, experiences can be created.

In addition to public and cultural settings, social innovation and cocreation are "magic concepts" (Pollitt & Hupe, 2011). It is not surprising that recent cultural heritage management literature builds on cocreation theory (Davies et al., 2013) or embeds the latter specifically in relation to museum value development (Pencarelli et al., 2017). There is still a lack of research on visitor-museum cocreation. Based on the same literature, museums have the capacity to build networks with their audiences and other stakeholders to cocreate value from cultural experiences (Minkiewicz et al., 2014). As Coffee (2008, p. 261) argues, "no Museum is an island," that is, social forces underlie the existence of museums, affecting (or excluding) various audiences through cultural programming. In this respect, a museum serves as a *locus* of social interaction between visitors and the museum itself. In light of this, accessibility is a critical value driver for museums, whose "organizational culture" can influence individual and collective behavior (Quinn et al., 1991; Hooper-Greenhill, 2007). Consequently, museum managers are commissioned by society to seek public value. Public value can only be created by engaging citizens in the creation process (Moore, 1995). It is true that understanding what citizens want and need without involving them provides merely results in public service (Scott, 2006). However, public value does not necessarily coincide with intrinsic value, which Holden (2006, p. 14) defines as follows:

> The set of values that relate to the subjective experience of culture intellectually, emotionally, and spiritually.

Museums, as well as cultural organizations, can provide intrinsic value to communities and a sense of belonging. The Museum Value Framework identifies four types of museums based on the focus (internal/external) as well as the knowledge and interpretative strategies (single narrative/formal source and multiple interpretation/informal sources), which include temples, clubs, visitor attractions, and forums. The latter typologies (visitor attractions and forums) focus on the perception of the museum's functions by external audiences/stakeholders. In contrast, the "visitor attraction" type of museum focuses on communication with visitors to satisfy their needs. The forum type, on the other hand, emphasizes museums' role in contributing to the development of civil society. This means that a visit to the museum is no longer an occasional outing but rather a drop-in service, and its fruition becomes a cognitive process in the mind stimulated by participation and dialog (Nielsen, 2015). Piber (2020) emphasizes that in the context of participatory cultural organizations, the audience, or a part of it, includes not only the visitors but also the actors in the cocreation process. An organization's functions and existence are legitimated by its audience. It occurs in any cultural organization that is responsible for creating value for the community by managing common resources, such as cultural heritage.

2.4 The Multidimensional Created Value: Measurement and Reporting

Providing services transforms cultural value directly into personal growth, making value creation processes an essential element of every organization (Bowman & Ambrosini, 2007). This implies that cultural organizations can provide emotional and cognitive experiences to visitors. The term "value-creation-ability" is used (Catturi, 2007):

> The ability to create value and to distribute it equally and harmoniously among the various 'stakeholders' or 'interested parties'. This is to satisfy, at least somewhat, the needs they perceive.

Depending on the nature of the stakeholders' need to be fulfilled, the created value could be broken down into the following typologies: economic value and sociocultural value.

2.4.1 *Economic Value: How to Measure and Report?*

Economic value is represented by the results achieved in terms of effectiveness, efficiency, and cost-effectiveness. These are framed in the so-called "3E model" (Adam et al., 2011). According to the managerial accounting approach, it can be applied by answering the following core questions:

1. Is the cultural organization doing "the right things"?
2. Is the cultural organization doing the "right thing"?

The answer to the first question can be given through effectiveness indicators; otherwise, the second question can be answered through the use of efficiency indicators. When the creation process is effective and efficient at the same time, economic value is achieved.

The 3E model includes the concept of economy understood as the ability to acquire production factors at the lowest cost, provided that their quality is guaranteed, a parameter that accompanies each phase of the value creation process (Fig. 2.7).

The model shown above highlights all the phases of the value creation process: from the acquisition of production factors (input) to the creation of the proposed value (output) to its perception by the user in terms of satisfaction of users' needs, up to effects, positive or negative, induced by the value created (outcome). To evaluate the cost-effectiveness, it is necessary to extrapolate the relative consumption of the production factors (inputs) based on purchase costs. In this regard, one of the following indicators can be calculated:

1. Inputs/Outputs
2. Outputs/Inputs

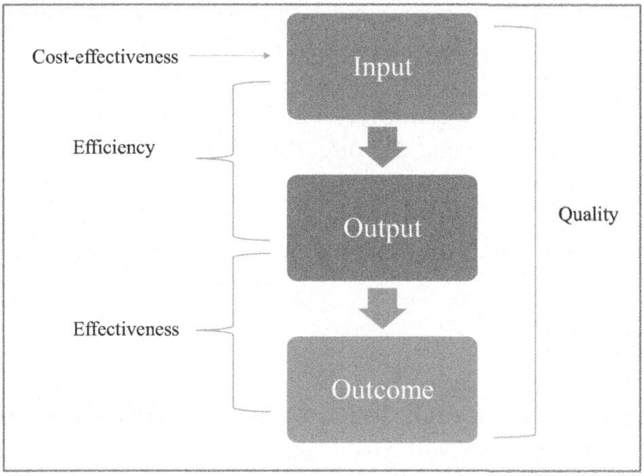

Fig. 2.7 The 3E model

The first indicator (Input/Output) provides a measure of the organization's ability to minimize the use of production factors for the same output. The level of efficiency increases as the value of the indicator decreases (e.g., Input = no. of guided tour operators; Output = number of guided tours), whose numerator and denominator must be calculated with respect to the same period of time.

The second indicator (Output/Input) measures the organization's ability to maximize the result for the same input. Efficiency increases as the ratio increases (e.g., Output = number of visitors; Input = weekly opening hours of the museum).

The quantities shown in the numerator and denominator must be logically connected and can be represented by financial and nonfinancial data expressed in numbers or as a percentage. It is evident that the indicators assume significance when compared with the relative estimated values or with respect to those calculated in previous periods as well as in relation to data considered benchmarks in the sector (e.g., descriptive statistics on culture at national level).

In relation to the short- and medium-term objectives, effectiveness can be distinguished in the following typologies (Mussari & Ruggiero, 2017):

- the operational effectiveness relating to the cost or revenue objectives assigned, in the short term, to the department, division, and project managers;
- An organization's social effectiveness refers to the ability to achieve strategic objectives that are directly connected to the organization's mission/vision.

The operational effectiveness is measured by the following ratio:

$$\frac{\text{Outputs}}{\text{Objectives}}$$

Clearly, the closer this indicator is to one or 100%, the more effective the value creation process will have been (e.g., Output = no. of actual visitors; objective = no. expected visitors).

Social effectiveness, on the other hand, is linked to the impact of the result on medium- to long-term objectives, that is, how performance contributes to the pursuit of the mission/vision. An example is the number of visitors with visual impairment out of the annual total (objective), taking into account the strategic objective of making the museum inclusive and accessible to specific visitor targets (outcome).

The aforementioned indicators provide an objective measure of operational effectiveness, even if to measure the outcome, that is, the effects of the value created on the community, it is advisable to adopt ad hoc tools that allow calculating the economic impacts of a cultural organization. A kind of tool should be a survey on users—tourists or excursionists—for whom it is possible to collect the information necessary to estimate the economic impact induced to their visit to the place of culture. The data necessary for the calculation of the indicators can sometimes be acquired from administrative sources, especially if they coincide with the information requested by institutional bodies for museum accreditation or for the reporting of financed or co-financed projects. However, measuring the created values may require a control dashboard necessary for the cultural organization to manage, rationally and responsibly, a portion of that common heritage, which is an expression of the cultural heritage of the community.

Economic value can be measured not only through indicators constructed on the basis of the 3E model but also by adopting economic quantities taken from the information-accounting system of the cultural organization. In fact, the legal form regulation obligates the organization to draw up a final account consisting of the balance sheet, income statement, or a specific accountability report.

The analysis of efficiency and effectiveness, from an accounting point of view, can be developed by processes based on the map of value creation processes (Fig. 2.6). Specifically, it is possible to measure the value created and consumed for each kind of activity included in this map to identify in which area it is necessary to improve.

The theoretical perspective assumed identifies in the added value the economic result that allows the encounter between supplier and consumer to be expressed in the context of the various cocreation processes developed by the organization. The added value is determined according to the following accounting approaches:

- Generation of Value Added
- Application of Value Added

According to the former approach, the value added is calculated as follows:

$$\text{Added Value} = \text{The Production Value} - \text{Cost of bought-in goods and services purchased}$$

The value of production is represented by all the revenues achieved by the cultural institution for each activity included in the value creation processes (i.e., ticket revenues, edutainment revenues, bookshop revenues). Value consumed to provide value to users is the cost of bought-in materials and components. This is the value added to recoup the consumption of assets in any category of environmental heritage, a portion of which is managed by cultural organizations (Fig. 2.8).

An organization's remuneration for personnel (A) is represented by the remuneration attributed to its internal stakeholders. Part of the fund is used to replenish the consumption of the heritage of knowledge. This heritage is formed by the coordinating and unitary set of skills, knowledge, and skills of the company personnel in this cultural case. A typical accounting item included in this macroaggregate is wages and salaries. The remuneration of the capital contributed by the owners (macroaggregate B) consists of the economic result achieved in the year, which can be

Generating Valued Added	Application Valued Added
Core Processeses	Heritage of Knowledge
Production Value (-) Cost of bought-in goods and services (A) Added Value generating by core processes	(A) Receipt by Workers/Employees (B) Receipt by Owners
Collateral Processes	Heritage of Historical Value
Production Value (-) Cost of bought-in goods and services (B) Added Value generating by core processes	(C)Receipt by Providers of Loan Capital (D) Receipts by Fixed Assets
Auxiliary Processes	Heritage of Natural and Cultural Value
Production Value (-) Cost of bought-in goods and services (C) Added Value generating by core processes	(E) Receipt by Government
Supporting Processes	
(D) Cost of bought-in goods and services Added Value generating by core processes	
Net Value Added [A+B+C-D]	Net Value Added [A+B+C+D+E]

Fig. 2.8 Value added statements

represented by a profit, which is reinvested in value creation processes where cultural organizations are legally regulated as nonprofit institutions. Otherwise, the operating loss will reduce the Global Added Value due to the increased consumption of that value that was created and recognized by the environment. The best approach in this case is to identify which processes absorb the most value and to improve their management. If the economic result for the year were represented by a breakeven, then in the displayed macroaggregate, the related accounting item would be found with a value equal to zero. It includes the restoration of the consumption of fixed acultural and natural heritage (F), which is linked to taxes and fees.

2.4.2 *The Sociocultural Value: How to Measure and to Report?*

The concept of sociocultural value is connected to the ability to create value to satisfy the needs of study, research, and edutainment.

A sociocultural value is quantifiable from the perspective of global (or social) effectiveness in terms of qualitative satisfaction. It makes it possible to measure the performances achieved from the perspective of stakeholders, thus overcoming the limits of quantitative indicators, which are unable to offer a holistic evaluation of the public value recognized by the users who cocreate it. In this respect, it is appropriate to proceed with the identification of stakeholders for the value creation process and subsequently adopt the tools of customer satisfaction analysis. The results must be treated objectively through the application of specific processing methods. It is unanimously acknowledged that the generation of value represents the *raison d'être* of any organization, just as the value created allows for a multiplicity of values intended for the various stakeholders. However, the need to improve relationship management has led the managerial literature to propose different taxonomies of stakeholders. These taxonomies can be applied to any type of organization, including cultural ones.

For purely sociological reasons, stakeholders can be classified based on direct or indirect relationships with the organization (Freeman, 1999) but also with respect to their actual influence and/or dependence on the organizational results achieved (Mitchell et al., 1997). A possible stakeholder-mapping proposal for cultural organizations combines the previous criteria, identifying the following categories:

- direct stakeholders, that is, subjects who relate, without the aid of intermediaries, to the cultural organization in the various value creation processes, who in turn can operate within the organizational structure of the same (internal direct stakeholders) or in third economies (external direct stakeholders);
- indirect stakeholders, represented by subjects influenced by the value created by the cultural organization even if they do not have direct relationships with it (external indirect stakeholders).

It should be stressed, however, that there are no series A or series B stakeholders but simply subjects who decide to participate in the cocreation of value because they expect to contribute to a better future than they would otherwise. As a result, some generic and standardized mappings have been questioned since a stakeholder can be an external user as well as a financier or partner.

Consequently, the mappings will have to be created ad hoc with respect to the cultural organization to identify the most suitable tools for verifying the degree of satisfaction from the point of view of social effectiveness. In fact, in the case of a museum, the customer satisfaction of users can be measured through the guest book. However, that of the staff operating in the same organizational structure requires the use of different techniques, such as questionnaires or direct interviews.

The managerial literature focused on the cocreation of value has directed scholars of cultural companies to explore which measurement tools are able to understand the contribution of stakeholders to the realization of these processes (Tomka, 2018). To create value with the user rather than for it, it is necessary to obtain knowledge about not only its stakeholders' needs but also their satisfaction with the experience they have lived there. From this point of view, the surveys conducted within this context are certainly relevant, aimed at verifying the effectiveness of audience development techniques (Coffee, 2008; Magliacani et al., 2018) as tools for the production of information concerning such perceptions. These tools have been proposed by international standard practice on measuring the value created by cultural organizations, with particular regard to museums (Foster, 2008).

The Evaluation Toolkit for Museum Practitioners contains an accurate description of the relative strengths and weaknesses of each component in terms of its suitability to the user and its availability to use. Among the most commonly used tools used in the Italian museum context are questionnaires, interviews, focus groups, guest books, and observations on visitor behavior.

Tools for measuring the degree of user satisfaction are also connected to the performance information framework (Kroll, 2013). It indeed contemplates the production of information through the application of various techniques for measuring results (performance measurement), as well as the use of the information produced from a management point of view (performance management) and the related connection with the decision-making process (performance steering). The same theoretical framework introduces the taxonomy between routine and nonroutine information, which are distinguished on the basis of specific elements that can be mainly traced back to the following:

- the source is prepared in a structured way (e.g., questionnaire) or not (e.g., guest book), which generates predefined information (routine information) or spontaneous information (nonroutine information), respectively;
- presentation and communication methods that can be formalized (routine information) or not (nonroutine information) in reports;
- the role of information in the decision-making process, which can be that of feeding and updating the information flows that form the company databases necessary for management control (routine information) or of enriching the information base, albeit in an unstructured way (nonstructured information routine).

Some audience development tools physiologically generate nonroutine information, just thinking about the data collected through guest books or focus groups, unlike those produced by questionnaires structured based on specific cognitive objectives, which are instead attributable to predictable ones.

After collecting the earlier (nonroutine) data sets, they can be considered relevant since they involve important performance improvements or nonpertinent and significant extraneous elements. It is therefore advisable to "selectively" manage the collection of all the information acquired using the methodologies chosen to measure the user's contribution to the cocreation of value. It implies avoiding neglecting data generated spontaneously, as sometimes happens when visitor comments reported in the guest book are not processed if not even read (Magliacani et al., 2018).

From the collection and selection of information, their processing requires a preliminary classification based on topics considered strategic for the improvement of performance in terms of social effectiveness (e.g., degree of appreciation of the museum itinerary, guided tour, cultural experience). The processing of classified information can be carried out by applying qualitative–quantitative methods chosen in relation to the cognitive objectives. Hence, the interpretation of the data proceeds in relation to their signaling capacity, which is closely linked to the organization's ability to perceive the meaning of the symbols used in the message, that is, to the "semantic dimension of communication." This implies the need to adopt, in institutional communication, a language that is understandable to both internal and external stakeholders.

Therefore, communication is critical to accountability, i.e., reporting to all stakeholders the results achieved through information accounting. In fact, the more reporting is able to satisfy the information needs of all stakeholders, the more it contributes to the social legitimacy of the organization considered.

With reference to the actors of cultural heritage, the managerial literature has referred to the various models of social reporting, based on the triple bottom line approach, that is, on the reporting of results from an economic, social, and environmental point of view (Stylianou-Lambert et al., 2014).

From the previous theoretical models, this research intends to offer an empirical contribution that can offer evidence of the processes underlying these applications to guarantee their internalization as managerial practices institutionalized for the pursuit of the mission/vision from a dynamic perspective, that is, that takes into account internal and/or contextual changes.

2.4.3 *The Case of the Civic Museums of Pavia (Lombardy)*

Overview

This case study was chosen because it was considered relevant in relation to the objective of identifying the processes that allow the implementation of tools for the production of information concerning the value created by cultural organizations from the user's point of view (Yin, 2017). In fact, in the period in which the survey was conducted (2014–2015), the Civic Museums of the Visconteo Castle in Pavia (Lombardy) were included in that small percentage of Italian public museums (14.3%) at the national level, having the characteristic of systematically monitoring visitors in the five-year period prior to the survey date (www.istat.it/it/archivio/musei). Specifically, the management of that cultural organization was interested in understanding the usefulness of audience development tools for measuring the value created, disseminated and perceived by users of the temporary exhibitions organized in the two-year period (2014–2016). This objective was connected to a much broader purpose, namely, that of activating visitor engagement processes functional to acquiring information useful for improving the management of events. In addition, the planning of arts initiatives that meet expectations.

Methodology

The Municipality of Pavia has engaged a team of research experts. They will account for the preparation of the tools necessary for customer satisfaction with each cultural initiative organized over the project period. The museum management had to prepare and implement a two-section questionnaire for each event. The first, made up of 12 multiple-choice questions, made it possible to detect the degree of visitor satisfaction with the exhibition by noting the motivation for the visit and possibly the appreciation of specific collections on display. In addition, the visitor was asked to express an opinion on the structure and on the additional services, as well as on the relative relationship with the Civic Museums of Pavia (if holders of the "My Museum Card" or *vice versa* if interested in acquiring information on the cultural initiatives of the museums themselves). It was also considered appropriate to examine the most common means of promotion among the public to support the cultural institution in question from a management point of view. With the second section, consisting of eight questions addressed to off-site visitors, an attempt was made to detect the impact of the exhibitions organized inside the Visconteo Castle on the local economy. At the provincial level, specific questions were formulated to determine the consumption of cultural and tourist services, especially catering and lodging.

The questionnaires were distributed by the front-office staff of the Civic Museums regarding the temporary exhibitions managed in-house.

The percentage of responses achieved (17%) represented a physiological result, since the stakeholder engagement process was only in the start-up phase and would certainly take some time before producing statistically significant results.

Regarding the exhibition "1525–2015. Pavia, the Battle, the Future" the guest book adopted was examined, in addition to the related questionnaire, to understand its effectiveness in terms of a tool for producing information useful for monitoring the visitor's contribution to the cocreation of value.

The data collected offered an initial representation of the behavior of users more inclined to dialog with the cultural institutions of the city. This representation was with the intention of offering ideas for maintaining if not improving the cultural offer, according to parameters of quality, efficiency, and effectiveness. From this perspective, the results obtained with the application of the 3E model in relation to the economic value created will be illustrated below. In terms of sociocultural values, an accurate analysis of the guest book will be proposed, concentrating on the exhibition.

The results of the survey on economic and sociocultural values were formalized in an accountability report, which was disclosed through a public event organized by the Civic Museums, which was also attended by the project team.

The discussion of the same will be proposed from the perspective of accountability. This perspective uses, metaphorically, the accountability report as a mirror that reflects and at the same time makes us reflect.

Results

The analysis of the performances achieved from the point of view of effectiveness, efficiency, and economy was carried out after the mapping of the value creation processes. This was done by the research team together with the staff employed in the Civic Museums.

For each process, indicators were identified with the aim of evaluating the efficiency of the "core" activities of conservation and promotion of the collections by comparing them with national data. In particular, the indicator was used:

$$\frac{\text{number of items exhibited}}{\text{number of items kept}}$$

The result achieved, constant for the three reference years (38%), highlighted the potential of the Civic Museums to organize new exhibitions through the rotation of the collections available in the deposits and, if necessary, having invested in recovery and conservation activities but also in research to make an appropriate enhancement.

Other indicators adopted concerned the technical effectiveness of the collections in terms of trends in the number of visitors, tickets sold, and their incidence on the total proceeds of typical cultural processes (revenue from ticketing/total annual proceeds). The ratio enables museum management to determine the value recognized by users *versus* the value proposed by the museum. This information is even more significant when it is provided with respect to temporary exhibitions (e.g., proceeds from exhibitions/total proceeds from ticketing).

The degree of appreciation of collateral processes (e.g., film festival proceeds/total proceeds) and auxiliary processes (bookshop proceeds/ total proceeds) was measured using the same logic.

Finally, regarding cost-effectiveness, the Civic Museums have opted for a measurement that highlights the social cost of all the value creation processes activated for the conservation, promotion, and enhancement of the city's cultural heritage. The indicator used was the following:

$$\frac{\text{Annual Proceeds}}{\text{Annual Expenses}}$$

Proceeds are the positive income components derived from the value exchanged as a counterpart (e.g., tickets, gadgets, workshop registration fees). Therefore, they do not include contributions from other funding agencies and sponsorships. Consequently, the value of the indicator, which will physiologically be less than the unit for public museums, such as those considered, expresses the direct contribution of users to the coverage of consumption. What remains, on the other hand, represents the cost of cultural heritage management borne by the entire community, which for the Pavia community amounted to approximately 70% in 2016.

This is a fascinating figure for various players, such as:

- the cultural organization is accountable toward its owning body (the Municipality of Pavia) and to the community, the social nature of the cultural services, thus guaranteeing their use to the maximum number of interested parties;
- the Municipality, which, on the basis of that data combined with that of the number of users observed on an annual level, can choose future cultural policies with increased rationality and responsibility;
- the local community that will be able to evaluate, with increasing awareness, the value created and disseminated by the Civic Museums on the basis of the contributions offered directly or through taxation;
- the users who will be able to judge whether the ticket price is appropriate with respect to the experience lived within the place of culture and, consequently, communicate their opinions on the matter to the Civic Museums, with a view to improving the quality of the service cocreated.

The Civic Museums of Pavia have always used the guest book for permanent collections even if the information is not processed, being non-routine, and therefore formally included in the information-accounting system given the particular relevance for the history of the territory narrated by the temporary exhibition "1525–2015. Pavia, the Battle, the Future," it was decided to experiment simultaneously with this audience development tool as well as a questionnaire dedicated to the same exhibition. The aim was to evaluate the effectiveness of both in producing information on the degree of satisfaction with the visit. This was done by the multimedia applications adopted and on the cultural experience in general.

First, between completing the questionnaire and using the guest book, the latter was much preferred by visitors to the exhibition. In fact, 90 pages of signs and comments were examined against a negligible percentage of completed questionnaires (less than 10%). From the analysis of the information collected through the guest book, it emerged that the increase in visitors was matched by an increase in signatures and comments (positive or negative). In addition to the origin of the visitors, the subjects of the comments and suggestions were detected (Fig. 2.9).

To determine the overall perception of the exhibition, sentiment analysis was applied to the information collected through the guestbook (Turney, 2002; Pang et al., 2002) (Fig. 2.10).

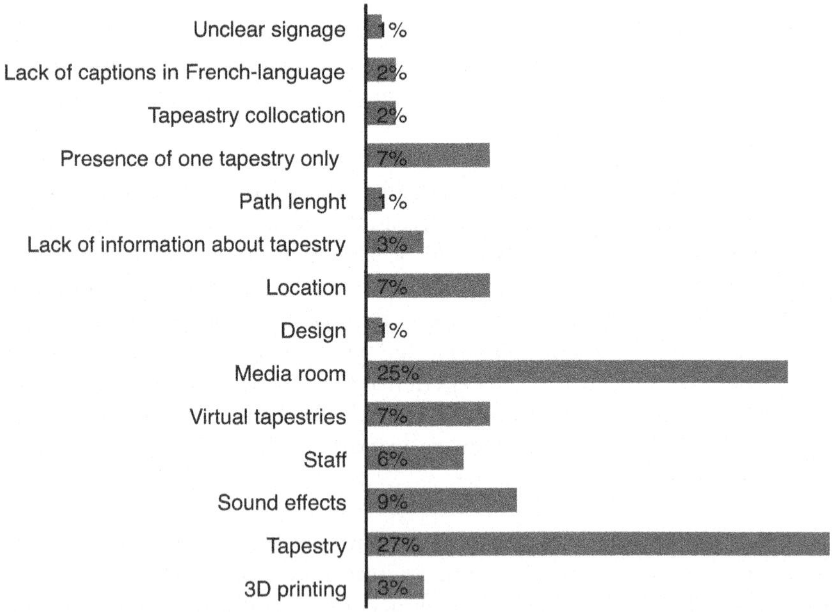

Fig. 2.9 Visitors' comments in the guest books Civic Museums of Pavia. (Source: Magliacani et al., 2018, p. 8)

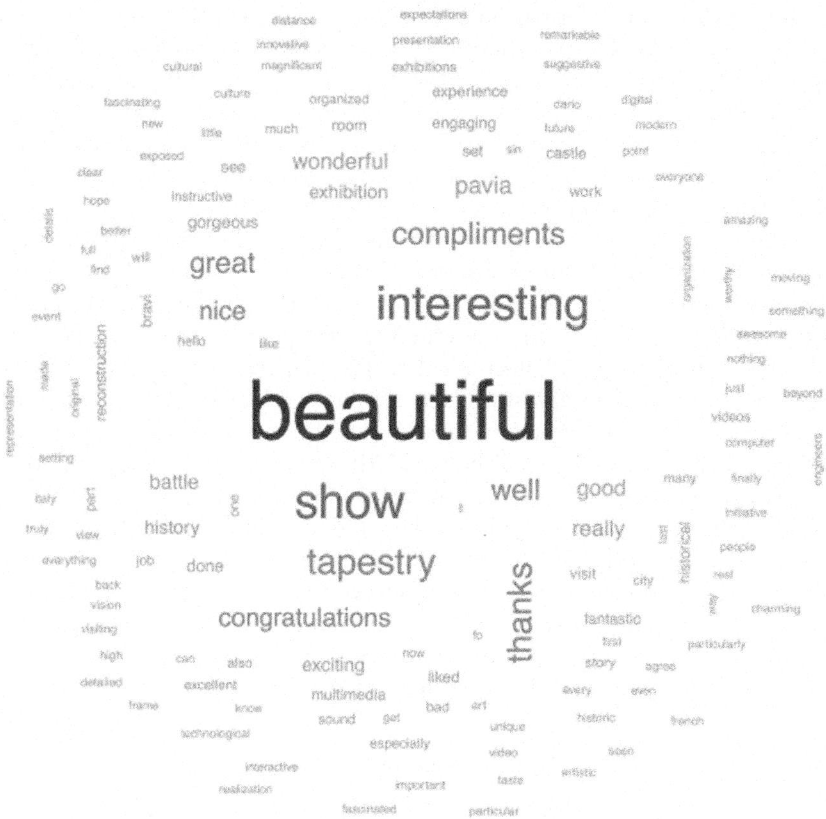

Fig. 2.10 Word cloud from the guest book sentiment analysis. (Source: Magliacani et al., 2018, p. 11)

From the experience of the Civic Museums of Pavia emerges how the culture of measurement is still in an experimental phase. This is because it is not mandatory except with respect to some parameters concerning the performances achieved in terms of the number of users.

Discussion

The analysis of the value created from a sociocultural point of view with reference to users has highlighted the usefulness of the guest book as a tool for producing information, albeit not routine, which assumes significance where it detects weaknesses to be overcome and points of strength to feed into. In addition is noteworthy the attempts to build information-accounting systems that allow the cultural organization to implement the management planning and control functions for continuous improvement in the management of historical heritage through the involvement of stakeholders in the typical processes of value creation.

A limitation of this research is certainly connected to the methodology adopted based on a single case study. This limits the validity of the results to the empirical context investigated. The experience of the Civic Museums of Pavia focused on sociocultural values with respect to users should in fact also be investigated in relation to other direct internal (staff) and external stakeholders (other local institutions, suppliers, lenders, etc.

The results of the research were, however, very compelling from an empirical point of view, since the Civic Museums still use audience development tools that feed into a database used by the Municipality of Pavia to guide the city's cultural policies. Through collaboration with academic research teams, skills have therefore been developed into institutionalized routines for controlling and monitoring cocreated value in typically cultural activities. This exchange of experience and skills with external professionals has activated capacity building within Civic Museums, thus increasing their wealth of knowledge.

2.5 The Cultural and Creative Production Ecosystem

Managerial studies point out that there cannot exist any organization detached from the environment. Therefore, interrelationships are indispensable to fulfilling the organizational function and achieving its mission.

Cultural organizations also create value by satisfying their users' cognitive and experiential needs. For this purpose, they have to interact with external stakeholders, represented not only by the public but also by suppliers of goods and services, as well as by lenders and the public administration, to carry out the value creation processes previously illustrated. By extending the perspective from the single cultural organization to all the relationships managed, it is possible to identify an ecosystem of actors—the so-called culture and creative production ecosystem—whose harmoniously integrated economic activities find their common denominator in cultural heritage (Imperiale et al., 2021). This is made up of different types of cultural organizations. They can be articulated in a "core cultural organization" or "cultural creativity-driven organization" in relation to their direct or indirect connection to the conservation and enhancement of tangible and intangible cultural heritage (Fig. 2.11).

To understand how this ecosystem operates in various territorial contexts, the managerial literature addresses research to investigate the antecedents, factors, processes and operating methods through which cultural organizations can contribute to the development of the quality of life of current and future generations (Throsby, 2017; Donato & Lohrasbi, 2017; Wiktor-Mach, 2020). This study responds to this call with the experience of a university museum. It shows how a project focused on accessibility can generate a network of relationships capable of stimulating the economy of the city and beyond.

Fig. 2.11 The cultural and creative production ecosystem. (Source: Our elaboration from Symbola "Io sono cultura," 2022, p. 20)

2.5.1 *The Museum of Electrical Technology of Pavia (Lombardy)*

Overview

The Electrical Technology Museum is part of the Museum System at the University of Pavia (Lombardy). In 2007, the University of Pavia, the Municipality, the Province and the Lombardy Region entered into a program agreement that led to the establishment of the Museum of Electrical Engineering. The purpose of this agreement was to conserve and enhance the collections honoring Alessandro Volta, inventor of the battery, who taught natural physics at the "Studium Pavese" (1795–1800), the current University of Pavia. This museum tour consists of five sections that correspond to the historical periods that tell about the major discoveries in this field of energy:

S1. The origins (until 1880)
S2. Electricity is established (toward the end of the nineteenth century)
S3. Electricity for everyone (early twentieth century)
S4. Electricity everywhere (second twentieth century)
S5. Electricity from now to the future

While wandering through the previous sections, located in an exhibition space of 2500 square meters, it is possible to reconstruct the main stages in the history of electrical technology. These stages range from the discovery of electricity to its use on an industrial scale and in the domestic field.

The museum's mission is to organize, safeguard, and promote the use of collections of significant historical-scientific interest, in support of research, teaching and training, adopting all initiatives aimed at enhancing them among the public, in collaboration with other university structures, and with local, national, and international cultural bodies.

In line with this institutional purpose, the museum promotes scientific research and innovation, with the involvement of all types of audiences.

From an organizational point of view, the management of the museum is entrusted, upon appointment by the rector, to a director chosen from among the professors of the University of Pavia, while conservation and maintenance activities, as well as scientific dissemination, are carried out by the curator, also in charge of security inside the building. A staff member also manages the inventory of the library works that include narration of the history of electrical technology from its origins to the present.

The *modus operandi* of the museum is characterized by intense networking activity with local stakeholders. This is primarily the various service areas of the University of Pavia, local public bodies, entrepreneurship, and the regional community.

To demonstrate a cultural organization's ability to create value in the relevant socioeconomic environment, this case study provides some evidence, answering the management literature calls for applied research to disseminate knowledge of successful practices (Thorkildsen & Ekman, 2013; Throsby, 2017; Wiktor-Mach, 2020). With respect to this literature call, the present study seeks to answer the following research question: which drivers allow a museum to generate specific outcomes for the reference community?

Methodology

To answer the aforementioned research question, this study adopted a qualitative research methodology using a relevant case study regarding the museum's ability to drive socioeconomic development in the area (Yin, 2018). A consideration was given to the limited experiences that are distributed by little-known museums that play a significant role in local communities, such as university museums. As part of the university's third mission, in addition to teaching (first mission) and research (second mission), they are institutionally obligated to provide knowledge transfer services (technological, scientific but also cultural) to the community they serve.

In the project called "Science at your hand," the museum adopted the ethnographic method based on direct observation of the facts (Dey, 2002; Spradley, 1979).

From the inside, it was possible to observe the entire development process, which lasted three years (2016–2019), from the articulation of the idea to the various milestones to the investigation of the generated results after one and a half years. Furthermore, several meetings were held for the preparation of two projects funded by the Lombardy Region on museum accessibility calls, as well as a number of initiatives to support the crowdfunding campaign (ten events spread over four months), and three workshops were arranged to assess the results achieved. The results were derived from ethnographic observation and are highlighted below.

Results

As part of its first decade of activities (March 2017), the museum organized and submitted a research project on social accessibility to the university crowdfunding platform. According to the project description on that website, the museum aimed to make the permanent exhibition accessible to all visitors, including people with visual disabilities.

Before launching the crowdfunding campaign, museum had already created a tactile map, in accordance with Lombardy Regional Law 39/74, 2016. Using 3D printing technology, a team of researchers and university labs (3DLab Centre and the Department of Civil Engineering and Architecture) designed and built the map. In addition, the Regional President of the Italian Union of the Blind and Partially Sighted has validated the functionality of the map. Further contributions and support were provided by the Rehabilitation Center for Visual Impairment of the Regional Hospital. Using their experience in solving the everyday problems of people with acquired visual impairment enabled the staging to be targeted and the effects to be verified. The museum exhibition spaces were first experienced by users and patients through touch, sensation, and, in general, a perception of the museum experience that extended beyond 3D printing to take on active roles during the preparatory stages of the project.

The objective of the crowdfunding project was to complete the exhibition path for blind or partially sighted people by means of cutting-edge technological devices. More specifically, these devices are museum map portions. They are linked to an app that enables visitors to listen to the story of the object that they can touch along the route. These devices are labeled "Museum Map of Tactile Experience" (MTE).

During the fundraising campaign, the platform updated the amount of financial resources received, the type of donors, and the remaining time within which it was necessary to achieve the goal of € 5000 by the end of June 2017. This amount of resources would have allowed the museum to complete the path for visually impaired and blind people, with the support of the university budget and the Lombardy region's contribution. As a result of the research team's work and the video-telling available on the platform, this was specified.

At the end of the campaign, the museum raised 134% of the resources requested from the crowd, thanks to the contribution of 21 stakeholders (event participants, industrial associations, local entrepreneurs, public institutions). Most of the donors who made it possible to achieve and exceed the minimum financial resources required from the crowd to co-finance the museum project visited or attended at least one of the events arranged by the museum during the four months of the crowdfunding campaign. The number of donors represented by visitors was 1204, whose contribution was enough to reach the goal. Participatory cultural initiatives consisted of three cultural workshops in March 2017, two performing art events for museum visits in April and May 2017, two Creative Labs for Kids and Families and two ateliers. All initiatives started with the presentation of the crowdfunding project, with the purpose to inform the audience to be aware of the objective of the fundraising as well as to stress the value that they would have contributed to cocreation for the welfare of the community. In that presentation, the museum staff stressed the importance of social inclusion. The curator declared, constantly, how the museum aims at feeding and satisfying curious visitors. This is because they want to know about the history of electrical technology and their inventions and inventors. Both children and adults perceive curiosity, whether they possess all five senses or not. The challenge has been emphasized to increase the awareness of the event participants regarding the project, which would enable blind and visually sighted adults and children to "touch" science in a manner that would be unique and exciting for them to experience at the museum.

Discussion

From the ethnographic observation of the Electrical Technology Museum with respect to the accessibility project "Science at hand," it was possible to deduce some elements that offer an answer to the research question pursued with this study.

Managerial skills were decisive for the design of an audience development proposal based on social inclusion. The presence of a financial fund call from the Lombardy Region on the theme of museum accessibility has certainly stimulated this idea. However, the museum has shown that it is pursuing a medium- to long-term vision, which has made it possible to carry forward the idea of a multisensory installation for the visually impaired and blind through the use of crowdfunding. Making the community aware of a museum accessibility project was the basic objective of the museum with respect to the public engagement function derived from being part of the University Museum System (Ferreira, 2018).

An attempt was made to transfer the scientific knowledge of the electrical technology collections to the community and nonlocal community, including the visually impaired, in compliance with the third mission

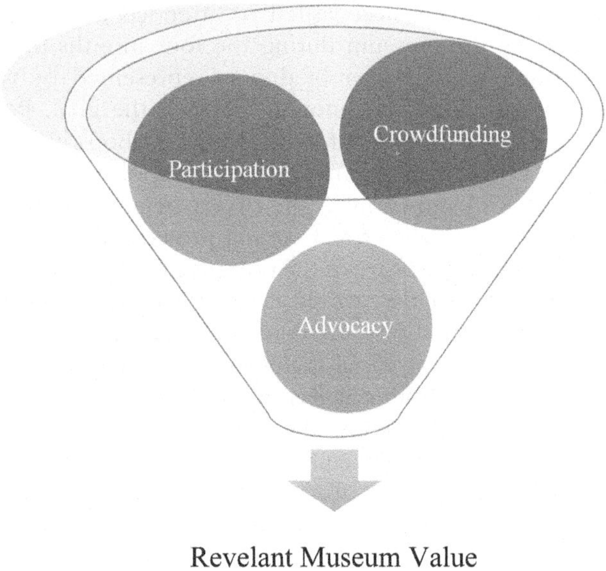

Fig. 2.12 The three components of the relevant museum value. (Source: Magliacani, 2020, p. 79)

function of the university's owner (Scott, 2006). The local community has assumed not only the role of user but also that of financier and promoter of the project. Compared to this last aspect, in fact, the museum has codesigned the MET and the pedotactile path, not only with the university department mentioned above but also with the Visual Rehabilitation Center of a hospital in Pavia and created both by engaging private companies operating in the cultural and creative production sector.

It was evident that direct interaction with the museum was important from observing the behavior of attendants after the visit. In other words, participation, advocacy, and crowdfunding have enabled the museum in co-financing public value creation, considered "relevant" by the crowd for the well-being of society (Fig. 2.12).

2.6 Final Remarks

The chapter attempted to answer two key questions to recognize the importance of culture for the economy and society as well as the managerial competences needed to manage cultural heritage.

Particularly, the exhibition activities aimed at spreading knowledge of the history of the local community (the case of the Civic Museums of the Visconteo Castle in Pavia) and the related attempt to stimulate dialog with visitors to understand their degree of satisfaction provide insights into the following: ***In what ways does cultural heritage affect the lives of current and future generations?***

The Civic Museums of Pavia have a very clear mission to contribute to the education and quality of life of current generations, and through the acquisition of technical-managerial competences, they can improve their offer over time, guaranteeing the conservation and enhancement of the collections for the benefit of future generations as well. To the same question, the case of the Electric Technical Museum provides some answers. The implementation of the project "Science at your hand" has made the fruition of the collections possible for a visually impaired audience. The welfare that museums can generate for current and future generations is evident from this case study.

With regard to the second question (***do cultural institutions recognize that they are organizations?***), both case studies demonstrated how the enhancement of collections makes it essential to implement managerial logics and programming and control techniques based on "conventional" accounting (i.e., accrual basis) for producing financial data and "unconventional accounting" (i.e., social basis) for producing nonfinancial data (Carnegie et al., 2022; Magliacani, 2022). This capacity building is triggered by partnerships that involve community participation in co-financing, coplanning, and corealization of a product and process innovation (Pollitt et al., 2006; Noya et al., 2009) (Fig. 2.13).

The experiences of the Civic Museums of the Visconteo Castle in Pavia and the Museum of Electric Technology identify the following skills as drivers capable of generating specific outcomes:

- *Ability to plan*, that is, to prepare development plans and to report them to the supplying bodies but also to other stakeholders (Lusiani & Zan, 2013);
- *Networking skills* that require knowledge of the internal skills of the organization and those that can be offered by the local economy with reference to the cultural and creative production ecosystem (Bäckstrand, 2006);
- *Fundraising and crowdfunding skills* consistent with the strategic budget drawn up in the project (Colasanti et al., 2016);

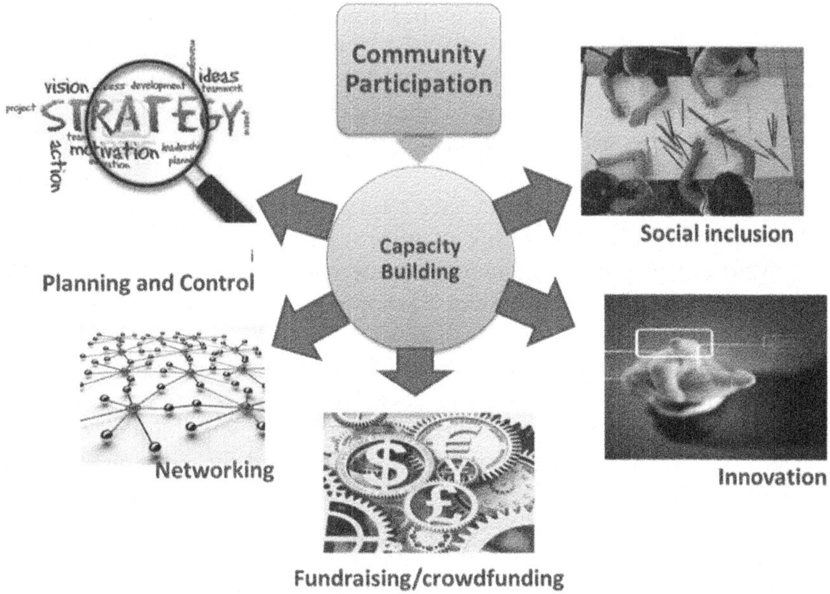

Fig. 2.13 The main driver of value creation in cultural organizations

- *Capacity for product and process innovation*, which requires openness to the environment on the basis of knowledge of what has already been tested to respond to new needs both in the national and international context (Thorkildsen & Ekman, 2013);
- *Ability to stimulate audience development* through specific partnerships (Tomka, 2018).

Cocreated value involves not only a new type of visitor target being reached by the cultural organizations examined but also the creation of an informal network and the stimulation of the cultural and creative production ecosystem. As a result of the involvement of local businesses and the community, the cultural heritage of Pavia has been enhanced significantly.

According to the interpretive model proposed in Fig. 2.13, other cultural organizations ought to become more aware of the value created by their management, which can be measured both economically and socioculturally by using traditional accounting tools or by creating them ad hoc according to their management and organizational characteristics.

References

Adam, B., Mussari, R., & Jones, R. (2011). The diversity of accrual policies in local government financial reporting: An examination of infrastructure, art and heritage assets in Germany, Italy and the UK. *Financial Accountability & Management, 27*(2), 107–133.

Alford, J., & Hughes, O. (2008). Public value pragmatism as the next phase of public management. *The American Review of Public Administration, 38*(2), 130–148.

Alonso, J. M., Andrews, R., Clifton, J., & Diaz-Fuentes, D. (2019). Factors influencing citizens' coproduction of environmental outcomes: A multilevel analysis. *Public Management Review, 21*(11), 1620–1645.

Bäckstrand, K. (2006). Multi-stakeholder partnerships for sustainable development: Rethinking legitimacy, accountability and effectiveness. *European Environment, 16*(5), 290–306.

Battilana, J., Besharov, M., & Mitzinneck, B. (2017). On hybrids and hybrid organizing: A review and roadmap for future research. *The SAGE Handbook of Organizational Institutionalism, 2*, 128–162.

Best, B., Moffett, S., & McAdam, R. (2019). Stakeholder salience in public sector value cocreation. *Public Management Review, 21*(11), 1707–1732.

Bowman, C., & Ambrosini, V. (2007). Firm value creation and levels of strategy. *Management Decision, 45*(3), 360–371.

Bovaird, T. (2007). Beyond engagement and participation: User and community coproduction of public services. *Public Administration Review, 67*(5), 846–860.

Bozeman, B. (2007). *Public values and public interest: Counterbalancing economic individualism*. Georgetown University Press.

Carnegie, G. D., Ferri, P., Parker, L. D., Sidaway, S. I., & Tsahuridu, E. E. (2022). Accounting as technical, social and moral practice: The monetary valuation of public cultural, heritage and scientific collections in financial reports. *Australian Accounting Review, 103*(32), 460–472.

Catturi, G. (2003). Valori etici e principi economici: Equilibrio possibile. *Studi e Note di Economia, 3*, 7–37.

Catturi, G. (2007). *La valorialità aziendale: Vol. I, La determinazione e la rilevazione del valore creato: Presupposti teorici e metodologici*. CEDAM.

Catturi, G. (2012). *Principi di economia aziendale: l'azienda universale: l'idea forza, la morfologia e la fisiologia*. CEDAM.

Coffee, K. (2008). Cultural inclusion, exclusion and the formative roles of museums. *Museum Management and Curatorship, 23*(3), 261–279.

Colasanti, N., Frondizi, R., Meneguzzo, M., & Santini, P. (2016). Esperienze di civic crowdfunding in Italia e in Europa: un modelo di classificazione e di benchlearning. *Azienda Pubblica, 29*(1), 59–80.

Davies, S. M., Paton, R., & O'Sullivan, T. J. (2013). The museum values framework: A framework for understanding organizational culture in museums. *Museum Management and Curatorship, 28*(4), 345–361.

Dey, C. (2002). Methodological issues: The use of critical ethnography as an active research methodology. *Accounting, Auditing & Accountability Journal, 15*(1), 106–121.

Donato, F., & Lohrasbi, A. (2017). When theory and practice clash: Participatory governance and management in Takht-e Soleyman. *Journal of Cultural Heritage Management and Sustainable Development, 7*(2), 129–146.

Edvardsson, B., Ng, G., Min, C. Z., Firth, R., & Yi, D. (2011). Does service-dominant design result in a better service system? *Journal of Service Management, 22*(4), 540–556.

Foster, H. (2008). Evaluation toolkit for museum practitioners. East of England Museum Hub.

Ferreira, T. C. (2018). Bridging planned conservation and community empowerment: Portuguese case studies. *Journal of Cultural Heritage Management and Sustainable Development, 8*(2), 179–193.

Freeman, R. E. (1999). Divergent stakeholder theory. *Academy of Management Review, 24*(2), 233–236.

Hodgkinson, I. R., Hughes, P., Hughes, M., & Glennon, R. (2017). Does ownership matter for service delivery value? An examination of citizens' service satisfaction. *Public Management Review, 19*(8), 1206–1220.

Holden, J. (2006). *Cultural value and the crisis of legitimacy*. Demos.

Hooper-Greenhill, E. (2007). *Museums and education: Purpose, pedagogy, performance*. Routledge.

Imperiale, F., Fasiello, R., & Adamo, S. (2021). Sustainability determinants of cultural and creative industries in peripheral areas. *Journal of Risk and Financial Management, 14*(9), 438.

Koontz, H. (1958). A preliminary statement of principles of planning and control. *Academy of Management Journal, 1*(1), 45–61.

Kroll, A. (2013). The other type of performance information: Nonroutine feedback, its relevance and use. *Public Administration Review, 73*(2), 265–276.

Lentz, S. S. (1996). Hybrid organization structures: A path to cost savings and customer responsiveness. *Human Resource Management, 35*(4), 453–469.

Lusch, R. F., & Vargo, S. L. (2006). Service-dominant logic: Reactions, reflections and refinements. *Marketing Theory, 6*(3), 281–288.

Lusiani, M., & Zan, L. (2013). Planning and heritage. *Journal of Cultural Heritage Management and Sustainable Development, 3*(2), 108–115.

Magliacani, M. (2020). How crowdfunding makes museum value relevant: An Italian university museum experience. *African Journal of Business Management, 14*(2), 73–85.

Magliacani, M. (2022). How the sustainable development goals challenge public. Action research on the cultural heritage of an Italian smart city. *Journal of Management and Governance*, 1–29.

Magliacani, M., Madeo, E., & Cerchiello, P. (2018). From 'listener' to 'speaker' museum visitors: Guest book as a means of dialog. *Museum Management and Curatorship, 33*(5), 467–483.

Minkiewicz, J., Evans, J., & Bridson, K. (2014). How do consumers cocreate their experiences? An exploration in the heritage sector. *Journal of Marketing Management, 30*(1–2), 30–59.

Mitchell, R. K., Agle, B. R., & Wood, D. J. (1997). Toward a theory of stakeholder identification and salience: Defining the principle of who and what truly counts. *Academy of Management Review, 22*(4), 853–886.

Moore, M. H. (1995). *Creating public value: Strategic management in government.* Harvard University Press.

Mussari, R., & Ruggiero, P. (2017). Merging for capacity and a capacity for merging: Politicians, citizens, and discourses in public administrations. *Financial Accountability & Management, 33*(1), 27–47.

Nenonen, S., & Storbacka, K. (2010). Business model design: Conceptualizing networked value co-creation. *International Journal of Quality and Service Sciences, 2*(1), 43–59.

Ng, I. C., & Vargo, S. L. (2018). Service-dominant logic, service ecosystems and institutions: An editorial. *Journal of Service Management, 29*(4), 518–520.

Nielsen, J. K. (2015). The relevant museum: Defining relevance in museological practices. *Museum Management and Curatorship, 30*(5), 364–378.

Niemann, L., & Hoppe, T. (2018). Sustainability reporting by local governments: A magic tool? Lessons on use and usefulness from European pioneers. *Public Management Review, 20*(1), 201–223.

Normann, R. (1977). *Management for growth.* John Wiley & Sons.

Normann, R. (2001). *Service management: Strategy and leadership in service business.* John Wiley & Sons.

Normann, R., & Ramirez, R. (1993). From value chain to value constellation: Designing interactive strategy. *Harvard Business Review, 71*(4), 65–77.

Noya A., Clarence E., & Craig G. (2009). Community capacity building. Creating a better future together, Local Economic and Employment Development (LEED). OECD Publishing, Paris.

Pang, B., Lee, L., & Vaithyanathan, S. (2002). *Thumbs up? Sentiment classification using machine learning techniques.* arXiv preprint cs/0205070.

Paolucci, A. (1996). *Museo Italia: diario di un soprintendente-ministro.* Sillabe.

Payne, A. F., Storbacka, K., & Frow, P. (2008). Managing the cocreation of value. *Journal of the Academy of Marketing Science, 36*, 83–96.

Pencarelli, T., Conti, E., & Splendiani, S. (2017). The experiential offering system of museums: Evidence from Italy. *Journal of Cultural Heritage Management and Sustainable Development, 7*(2). https://doi.org/10.1108/JCHMSD-02-2017-0009

Peters, B. G. (2021). *Administrative traditions: Understanding the roots of contemporary administrative behavior.* Oxford University Press.

Petrescu, M. (2019). From marketing to public value: Toward a theory of public service ecosystems. *Public Management Review, 21*(11), 1733–1752.

Piber, M. (Ed.). (2020). *Management, participation and entrepreneurship in the cultural and creative sector.* Springer.

Pinho, N., Beirão, G., Patrício, L., & Fisk, R. P. (2014). Understanding value cocreation in complex services with many actors. *Journal of Service Management, 25*(4), 470–493.

Pollitt, C., & Hupe, P. (2011). Talking about government: The role of magic concepts. *Public Management Review, 13*(5), 641–658.

Pollitt C., Bouckaert G., & Löffler E. (2006). Making quality sustainable: Co-design, co-decide, co-produce, coevaluate, Report by the Scientific Rapporteurs of the 4th Quality Conference, Ministry of Finance, Finland.

Prahalad, C. K., & Ramaswamy, V. (2004). *The future of competition: Cocreating unique value with customers.* Harvard Business Press.

Quinn, R. E., Hildebrandt, H. W., Rogers, P. S., & Thompson, M. P. (1991). A competing values framework for analyzing presentational communication in management contexts. *The Journal of Business Communication (1973), 28*(3), 213–232.

Scott, J. C. (2006). The mission of the university: Medieval to postmodern transformations. *The Journal of Higher Education, 77*(1), 1–39.

Spradley, J. P. (1979). *The ethnographic interview.* Holt Rinehart and Winston.

Stylianou-Lambert, T., Boukas, N., & Christodoulou-Yerali, M. (2014). Museums and cultural sustainability: Stakeholders, forces, and cultural policies. *International Journal of Cultural Policy, 20*(5), 566–587.

Symbola-Unioncamere, "Io sono cultura." (2022). https://www.symbola.net/ricerca/io-sono-cultura-2022.

Thorkildsen, A., & Ekman, M. (2013). The complexity of becoming: Collaborative planning and cultural heritage. *Journal of Cultural Heritage Management and Sustainable Development, 3*(2), 148–162.

Throsby, D. (2017). Culturally sustainable development: Theoretical concept or practical policy instrument? *International Journal of Cultural Policy, 23*(2), 133–147.

Tomka, G. (2018). The orthodoxy of cultural management research and possible paths beyond it. In *Arts and cultural management* (pp. 108–128). Routledge.

Turney, P. D. (2002). *Learning to extract keyphrases from text.* arXiv preprint cs/0212013.

Vargo, S. L., & Lusch, R. F. (2004). Evolving to a new dominant logic for marketing. *Journal of Marketing, 68*(1), 1–17.

Vargo, S. L., & Lusch, R. F. (2016). Institutions and axioms: An extension and update of service-dominant logic. *Journal of the Academy of Marketing Science, 44*, 5–23.

Wiktor-Mach, D. (2020). What role for culture in the age of sustainable development? UNESCO's advocacy in the 2030 Agenda negotiations. *International Journal of Cultural Policy, 26*(3), 312–327.

Yin, R. K. (2017). *Case study research and applications: Design and methods.* Oaks.

Yin, R. K. (2018). *Case study research and applications.* Sage.

Zappa, G. (1956). *Le produzioni nell'economia delle imprese: tomo primo.* Giuffrè.

CHAPTER 3

Using Accounting for Managing Cultural Heritage

Abstract How does accounting contribute to the management of cultural heritage? In cultural organizations, how can accounting systems be designed to facilitate rational and responsible decision-making? What are the preconditions for starting such a process of building inter- and intra-organizational accounting knowledge? A theoretical and practical approach is adopted to answer these questions. Through simulations for cultural organizations, the basic concepts of managerial control, budgeting, and cost accounting are described and applied. The use of accounting for the start-up of cultural networks will be examined through a critical case study.

Keywords Strategic planning and thinking • SWOT analysis • Cultural budgeting • Cultural cost accounting • Balanced scorecard

3.1 Introduction

It is imperative that managerial accounting practices are used to govern and manage cultural heritage from a perspective of continuous improvement to ensure sustainability and resilience. They are tools that enable organizations to acquire information on the current situation to plan more effectively and responsibly. Nevertheless, these managerial control practices require accounting skills that are still not widespread in cultural

M. Magliacani, V. Toscano, *Accounting for Cultural Heritage Management*, https://doi.org/10.1007/978-3-031-38257-4_3

organizations, especially in the Italian context. However, the necessity to acquire this technical knowledge is felt to be more urgent by these organizations operating with increasingly rare and scarce resources. This is in light of context changes that can bring new needs and new opportunities/criticalities.

Based on these observations, this chapter proposes managerial accounting models and tools that enable organizations to plan how to enhance their cultural heritage and to measure and control whether their strategies and actions are achieving their intended goals. This study focuses particularly on the logic behind the use of *ex ante* and *ex post* managerial control tools in cultural organizations. Specifically, the balanced scorecard model will be discussed, which originated in the management culture of companies and has been adapted to cultural organizations. It presents an empirical study of a rural organization's attempt to create a cultural network. In this instance, we are dealing with a *suis generis* experience, since the organizations investigated are not cultural ones in the classical sense, but businesses that manage a rural heritage that is an expression of the cultural heritage (tangible and intangible) of the local communities.

Creating a cultural network among rural organizations to preserve the historical memory of a particular region's productive tradition represents an interesting case study from a variety of perspectives. On the organizational level, it is evident that many private organizations are willing to enhance cultural heritage as a common good through networking and partnership. Identifying the opportunity to establish a network and putting it into action is the key to success. Moreover, from the capacity point of view, this project-case study is relevant because it has been able to increase entrepreneurs' awareness of the value of cultural heritage, as well as to activate knowledge-sharing processes to create economies of scale and scope. Methodologically, ethnographic research emphasizes the importance of developing a continuous improvement culture in management. Essentially, planning involves governing internal and contextual dynamics to achieve a successful outcome from a social, cultural, and economic perspective on a local level.

As part of this study, some simulations are presented on budgeting and cost accounting applied to cultural organizations (so that budgeting and cost accounting are labeled with the adjective "cultural"). They may assist practitioners in making rational and responsible decisions regarding the management of cultural heritage. Toward the end of the chapter, some thoughts about capacity building in the accounting field for cultural organizations are provided.

3.2 Strategic Thinking and Planning

The purpose of planning is to consciously determine the course of action that should be taken to achieve the goals. Therefore, planning involves making decisions (Koontz, 1958). The process cannot ignore the institutional aim (mission) through which any organization derives its legitimacy to operate in a particular socioeconomic context. Planning consists of actions that must be taken today to achieve tomorrow's objectives, aligned with the corporate mission (Drucker, 1973).

It is important to note that an organization cannot plan rationally and, therefore, in a conscious manner if it does not acquire information about the external dynamics to predict the effects they may have on the internal perimeter. In view of the homeostatic relationship between the organization and its environment, a context analysis is essential. For an organization to remain competitive, it must be constantly updated. It is essential to possess this knowledge to be able to dominate both the changes in the context that can be reflected within the organizational perimeter and those that affect the external environment, which is subject to constant change in this perspective. It is therefore necessary to adopt proactive or reactive behaviors to respond to changes in the scenario after taking into consideration the effects that some decisions may have inside and outside the organization, rationally and responsibly. A strategic approach to planning takes on a new meaning when it is carried out with a deep understanding of the close relationship between the organization and its environment, with which it is mutually dependent (Normann, 1977).

To fully comprehend the role of strategic planning in the management of change (organizational/environmental), it is necessary to clarify the meaning of the adjective "strategic." In the military field, "strategy" refers to the general plan of how resources are allocated to achieve a competitive advantage (Grant, 1994). An organizational strategy is also based on three fundamental elements: objectives, internal resources (human and material), and external factors. Even though a strategic approach is primarily characteristic of firms operating under market conditions, it should be applied to any organization with a desire to improve continuously.

With this orientation, the organization is able to identify the operational areas where it can create value for stakeholders, thereby ensuring its survival and growth in the long run (Normann, 2001).

With the environment in continuous transition, it is necessary to strategically plan corporate management to keep the organization in a state of dynamic balance. A strategic plan identifies objectives and actions with a medium- to long-term perspective. Indeed, strategic planning is included in managerial control, a process through which organizations ensure that resources are obtained and used effectively and efficiently to achieve corporate objectives (Bryson, 1988).

The strategic planning process is an essential ex ante control that allows organizations to compare the results achieved after a defined period of time with the objectives set during the planning process. Based on this perspective, strategic planning aims to determine "controlled" changes in the socioeconomic scenario (Ozbekhan, 1969).

The process of strategic planning begins with the definition of a mission-vision and strategic objectives, that is, the goals that an organization intends to attain in a medium-long period of time in terms of growth, development, and reputation. Among the identifying features of an organization is its mission, the formulation of which is a prerequisite to the commencement of decision-making. A SWOT analysis could be useful in this regard. This involves assessing the strengths and weaknesses of the organization (internal analysis), as well as opportunities and threats related to the environment in which it operates (external analysis) (Fig. 3.1).

Based on the SWOT analysis, it is possible to identify the critical success factors in the context of the external analysis and the specific skills that are needed to improve value creation processes. This analysis is followed by the formulation of strategies for which it may be helpful to address the following three questions of strategic thinking:

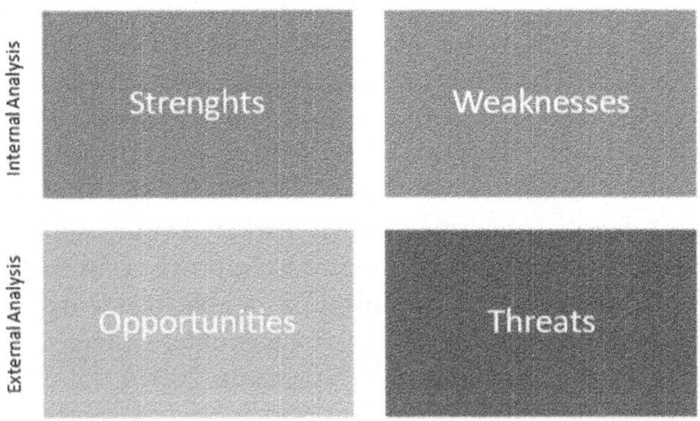

Fig. 3.1 SWOT analysis model. (Source: Adaptation by Leigh (2009))

1. What value to create? 2. For whom? 3. How?

To formulate favorable strategies, it is necessary to take into account the external conditions and the internal capabilities with respect to each value creation process. External challenges can be faced by applying an "adaptive" approach. This is typical of the behaviorist school, such that the deliberate strategy emerges as a result of behaviors capable of responding to environmental changes (Mintzberg, 1987). Conversely, the rationalist school proposes formulating strategies based on a proactive approach capable of anticipating changes in the context (Simon, 1979). The theoretical model that combines these two approaches is that of the design school (Mintzberg, 1990) (Fig. 3.2).

From the SWOT analysis, the design school formulates strategies. The strategic decision is made taking into consideration the organizational ethics encompassed in the mission/vision and the social responsibility of the organization (Parisi & Hockerts, 2008). The strategy is implemented if it is considered economically sustainable.

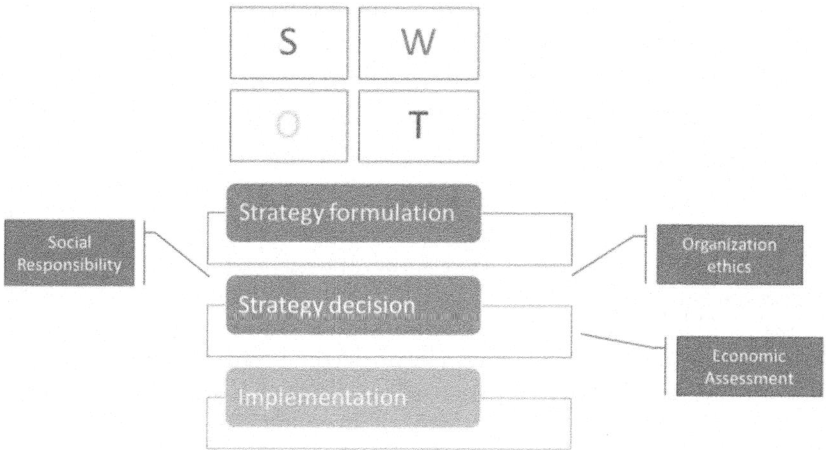

Fig. 3.2 Design school model. (Source: Adaptation by Mintzberg (1990, p. 174))

3.3 The Balanced Scorecard for Cultural Organizations

A theoretical model that fits well with the strategic approach, allowing organizations to prefigure their actions in different perspectives of value creation, is the one underlying the use of the balanced scorecard tool, known by the acronym BSC (Kaplan & Norton, 1992). It facilitates reasoning on how to align vision/mission with strategies and lines of action, applying the principle according to which (Kaplan & Norton, 2000, p. 14):

> *"You cannot manage what you cannot measure and you cannot measure what you cannot describe."*

The implementation of the BSC begins with the description of the objectives to be achieved, that is, the mission/vision broken down into strategic objectives, actions, and results. During this phase, a strategy map is constructed with the identification of drivers (value generators) based on the cause-effect relationships between variables that are aligned with the objectives to be pursued (Kaplan & Norton, 2004). In the classic model of Kaplan and Norton (1992), these drivers are identified in relation to value creation. The following are their representations:

- Financial Perspective
- Customer Perspective
- Internal Perspective
- Learning and Growth Perspective

By using value creation processes, the strategic map must describe how the organization attempts to achieve the objectives that operationalize the mission. To achieve this, it is important to measure value based on economic-financial sustainability (Financial Perspective), customer satisfaction (Visitors' Perspective), internal productivity (Internal Perspective), and the improvement and growth of personnel skills (Learning and Growth Perspective). To create value for the organization, these perspectives must correspond to the strategic areas in which the organization creates value. For this reason, the BSC model must be adapted to the morphological and physiological characteristics of each organization. In addition, cultural organizations need another perspective of value creation aligned with their mission to serve society by providing a variety of

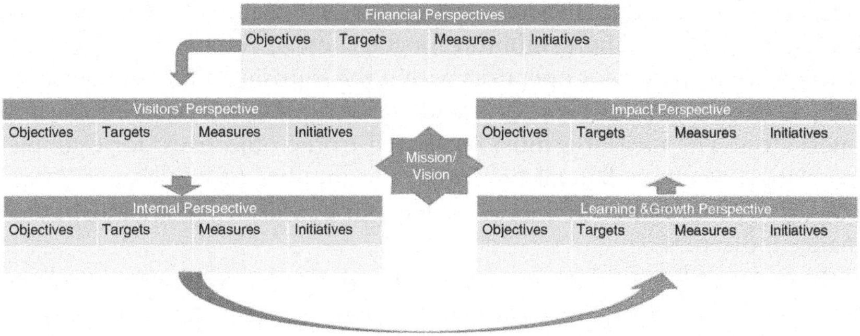

Fig. 3.3 BSC model applied to cultural organizations

educational, enjoyment, reflection, and knowledge-sharing experiences. In terms of impact, this perspective is related to the community relationship (Fig. 3.3).

The BSC model is structured in the following elements regardless of the number of perspectives:

- the objectives are derived from the mission and vision of the organization;
- measures such as indicators that can be used to evaluate the identified performance results;
- a target is defined as a quantity value that provides a concrete expression of the objectives expressed in the preselected measures;
- To accomplish the objectives, initiatives must be implemented.

To breakdown the mission into objectives and measures, specific questions should be referred to for each perspective. If museums are considered examples of cultural organizations, the management should ask itself: how should the cultural organization approach its visitors to achieve its mission? Increasing visitor satisfaction is a related goal, although vague. As an example, it can be measured by the annual variation in the number of visitors, the ratio of visitors under 18 to the total number of visitors, and the weight given to positive opinions over negative ones.

Regarding the internal perspective, the question to be asked is: which processes should cultural organizations develop to meet the needs of visitors? A few objectives can be identified within the context of core cultural activities (improve the efficiency and quality of restoration works, enhance the effectiveness of the exhibition itinerary, etc.), collateral (agreements with institutions and/or operators within the tourism and cultural sectors, etc.) or auxiliary (provision of "new" services, improvement of existing ones, etc.). The measures must be related to the objectives: for example, in relation to the collateral processes, the number of conferences organized, or the number of rooms rented out could be considered performance indicators.

In terms of financial performance, when formulating objectives related to strategic guidelines, management will have to ask the following: *How should cultural organizations improve financial performance to achieve their mission?* The objective may be to increase the efficiency of value creation processes. Examples of actions that can be implemented include the promotion of collateral activities, such as film festivals organized within the museum or theatrical performances. The following indicator can be used to assess the effectiveness of this action: revenues from collateral activities as a percentage of total income, as well as total revenues as a percentage of total costs. To ensure accurate monitoring, both indicators must be calculated over the period of management control that cannot exceed 12 months to avoid running into situations in which it is difficult to correct the shot, that is, by containing the adverse effects on performance.

In light of the learning and growth perspective, management should ask the following questions: *what skills are needed to achieve the mission?* Objectives can be defined in terms of enhancing organizational knowledge or developing internal and/or external synergies among professionals, depending on the circumstances. A number of parameters should be considered in alignment with these initiatives, including the number of training hours per year, the incidence of training costs on total operating costs, the percentage of internal team projects on total projects, and the level of staff satisfaction.

For the museum to define its mission in terms of relations with the local community, management must consider: how is it to fulfill its function as a center for disseminating local culture and, above all, *what kind of inter-institutional relationships should be developed?* Increasing the socioeconomic impact of cultural activities could contribute to the development of the knowledge economy within the territory as one objective. In the operational hypothesis just mentioned, some measures that can be adopted include the number of initiatives with school groups, participation in cultural projects in collaboration with research centers, and the number of relationships with trade associations and enterprises that operate in the cultural production ecosystem.

3.4 The Roadmap of Cultural Value Creation

By presenting a strategic plan, which can take the form of a business plan, if the organization is preparing it for the first time for a specific funding call, formal communication will be addressed to the staff regarding the implementation of the strategies and related actions. For managerial control, the strategic plan outlines the organization's objectives, the actions that will be taken to achieve them, the evolution of the key value drivers, and the expected results in the short and medium term. Although this document does not follow a standard format, it consists primarily of two sections: one qualitative, which describes the organization, the mission and vision, and the business model, and the other quantitative, which includes economic, financial, and equity forecasts. As the first section outlines, "in prose," the project idea for which the feasibility plan was prepared, the second section consists of a strategic budget. A good practice is to accompany the numbers with an explanation of the actions underlying them by illustrating the management model (the "business model"). It is addressed to both internal and external stakeholders. Members of the internal decision-making body are those who have the authority to approve the plan's implementation. External stakeholders are funding organizations (e.g., banking foundations, the EU, local public bodies) from which organizations plan to request funding for the implementation of the project.

An operational logic is required to transform a business idea into a feasibility project that is innovative, reliable, and above all sustainable (DaSilva & Trkman, 2014). As a result, managers are able to answer the following strategic questions: (a) Where are we? (b) Where would we like to be? (c) How to get there?

As a result of the logic of the business model, it is possible to develop a roadmap for the creation of value that is useful for answering the previous questions as well as developing a project that should be sustainable (Amit & Zott, 2015). The process begins with the analysis of the needs of the customers or users to whom the organization is proposing value. This exploration can be carried out through recourse to the empirical literature of the sector or through research conducted through surveys, focus groups, and direct interviews. In this analysis, you will gain a deeper understanding of what the unexpressed desires of one's visitors or users are or how to attract a new audience with different sociodemographic, economic, geographical characteristics than the existing ones. It is necessary to collect information from existing and/or potential visitors/users if the organization plans to innovate its products or make them more usable or to provide new collateral services and accessories.

After collecting these data, cultural organizations will have to design the product/service with which they can satisfy the intercepted needs. The creation of this value leads the organization to analyze its current situation (*where are we?*) through SWOT analysis and formulate appropriate decisions to achieve strategic objectives (*where would we like to be?*). Indeed, it has to understand which production processes to enhance or activate from scratch, which skills are necessary to implement them, how to acquire these skills, if necessary, which resources can be invested in, and which ones to look for and who to contact.

Activities can be analyzed by adopting the mapping of value creation processes (core, collateral, auxiliary, and supporting). To achieve this, the organization has to choose the tool or mix of tools that may be appropriate for the type of target considered, for example, social media if the target audience is represented by millennials. This decision must be made after having carried out an internal analysis relating to human capital and related skills. This analysis must evaluate, if necessary, the opportunity to acquire or outsource those not currently available.

An alternative to these options could be the use of partnerships with other organizations or institutions that may be interested in creating the product/service.

The value creation process results in direct relationships with partners, suppliers, lenders, and users with whom the organization has interacted since the first phase of the roadmap and indirect relationships with the wider community, potential users, and institutions.

Management of these relationships involves the incurrence of costs, which will be recorded, such as economic-financial and asset forecasts, in the strategic budget of the feasibility plan. In addition to costs, revenue forecasts and investment requirements are calculated for each project idea.

At this stage, the roadmap allows us to develop the strategic budget that makes up the feasibility plan and, therefore, to answer the last strategic question (*How do we get there?*)

To make this project sustainable, it is important to highlight, within the same document, the value created in terms of economic, social, and cultural outcomes (i.e., the benefit brought to users as an experience achieved through the use of this value and the contribution to the development of the economic context) (Fig. 3.4).

As a means of operationally understanding how to implement a project in accordance with the logic of the business model, thus developing all the steps of the roadmap that lead to the creation of value, an ethnographic research project is proposed below. The research was conducted by the author as part of a partnership formed by universities, local public bodies, associations, and individuals under the coordination of a forest industry body of the Lombardy Region. The objective of this study is to draw attention to the critical issues that can arise during the preparation of cultural enhancement projects while also emphasizing the process of creating the knowledge that can result from such experiences.

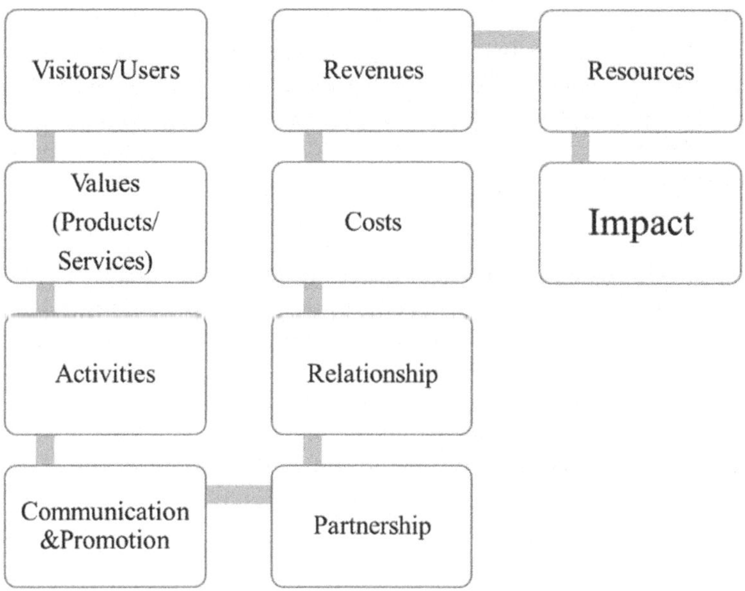

Fig. 3.4 The value creation roadmap for cultural organizations

3.4.1 The Case of the Cultural Rural Network Project

Overview
The project experience proposed has been experienced by an interdisciplinary research group made up of academics of the economic-business discipline (including the writer), by institutional representatives of the Lombardy Region, by an association of rural tourism entrepreneurs and by six pilot organizations belonging to the same rural association.

The objectives of the project, financed by the "Cariplo" Foundation, are as follows:

1. to enhance the tangible and intangible cultural heritage of a Lombard rural area;
2. to create networks between rural organizations that manage that heritage in the area located along the canal "Naviglio Pavese," between Milan and Pavia;
3. to define a management model capable of enhancing the cultural heritage of that area from a sustainable perspective.

To pursue these aims, the research team selected six pilot rural organizations, among those belonging to the partner (Association of Rural Tourism Entrepreneurs), based on their location on the "Naviglio Pavese" and with respect to the value creation processes based on rural activity and on the enhancement of the related culture made usable through hospitality and guided tours.

Methodology
Using an ethnographic approach, the study adopted a constructivist logic based on the sharing of experiences, values, and information related to their morphological and physiological characteristics among rural pilot organizations.

The operational phases of the project were structured as follows:

1. knowledge sharing between research teams and pilot organizations;
2. construction of the strategic map of the cultural rural network;
3. design of a business model.

To implement a project, knowledge sharing was the first step. A qualitative research method such as interviews and focus groups was adopted to develop this stage. To obtain detailed information about their own rural cultural environment, the entrepreneurs of each rural organization were interviewed first. A minimum of 1 h 30 and a maximum of 3 h were allotted for interviews, which were unstructured so that answers could not be conditioned by the project's strategic themes (i.e., the role of rural organizations in enhancing the culture of local communities, the objectives, and the advantages, and the criticalities presupposed by the network's creation). In this study, interviews are recorded and processed using the logic of content analysis (Ahmad et al., 2017; Elo & Kyngäs, 2008) as follows:

1. transcription of interviews' text;
2. text encoding by identifying keywords;
3. abstraction, providing a general description of the search results.

The text analysis of the interviews was carried out using, as keywords for coding, those attributable to strengths, weaknesses, opportunities, and threats.

Results

Through a focus group conducted by the project leader and team members, a SWOT matrix was developed (Fig. 3.5).

During the same focus group, the Strategic Map was built to define common objectives and then the relative key value drivers (Fig. 3.6).

Fig. 3.5 Results phase 1 of the project: knowledge sharing

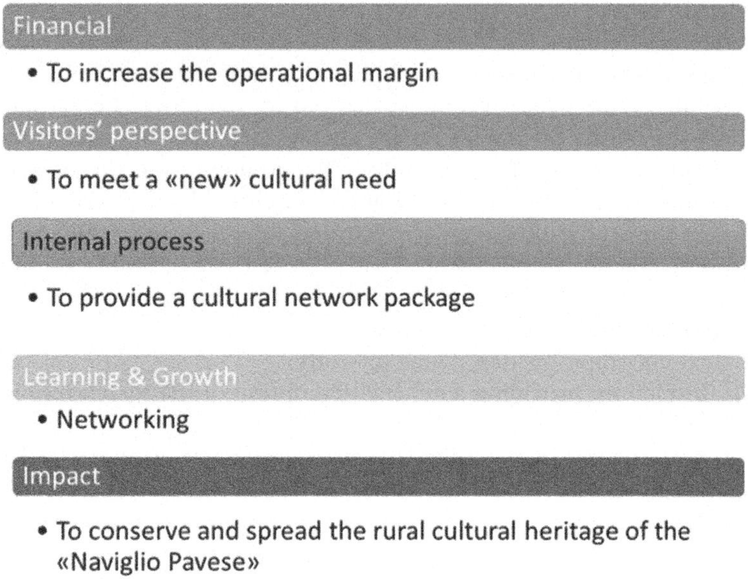

Fig. 3.6 Results phase 2 of the project: the strategic map of the cultural rural network

A strategic map was prepared by the research group, and an action plan was proposed for launching a network to enhance the Pavia canal, the "Naviglio Pavese."

Based on the study of the territory from the standpoint of its attractiveness as a tourist destination, an action plan was developed. It is possible to enjoy the Pavia canal from the cycle path that is used by hikers and cyclists. In the rankings of the most attractive countries for cycle tourism, Italy ranked eighth in the ranking of the most attractive countries by the CISET (Centro Internazionale Studi sull'Economia Turistica—International Centre for Studies on Tourism Economics). Cycle tourism represented almost 12% of the GDP in Italy. Meanwhile, according to the National Tourism Agency, bikers who prefer to spend their holidays in Italy by bike opted most often for the northern regions due to the many kilometers of quality cycle paths and numerous ancillary services available in these regions. Sixty-one percent of these individuals were foreigners, and 39% were Italians. Additionally, Pavia is a member of the FIAB (Federazione

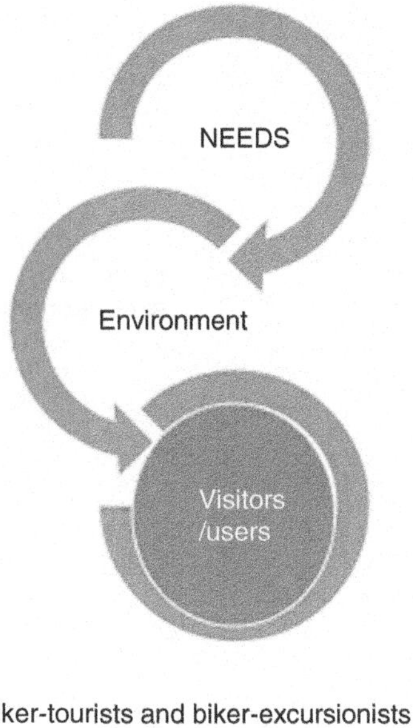

Fig. 3.7 Results phase 3 of the project: business model design (target)

Italiana Ambiente e Bicicletta—Italian Federation Environment and Bicycle), a network of arts cities, which led the research group to focus on the customer target of biker-excursionists (Fig. 3.7).

Following the value creation roadmap (Fig. 3.4), we identified the consumers' (visitors'/users') needs and utilized information available from the Association of Rural Tourism Entrepreneurs, project partners, and the website of the Italian bike promoter (Fig. 3.8).

As far as specific activities are concerned, the core cultural activities of rural organizations (catering and hospitality) as well as support activities that could be implemented with economies of scale were identified, for example, communications and promotion conducted by an organization for the entire network, such as providing technical assistance services for motorcycles. Communication and promotion channels, which were to be used to make the network visible, were primarily institutional sites of bike promoters (Fig. 3.9).

To guarantee all the collateral and auxiliary services, partnerships with physiotherapists, sports medicine doctors, bike mechanics, schools, and excursion guides are envisaged. Hence, the management of two types of relationships is proposed (Fig. 3.10).

Target	biker-tourists
biker-excursionists	Cafeteria/Restourant
	Packed lunch
	Info on energy value of food provided
	Wi-fi
	Bike Parking
	Bike Repair shop
	Bike washing tap
	Physician/Physiotherapist
	Brochures
	bike sharing
	Accomodations
	Bike room
	B&B
	Laundry

Fig. 3.8 Results phase 3 of the project: business model design (product/service)

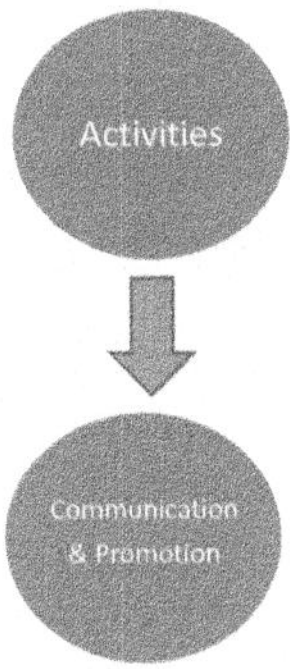

Specific activities provided by the rural organizations (i.e. catering, hospitality)

Cross-cutting activities provided by the organization for the entire network (i.e. communication & promotion)

- http://www.bikeitalia.it/bike-hotel/agriturismo-cascina-santa-brera/
- http://www.bikeitalia.it/itinerario-in-bici-da-milano-alla-certosa-di-pavia-lungo-il-naviglio/
- http://www.bicimilano.it/elenco.htm
- http://fiab-onlus.it/bici/turismo-in-bici/viaggiare-in-bicicletta/itinerari-e-resoconti-di-viaggio.html
- http://www.ilcicloviaggiatore.it/
- http://www.bikeitalia.it/category/itinerari-cicloturismo/italia/lombardia/
- http://www.turismo.regione.lombardia.it
- http://www.100cascine.it/
- http://www.activesporttours.com/
- http://www.albergabici.it/

Fig. 3.9 Results phase 3 of the project: business model design (activities and communication and promotion)

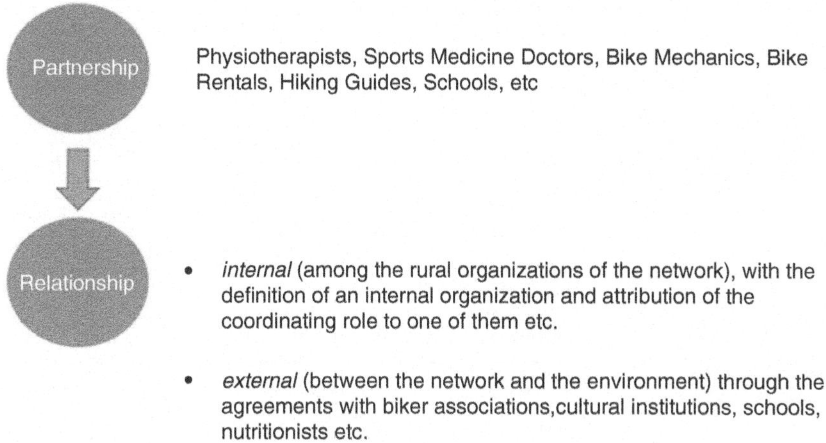

Fig. 3.10 Results phase 3 of the project: business model design (partnerships and relationships)

In the future model of the strategic budget, the value creation roadmap led to the formulation of costs, the estimation of revenues, and the determination of operating margins. An excursion along the Pavia canal on a bicycle rented from the first rural organization at the beginning of the path represented the value provided. For the entire network to use the bicycles, 50 bicycles must be purchased at an average cost of € 200.00 each, and they must be rented at an average cost of € 12.00 per day. For the five-year period following the project (2016–2020), simulation data were proposed. Based on varying the number of rental days and bicycles rented, three scenarios (base, best, worst) were envisaged (Fig. 3.11).

A previous simulation demonstrated that a nondepreciable investment of 50 bicycles for the entire network would have been able to generate profits as early as the first year. The hypothesis of renting ten bikes per day for 80 days, distributed throughout the year, is an exception. Finally, the impacts generated in terms of outcome would be identified in the achievement of a positive operating margin that will be distributed among rural organizations of the network (economic impact), as well as the greater ability to attract targets (social impact) interested in cultural heritage. The value package offered by the cultural network, based on eco-sustainable means of mobility (environmental impact), aligns with the triple bottom line approach to sustainability (Fig. 3.12).

Network bike sharing – strategic budget

Assumptions: Number of the bikes = 50; average cost per bike = £ 200; renting bike price = £ 12 per day

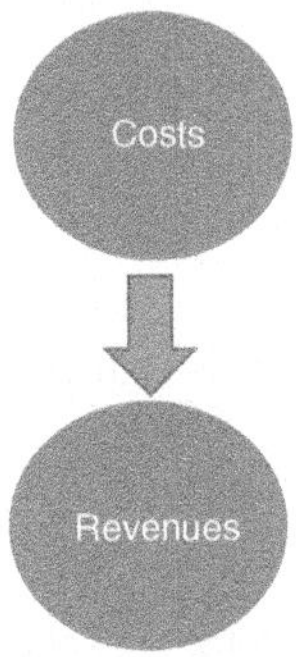

Costs	Year 1	Year 2	Year 3	Year 4	Year 5	Sources
Bikes costs	£ 10.000	£ -	£ -	£ 6.000	£ -	http://www.awsbici.com
Ordinary Mantainance		£ 1.250	£ 500		£ 750	
Bike toolkit	£ 240					Decathlon
Bike racks	£ 460					Amazon
Helmets	£ 1.400			£ 600		
Child bike seatsl	£ 750			£ 600		
Bike locksi	£ 300					Amazon
Total	**£ 13.150**	**£ 1.250**	**£ 500**	**£ 7.200**	**£ 750**	

Revenues	Year 1	Year 2	Year 3	Year 4	Year 5
Base scenario: 25 rent bikes 115 days a £12 per day	£ 34.500	£ 34.500	£ 34.500	£ 34.500	£ 34.500
Operating Margin	**£ 21.350**	**£ 33.250**	**£ 34.000**	**£ 27.300**	**£ 33.750**

Base scenario: 50 rent bikes 120 days a £12 per day	£ 72.000	£ 72.000	£ 72.000	£ 72.000	£ 72.000
Operating Margin	**£ 58.850**	**£ 70.750**	**£ 71.500**	**£ 64.800**	**£ 71.250**

Worst scenario: 10 rent bikes 80 days £12 per day	£ 9.600	£ 9.600	£ 9.600	£ 9.600	£ 9.600
Operating Margin	**£ 3.550**	**£ 8.350**	**£ 9.100**	**£ 2.400**	**£ 8.850**

Fig. 3.11 Results phase 3 of the project: strategic budgeting of the cultural rural network

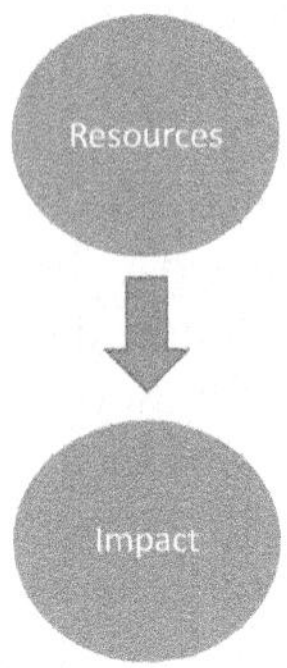

non-depreciable investment

- Economic impact = investment cost/operating margin equally allocated in the network
- Social impact= to provide a new experience on natural and cultural heritage of the «Naviglio pavese»
- Environmental impact= to enhance the «Naviglio pavese» through a sustainable escursionism and tourism

Fig. 3.12 Results phase 3 of the project: the impact of the cultural rural network

Discussion

The experience of the "Naviglio Pavese" network project was interesting from both theoretical and practical points of view.

The rural organizations involved in the project have experimented with knowledge sharing, strategic thinking, and business modeling. That experience has validated their effectiveness also for the creation of complex socioeconomic ecosystems such as a network aimed at enhancing cultural and rural heritage.

Ethnographic research has favored the activation of organizational learning processes by organizations that have welcomed the accompaniment of the research group, making themselves available for interviews and focus groups. The sharing of their specific knowledge that was tacit became explicit in preparing the network construction process (Magliacani & Madeo, 2018). It started with the definition of the mission and a strategic map of the cultural rural network.

However, the proposal for the action plan was accepted as a simulation of what the rural partners could have achieved together. This was developed as one of the strategic objectives of the BSC for cultural organizations. Even in this version, the business model has been learned from rural organizations as a social practice. This is to be internalized as a guide and direction tool for managing the available heritage in a sustainable way.

Strategic thinking and planning provide interesting ideas for understanding how to operate in the formulation phase of the project, in its operational translation and in measuring the value created not only from the internal perspective but also in the external one, with reference to visitors' satisfaction and the social, cultural, and environmental impact.

3.5 The Budgeting and Cost Accounting for Cultural Organizations

3.5.1 Cultural Budgeting

A budget is a useful ex ante monitoring tool for all activities carried out to create value within the processes activated by cultural organizations. The purpose of this document is to direct the behavior of those in charge of carrying out activities in a manner consistent with the objectives assigned by the governing bodies with the approval of this document. Accordingly, the relative performance will be evaluated based on the timing (annual or interim) of management control.

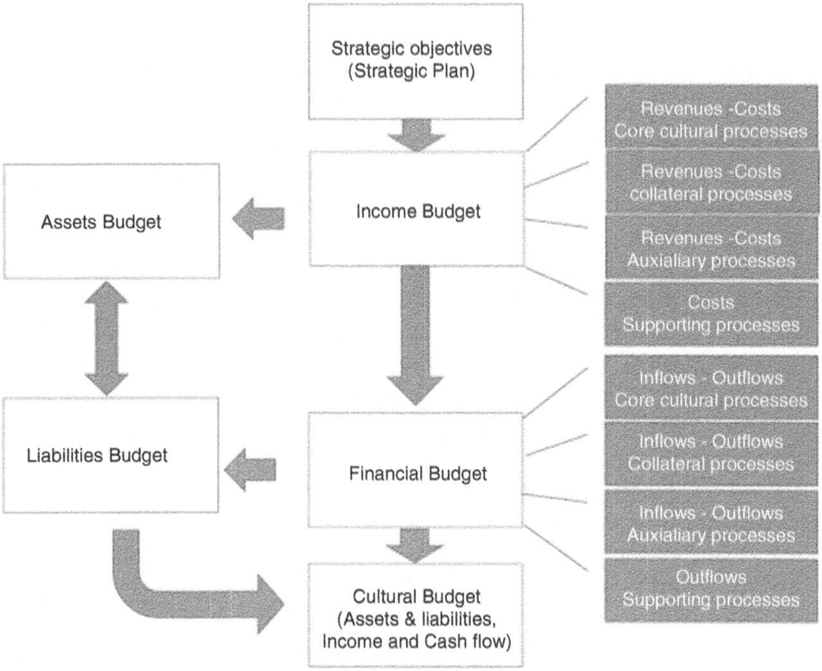

Fig. 3.13 Cultural budgeting

The main budgeting model proposed by accounting theory and widely used in practice involves the consolidation of sectoral budgets organized by functions or operations. Value creation processes can effectively articulate that model in cultural organizations. As shown in Fig. 3.13, the cultural budget consists of three budgets: the income budget, the assets and liabilities budget, and the financial budget (or cash flow budget) (Fig. 3.13).

The income budget, aligned with the strategic objectives, consists of the sectoral budget related to the estimated revenues and costs of "core" cultural processes (conservation, exhibitions, etc.), collateral processes (edutainment labs, copyrights, events, etc.) and auxiliary processes (bookshops, parking lots, cafeterias, etc.). The total operating margin is calculated by adding the costs of supporting activities (Table 3.1).

Table 3.1 The income budget for cultural organizations

Income budget	*Year 1*	*Year 2*	*Year 3*
Core cultural processes			
Revenues			
Tickets			
Public contributions			
Sponsorships			
...			
Costs			
Wages			
Collection rent			
Ammortization & depreciation			
(A) Operating margin			
Collateral processes			
Revenues			
Tickets			
Sponsorships			
...			
Costs			
Wages			
Transportation			
...			
(B) Operating margin			
Auxiliary processes			
Revenues			
Merchandising			
Cafeteria			
...			
Costs			
Wages			
Good and service			
(C) Operating margin			
Supporting processes			
Costs			
Communication & promotion			
Wages			
Utilities			
Taxations			
(D) Total cost			
(A+B+C-D) OPERATING MARGIN			

Since some tangible assets (e.g., totems, equipment, etc.) and intangible assets (e.g., software, ICT contracts) are used in value creation processes over a period greater than a year (fixed assets) or within the year (current assets), the income budget is closely related to the investment budget. An investment budget can be prepared using incremental budgeting or zero-based budgeting techniques. It is logical to increase investment costs in comparison to the past. Alternatively, zero-based budgeting involves forecasting investment costs as if management were starting from scratch every year. It is suitable for the management of projects. For the investment estimate to be valid, it must be consistent with the strategic plan's objectives. The cost of investments relating to value creation processes, which will increase the stock of assets, is included in this category. In addition to these values, financial resources are usually used for the restoration of works of art, an activity that generates extraordinary maintenance costs.

An asset budget is linked to a liability budget from which funds will be drawn for investments. To avoid equity and liquidity problems, they must be structured in accordance with the principle of time correlation: to avoid equity and liquidity problems (Table 3.2), fixed assets must be covered with equity or loans to be repaid over the long term (more than 12 months) and current assets with short-term resources (within 12 months).

Upon closing the cultural budget represented by the assets and liabilities statement (cash flow), the financial budget (or cash flow) results are merged into the bottom-line budget (Table 3.3). The operating margin is calculated as a function of the income budget and the expected changes in the active (assets) and passive (liabilities and equity) stocks over the strategic plan period.

Finally, the budget of a cultural organization can take the form specified by the legislation that governs its activities. Scholars and professionals continue to debate the issue of the valuation of heritage assets in financial statements (Carnegie & Wolnizer, 1995; Carnegie, 1996; Imperiale, 2018; Carnegie & West, 2005; Ferri et al., 2021).

3.5.2 *"Cultural" Cost Accounting*

For cultural organizations to achieve their mission to preserve, enhance, and promote tangible and intangible heritage for society, they must combine the parameters of infra-intergenerational equity with economic criteria (effectiveness, efficiency, and cost-effectiveness). From this perspective,

Table 3.2 The assets and liabilities budget for cultural organizations

Assets budget	*Year 1*	*Year 2*	*Year 3*
Current assets			
Cash			
Investments			
Inventories			
Account receivables			
Others			
Total current assets			
Property & equipment			
Furniture & furnishings			
License			
Less accumulated depreciation			
Total fixed assets			
Total assets			

Liabilities budget	*Year 1*	*Year 2*	*Year 3*
Current liabilities			
Account payables			
Accrued wages			
Others			
Total current liabilities			
Long-term liabilities & equity			
Mortgages payable			
Equity			
Total long-term liabilities & equity			
Total liabilities & equity			

cost accounting should be included in the management control toolbox. The main purpose of this accounting method, indeed, is the determination of the cost of the product (i.e., digital device for collection fruition, digital library, etc.) or service (temporary exhibition, events, etc.). Therefore, it provides useful information for determining the following:

- the proceeds to totally or partially cover the created value, according to the chosen trade off (sociability vs economy);
- the convenience to make or outsource some activities or functions such as the provision of specific service;
- the identification of responsibilities in the use of resources;

Table 3.3 The financial budget for cultural organizations

Financial budget	*Year 1*	*Year 2*	*Year 3*
(a) Cash and cash equivalent, beginning of the year			
Operating margin			
(+) Amortization & depreciation			
Changes in operating assets and liabilities			
(+/-) Accounts receivable			
(+/-) Inventories			
(+/-) Accounts payable			
(A) Cash generated by operating activities			
Investing activities			
Purchase (-) or proceed from sales (+) of			
Properties and equipment			
Intangible assets			
Securities			
others			
(B) Cash generated by investing activities			
Financing activities			
Dividend paid (-)			
Proceeds from issuance of long-term debts (+)			
Increase (+) or decrease (-) of liabilities			
Increase (+) or decrease (-) of equity			
(C)Cash generated by financing activities			
(A+/-B+/-C) CASH FLOW (b)			
Cash and cash equivalent, end of the year (a+/-b)			

- the attribution of benefits if a managerial incentive system is set up linked to the assessment of performance with respect to cost or revenue objectives.

Keeping cost accounting separate from general accounting ("dual mixed system") could be appropriate, especially for cultural organizations such as museums, archives, and parks, which mostly adopt financial-based rather than accrual accounting systems (Adam et al., 2011; Anessi-Pessina et al., 2020; Carnegie et al., 2022).

The following are the basic principles of cost accounting that also apply to cultural organizations:

1. the cost of cultural services/products is determined by the stratification of utilities transferred by the productive factors that are used to produce them;

2. the choice of the period of analysis should be correlated with the production cycle and, therefore, with the time frame envisaged for management control (interim or at most annual);
3. cost data are obtained from nonaccounting documents (invoices, pay slips, etc.);
4. the immediate objects of detection are the accrual costs, that is, the consumption of production factors, while the final one is the cost of the output of each production process.

To calculate the cost of a cultural service or product, the following traditional classification of consumption of production factors must be assumed:

- as output levels change, fixed costs and variable costs change as well;
- the costs of production factors attributed to the final cost unit (product/service or responsibility center) can be categorized as direct costs or indirect costs.

To address the accounting issues arising from the allocation of costs common to several services, such as temporary exhibitions in the case of a museum, a simulation is presented below. It relates to the calculation of the cost of the temporary exhibition arranged for three months (Table 3.4).

An organization's cost accounting system is structured in accordance with its map of responsibilities (organizational structure). This implies that the direct and indirect costs of common inputs should be allocated to different accountability positions (responsibility centers). The map of responsibility can be composed of the following types of centers:

1. the operational centers are represented by the organizational units in which the core, collateral, and auxiliary value creation processes are carried out;
2. the *crosscutting centers* are organizational units that carry out supporting processes;
3. the *dummy centers*, unlike the previous ones, are not correspondent to an organizational position since they constitute accounting devices created by the controller to aggregate costs for which responsibility cannot be attributed to a single person.

Table 3.4 Cost account of cultural organizations

Cost accounting data

Costs

- Amortization of audio guides: € 1200 (annual fee)
- Cost of technical-scientific personnel: € 5000
- Commercial costs (quarterly): € 2.016
- Set-up costs: €700
- Electricity (quarterly): €800
- Administrative costs (quarterly): €1600

Bases of indirect cost distribution

- Number of invoices issued in the quarter: 40
  - for the exhibition: 25
- Number of counter clicks in the quarter: 200
  - for the exhibition: 120
- Annual depreciation broken down according to the duration of the event
- Total hours of personnel involved in promotion per quarter: 672 h
  - for the exhibition: 383 h

The cost of the temporary exhibition

Direct cost: € 5700

- Cost of technical-scientific personnel: € 5000
- Set-up costs: € 700

Indirect cost ascribed to the temporary exhibition: €2929

- Amortization of audio guides: (€ 1200/12)*3 = € 300
- Electricity: (€ 800/200)*120 = € 480
- Administrative costs: (€1600/40)*25 = €1000
- Commercial costs (€ 2016/672)*383 = €1149

  Cost of the temporary exhibition: € 8.629

After identifying an appropriate basis of distribution, the cost accounting methodology proceeds with the preparation of cost accounts for any center by allocating specific costs to operational centers and indirect costs to responsibility centers. Following the identification of an appropriate allocation basis for the operating center, the cost of the core cultural value created by the operating center needs to be transferred to the operational centers. Figure 3.14 summarizes the above procedure.

To clarify the application of the methodology for determining the costs of cultural services/products based on the centers of responsibility and to demonstrate how the information deduced from the same can be useful for making strategic decisions (make or buy activities or services), a simulation is presented below (the "Alpha" case).

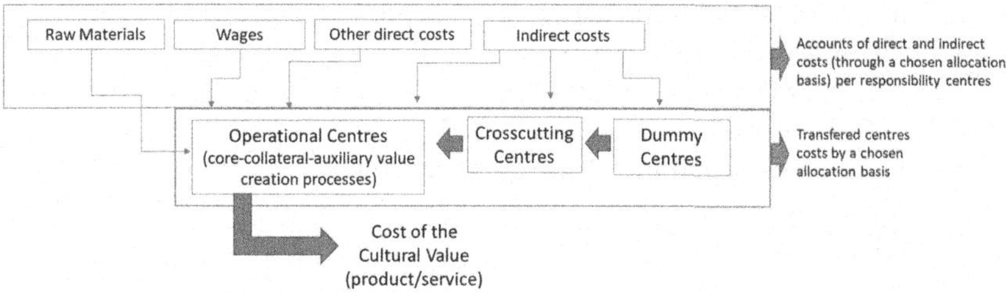

Fig. 3.14 Cost accounting methodology for cultural organizations

The Alfa Case

In addition to the conservation and exhibition of the collections, the cultural organization "Alfa" also carries out printing and publishing activities. The printers have also been used for publishing research books. The responsibility centres are the following:

- C&E: Conservation and Exhibition (Operational "core" Centre)
- P&P: Printing/Publishing (Operational "collateral" Centre)
- Administration (Crosscutting Centre)
- M&R: Maintenance & Repair (Dummy Centre)

The costs of the production factors used in the analysis period and recorded in the supporting accounting documents are as follows:

- Revenue from ticketing: € 13,200
- Publication revenue: € 2300
- Utilities: € 900
- Fixed term staff (i.e., Interns): € 1500 (P&P), € 2200 (C&E)
- Raw materials: € 700 (P&P), € 1000 (C&E)
- Equipment depreciations: € 2000 (M&R), € 300 (Administration), € 1000 (P&P for Printer depreciation), € 2000 (C&E)
- Permanent personal (i.e., Curator): € 800 (M&R); € 1800 (Administration); € 1000 (C&E)

Supporting information for the purpose of "transferring" the dummy and crosscutting centers' costs on the operational ones is reported in the following points:

- 560 hours of maintenance:
  - Administration: 140 h
  - P&P: 280 h (for printers, etc.)
  - C&E. 140 h
- 400 invoices issued in the analysis timespan.
  - P&P: 50
  - C&E: 350

The cost accounting report is shown below (Table 3.5).

According to the previous control report, an operating margin of € 300 is derived from the core cultural processes as well as from printing/publishing and other value-creating activities. It is unclear whether Alfa should continue to carry out collateral activities. The cost of the printer and the M&R allocated to printer activities are charged to the C&E in the event of quit publishing. According to the Alfa cost accounting report, it is best to continue with the collateral activities. Without them, the operational margin is lower (Table 3.6).

Table 3.5 "Alfa" cost accounting report

Responsibility centers	*Dummy Centre*	*Crosscutting Centre*	*Operational centers*		
"Alfa"	*M&R*	*Administration*	*P&P (collateral)*	*C&E (core)*	*Total*
Revenues			2300	13,200	15,500
Direct costs					
Utilities				900	900
Fixed term staff			1500	2200	3700
Raw materials			700	1000	1700
Contribution Margin			100	9100	9200
Indirect costs					
Equipment depreciations	2000	300	1000	2000	5300
Permanent personnel	800	1800		1000	3600
Total	*2800*	*2100*	*1000*	*3000*	*8900*
M&R transfer cost		*+700*	*+1400*	*+700*	
		2800	*2400*	*3700*	
Administration			*+350*	*+2450*	
transfer cost			*2750*	*6150*	
Operating margin			*−2650*	*2950*	*300*

Table 3.6 "Alfa" cost accounting report (without P&P)

Responsibility centers	*Dummy Centre*	*Crosscutting Centre*	*Operational centers*	
"Alfa"	*M&R*	*Administration*	*C&E (core)*	*Total*
Revenues			13,200	13,200
Direct costs				
Utilities			900	900
Fixed term staff			2200	2200
Raw materials			1000	1000
Contribution margin			9100	9100
Indirect costs				
Equipment depreciations	2000	300	3000 (including printers' depreciation)	5300
Permanent personnel	800	1800	1000	*3600*
Total	*2800*	*2100*	*4000*	*8900*
M&R transfer cost		*+700*	*+2100*	
		2800	*6100*	
Administration transfer cost			*+2800*	
			8900	
Operating margin			*200*	*200*

3.6 Final Remarks

This chapter has shed light on relevant managerial accounting issues for cultural organizations. Relating to ***how accounting contributes to the management of cultural organizations***, simulations have demonstrated the effectiveness of traditional accounting practices in enabling cultural organizations to gain a deeper understanding of and control over their internal dynamics. These results produce meaningful information for decision-making, considering the opportunities and critical issues resulting from changes in the socioeconomic environment.

Furthermore, the morphological and physiological characteristics of cultural organizations must be taken into account, whereas the challenge to face is ***how to design accounting systems to facilitate rational and responsible decision-making***. This requires teamwork between different professionals (such as accountants, consultants, curators, archive managers, social media managers, etc.) within or outside the organization's underpinned.

The empirical evidence analyzed has demonstrated that the managerial accounting system needs to be implemented gradually within the cultural organization to make its usefulness and functionality more understandable while taking into account the information needs of the stakeholders to whom the information flows are addressed. Moreover, managerial accounting knowledge should be extended to the various levels of the organizational structure so that useful ideas can be drawn from each of them to improve their efficiency and effectiveness. Within cultural organizations, engaging personnel in the refinement of the managerial accounting system and sharing its usefulness are critical to growing the managerial culture.

In relation to *the preconditions for starting such a process of building inter- or intraorganizational accounting knowledge*, the commitment of organizational leadership is a *conditio sine qua non* for the effectiveness of any managerial control system. It is essential to disseminate authoritatively the need to adopt managerial logics and technicalities to ensure good governance for any cultural organization. Therefore, capacity building on accounting must involve all the human resources responsible for governing and managing cultural heritage. For managerial accounting logic and tools to be institutionalized as social practices within the ecosystem of cultural heritage organizations, this is a fundamental precondition.

References

Adam, B., Mussari, R., & Jones, R. (2011). The diversity of accrual policies in local government financial reporting: An examination of infrastructure, art and heritage assets in Germany, Italy and the UK. *Financial Accountability & Management, 27*(2), 107–133.

Ahmad, U., Zahid, A., Shoaib, M., & AlAmri, A. (2017). HarVis: An integrated social media content analysis framework for YouTube platform. *Information Systems, 69*, 25–39.

Amit, R., & Zott, C. (2015). Crafting business architecture: The antecedents of business model design. *Strategic Entrepreneurship Journal, 9*(4), 331–350.

Anessi-Pessina, E., Caruana, J., Sicilia, M., & Steccolini, I. (2020). Heritage: The priceless hostage of accrual accounting. *International Journal of Public Sector Management, 33*(2/3), 285–306.

Bryson, J. M. (1988). A strategic planning process for public and nonprofit organizations. *Long Range Planning, 21*(1), 73–81.

Carnegie, G. D. (1996). Enabling accountability in museums. *Museum Management and Curatorship, 15*(4), 371–386.

Carnegie, G. D., Ferri, P., Parker, L. D., Sidaway, S. I., & Tsahuridu, E. E. (2022). Accounting as technical, social and moral practice: The monetary valuation of public cultural, heritage and scientific collections in financial reports. *Australian Accounting Review, 103*(32), 460–472.

Carnegie, G. D., & West, B. P. (2005). Making accounting accountable in the public sector. *Critical Perspectives on Accounting, 16*(7), 905–928.

Carnegie, G. D., & Wolnizer, P. W. (1995). The financial value of cultural, heritage and scientific collections: An accounting fiction. *Australian Accounting Review, 5*(9), 31–47.

DaSilva, C. M., & Trkman, P. (2014). Business model: What it is and what it is not. *Long Range Planning, 47*(6), 379–389.

Drucker, P. F. (1973). Managing the public service institution. *The Public Interest, 33*, 43.

Elo, S., & Kyngäs, H. (2008). The qualitative content analysis process. *Journal of Advanced Nursing, 62*(1), 107–115.

Ferri, P., Sidaway, S. I., & Carnegie, G. D. (2021). The paradox of accounting for cultural heritage: A longitudinal study on the financial reporting of heritage assets of major Australian public cultural institutions (1992–2019). *Accounting, Auditing & Accountability Journal, 34*(4), 983–1012.

Grant, J. (1994). On some public uses of planning 'theory': Rhetoric and expertise in community planning disputes. *The Town Planning Review, 65*, 59–76.

Imperiale, F. (2018). Il valore dei beni culturali nel patrimonio dello Stato Italiano. Angeli, Milano.

Kaplan, R. S., & Norton, D. P. (1992). The balanced scorecard—Measures that drive performance. *Harvard Business Review, 70*(1), 71–79.

Kaplan, R. S., & Norton, D. P. (2000). Having trouble with your strategy? Then, map it. *Focusing Your Organization on Strategy—With the Balanced Scorecard, 49*(5), 167–176.

Kaplan, R. S., & Norton, D. P. (2004). The strategy map: Guide to aligning intangible assets. *Strategy & Leadership, 32*(5), 10–17.

Koontz, H. (1958). A preliminary statement of principles of planning and control. *Academy of Management Journal, 1*(1), 45–61.

Leigh, D. (2009). SWOT analysis. In *Handbook of improving performance in the workplace: Volumes 1–3* (pp. 115–140). Wiley.

Magliacani, M., & Madeo, E. (2018). Exploring "culturalization" in rural entrepreneurial context through content analysis. *Knowledge and Process Management, 25*(4), 292–301.

Mintzberg, H. (1987). Crafting strategy. *Harvard Business Review, 65*, 66–75.

Mintzberg, H. (1990). The design school: Reconsidering the basic premises of strategic management. *Strategic Management Journal, 11*(3), 171–195.

Normann, R. (1977). *Management for growth*. John Wiley & Sons.
Normann, R. (2001). *Reframing business: When the map changes the landscape*. John Wiley & Sons.
Ozbekhan, H. (1969). Planning theory. *Ekistics, 28*, 296–299.
Parisi, C., & Hockerts, K. N. (2008). Managerial mindsets and performance measurement systems of CSR-related intangibles. *Measuring Business Excellence, 12*(2), 51–67.
Simon, H. A. (1979). Rational decision making in business organizations. *The American Economic Review, 69*(4), 493–513.

CHAPTER 4

Cultural Heritage and Sustainable Development: How Does Accounting Matter?

Abstract Cultural heritage and sustainability are two concepts increasingly associated in the literature. Reporting plays a significant role in monitoring the pursuit of goals, but what are the most efficient ways of reporting cultural performance? What accounting tools could be used to measure the degree of current achievement of sustainability goals? Is there a universally adoptable framework? Through a review of the literature, an analysis of the UNESCO Culture 2030 Indicators framework, and an analysis of the reporting tools used to measure the achievement of sustainability goals, these research questions will be addressed in this chapter through the analysis of five initiatives—Italian or European Capitals of Culture—as an example.

Keywords Cultural heritage • Sustainability • Accounting • Culture indicators • Capital of Culture

4.1 Introduction

Cultural heritage refers to the legacy left to future generations by a cohesive group of people who share identities, values, and symbols (Blake, 2000). It consists of material evidence, such as monuments,

M. Magliacani, V. Toscano, *Accounting for Cultural Heritage Management*, https://doi.org/10.1007/978-3-031-38257-4_4

archaeological sites, and objects, as well as intangible evidence, such as knowledge, techniques, and skills acquired over time (Prott & O'Keefe, 1992).

Although the contribution of cultural heritage to the socioeconomic development of a country is still often underestimated, and its potential is not always exploited effectively (Sciacchitano, 2015), due to the activities generated by it and the policies that protect and support it, it can also contribute to other sectors, such as education, employment, and tourism (Council of Europe, 2017). Consequently, protecting cultural heritage is considered crucial for the community. In any case, the active involvement of experts in the field or of public authorities is not sufficient: it needs to be complemented by the participation of the whole community (Fitri et al., 2015).

In addition, the role of culture is increasingly studied in the field of sustainability, where "*culture sustainability*" has begun to be addressed. The pursuit of Sustainable Development Goals must rely on the actions performed by humans, which are influenced by their culture. Therefore, sustainability studies must consider the latter (Soini & Dessein, 2016).

However, to evaluate the effectiveness of human-implemented processes in achieving these objectives, actions must be taken, and the results must be reported (Behn, 2003). Therefore, it is necessary to identify methods for measuring the performance of the cultural sector, including its contribution to sustainability.

The purpose of this chapter is to examine the relationship between the cultural sector and sustainable development and to identify its potential contribution to sustainability goals. Furthermore, it will critically analyze some of the existing and proposed methods of measuring sustainable cultural performance—both locally and internationally—to ascertain the most effective.

To achieve this goal, the sustainability indicators proposed by UNESCO will be presented, and the reporting methodologies used to represent the effectiveness of Italian and European Capitals of Culture projects will be discussed. Based on the analysis of five case studies, a conceptual model will be developed. Through the use of accounting, the factors deemed most important to improving the actions performed for achieving sustainability goals will be highlighted.

4.2 Culture for the Agenda 2030

In 2015, there was an agreement between all UN Member States to adopt the 2030 Agenda for Sustainable Development. It established a framework for action to combat poverty and inequality, promote peace and justice, and protect the environment. It consists of 17 Sustainable Development Goals (SDGs) and 169 subgoals that provide guidelines for achieving the main goals. The 2030 Agenda emphasizes the need for governments, citizens, businesses, organizations, the scientific community, and all stakeholders to participate actively in achieving sustainability (Carpentier & Braun, 2020; United Nations, 2015).

Although UNESCO advocated for the establishment of an SDG dedicated to culture within the 2030 Agenda—since it believed there was a need for a goal that would consider the importance of cultural heritage, diversity, creativity, and knowledge transmission and that would include and highlight the relationship between culture and the different dimensions of sustainable development—this did not happen (Culture 2030 Goal Campaign, 2019). Despite that, culture was considered in some of the other SDGs, as summarized in Table 4.1.

Table 4.1 Culture in 2030 Agenda

SDG	*Target*	*Content*
Sustainable cities and communities (SDG#11)	4	Strengthen efforts to protect and safeguard the world's cultural and natural heritage.
Quality education (SDG#4)	7	By 2030, ensure that all students acquire the knowledge and skills needed to promote sustainable development through education for sustainable development and sustainable lifestyles, human rights, gender equality, the promotion of a culture of peace and non-violence, global citizenship, the valorization of cultural diversity and the contribution of culture to sustainable development.
Decent work and economic growth (SDG#8)	9	By 2030, develop and implement policies to promote sustainable tourism, which creates jobs and promotes local culture and products.
Responsible consumption and production (SDG#12)	8b	Develop and implement tools to monitor the sustainable development impacts for sustainable tourism, that creates jobs and promotes local culture and products.

As a result, cultural heritage was only briefly mentioned, along with natural heritage, in objective #11. In addition, only the issue of its protection and preservation was discussed, without any consideration of its enhancement or regeneration (Nocca, 2017).

Due to this lack of inclusion in the 2030 Agenda, in 2015 UNESCO launched the "Culture for Sustainable Urban Development Initiative" to demonstrate the relevance of the implementation of the Conventions on Culture to the pursuit of global sustainability goals. A series of analyses and recommendations were presented in the UNESCO "Global Report on Culture for Sustainable Urban Development" to highlight the crucial role that culture plays in sustainable urban development. In fact, the document provides a comprehensive analysis of the relevance of safeguarding, preserving, and managing urban heritage, promoting creative and cultural industries, and emphasizing their value as resources for achieving the Sustainable Development Goals (Culture 2030 Goal Campaign, 2019).

In addition, it is believed that the absence of a specific SDG on culture is due to the contrasting views of different states regarding its role in sustainable development. It should be noted that not everyone agrees with the definition of culture presented by UNESCO, which sees it as a positive factor naturally predestined to make the world a better place. We can conclude from the analysis of reality that culture is not only associated with peace and harmony but also has a close relationship with conflicts. For example, not all cultures are accepted and recognized, as there are still groups of people who are forbidden to express themselves or indigenous people who are asked to forget and deny their cultural identity and to conform to a different national culture. It is, therefore, necessary to emphasize that there are indeed many aspects of sustainable development that involve and are positively influenced by culture but also that there are some in contrast. This paradox led to the skepticism of some states regarding its inclusion in the 2030 Agenda (Wiktor-Mach, 2020).

Therefore, it can be stated that there is a relationship between culture and sustainable development. Three main ways of relating the two factors have been identified in the literature. The first is the so-called culture in sustainable development, according to which culture is considered the fourth autonomous pillar of sustainable development, separate from the environmental, social, and economic aspects. In the second mode, culture is viewed as a force operating independently from the other three pillars, contextualizing them and acting as a mediator between them. The concept guides sustainable development between economic, social, and environmental needs arising from people's expectations and actions, which are influenced by their culture. According to the third mode, "culture as sustainable development," culture is a necessary foundation for achieving sustainable development. All decisions, actions, and mentalities of a community are rooted in its approach to sustainable development, thus negating the need for a distinction between economic, social, and environmental elements. However, these three relationships do not necessarily represent mutually exclusive approaches to interpreting and organizing values, meanings, and strategic norms concerning the relationship between culture and sustainable development (Dessein et al., 2015).

Culture plays a significant role in achieving the goals set out in the 2030 Agenda, which is why UNESCO has developed the "Thematic Indicators for Culture in the 2030 Agenda" (also referred to as "Culture 2030 Indicators"). This framework was designed to identify an appropriate methodology to demonstrate the role and contribution of culture to achieving the SDGs while providing policymakers with evidence and tools that can be used when making decisions and structuring policies and plans (UNESCO, 2019).

4.3 The European and Italian Guidelines

Over the past few decades, the importance of safeguarding and enhancing cultural heritage has grown at the EU level since it is associated with both people's cultural identity and their social values. There are several examples of this, including the 1954 "European Cultural Convention," which was approved by the Council of Europe, the 2003 UNESCO "Convention for the Safeguarding of Intangible Cultural Heritage," and the 2005 "Framework Convention on the Value of Cultural Heritage for Society," issued by the Council of Europe, which was also referred to as the "Faro Convention" (Montella et al., 2016).

The Faro Convention, in particular, defines cultural heritage as a complex system of resources inherited from the past that people identify, irrespective of ownership, as reflecting and expressing the constant evolution of values, knowledge, and traditions and that includes aspects of the environment that arise from the interaction between people and places over time. Specifically, the Convention acknowledges the presence of European cultural heritage and stresses the responsibility of the entire community, from governments to citizens, to protect and develop this heritage (Council of Europe, 2005). Moreover, it emphasizes that cultural heritage must be protected not only for its intrinsic value but also for its potential to generate economic and social value for the whole community if it is exploited. In this context, economics and sociology are not in opposition but rather converge, united by a desire to derive utility from the value of the assets that make up heritage. In addition to its relevance to the improvement of the quality of life, its value also derives from its importance in achieving the objectives of sustainable development (Montella et al., 2016). Nevertheless, the most significant novelty of the Faro Convention remains the right of everyone, by their personal choice, to encounter cultural heritage and to participate in the cultural life of their community. In this way, culture becomes a tool for collective engagement (Zagato, 2015).

Following the spirit of the Faro Convention, the European Commission has prepared the "New European Agenda for Culture," which aims to enhance society's understanding of cultural heritage by putting people and communities at the center and involving them in the decision-making process. Through research, experimentation, and practice, an increasing number of users have become interested in cultural heritage. This enables the development of creative methods for participation in the governance and management of cultural heritage. As a result, the Faro Convention can serve as a starting point for creating synergies between the various stakeholders involved in the process of cultural heritage regeneration. By identifying the process tools needed to activate and promote cultural heritage, we can implement behaviors that support the sustainable development of local territories and their communities (European Commission, 2020; Cerreta & Giovene Di Girasole, 2020).

However, it is important to note that there is still a lack of tools to assist in the evaluation of these processes, which should be able to enable communities to test the extent to which they can adapt to the principles enshrined in the Convention and to monitor their progress over time (Cerreta & Giovene Di Girasole, 2020). There is a digital platform, the Faro Convention Network, on which communities can check the progress of their objectives against the principles enshrined in the Convention and thus carry out a self-assessment. This provides for the analysis of both the actions implemented and the proactive involvement of the actors and allows for the adjustment of strategies if they are not proving efficient. The effectiveness of the evaluation depends on many subjective factors, among which can be identified issues related to the independence and representation of the actors involved in the process; therefore, it cannot be considered a suitable tool for evaluation purposes (Di Capua, 2021).

The Faro Convention was followed by further frameworks, documents, or recommendations on the management or protection of cultural heritage. For example, the European Parliament and the Council decided in May 2017 that 2018 should be the "European Year of Cultural Heritage." As part of the project, the European community was made aware of the importance of culture and cultural heritage from an economic and social perspective. Following the Commission's 2018 Communication "A New European Agenda for Culture," the "European Framework for Action on Cultural Heritage" was adopted. It aimed to include actions related to cultural heritage that have a common direction for all member countries in EU policies and can be considered to be in line with the "Recommendation of the Committee of Ministers to Member States on the European Cultural Heritage Strategy for the 21st Century," Agenda 2030, and "Sendai Framework for Disaster Risk Reduction 2015–2030" (European Commission, 2019).

Due to the outbreak of the COVID-19 pandemic, the European Union devised a recovery plan called *NextGenerationEU* (NGEU) to assist entrepreneurs and citizens of the EU or partner countries. To facilitate economic recovery and to repair social damage caused by the pandemic, this plan aims to make Europe more modern, sustainable, and resilient (European Commission, 2021). To be able to access *NextGenerationEU* European funds, Italy was required to prepare the National Recovery and Resilience Plan (PNRR), which set out the objectives, reforms, and investments that the state intended to implement thanks to European funding (Governo Italiano, 2021).

The Italian PNRR consists of 16 Components, which are grouped into 6 Missions. The latter are designed based on the pillars indicated in the PNRR Regulation and are (PNRR):

- Mission 1: Digitization, Innovation, Competitiveness, Culture, and Tourism;
- Mission 2: Green Revolution and Ecological Transition;
- Mission 3: Infrastructure for Sustainable Mobility;
- Mission 4: Education and Research;
- Mission 5: Cohesion and Inclusion;
- Mission 6: Health.

In this regard, Culture is a specific objective of Mission 1, which strives to relaunch the country economically and productively by increasing investment in the public administration, production system, tourism, and cultural sectors (PNRR).

The mission is in turn subdivided into three Components (PNRR):

1. Digitization, innovation, and security in PA;
2. Digitization, innovation, and competitiveness in the productive system;
3. Tourism and Culture 4.0.

The third Component, therefore, aims to modernize the infrastructure of the historical and artistic heritage, to make culture more usable and accessible—also through promotion and digitization activities—and to support the recovery of the cultural industry, always supporting the green and digital transition through works to increase energy efficiency and improve the organization of cultural events in terms of sustainability (PNRR). In addition, it is envisaged in the plan that interventions with the aim of digitizing cultural heritage will be prepared to make resources more accessible for all stakeholders (Ippolito, 2021). In the pursuit of this objective, the strong role to be played by public authorities will be flanked by that of the private sector, citizens, and the community, both in terms of funding, offering support through sponsorship, and the implementation of proactive, integrated, and participatory behaviors (PNRR). For example, innovative start-ups are envisaged to improve digital infrastructures at the national level (Ippolito, 2021).

The PNRR, however, indicates that only 455 million euros (from the total 222.1 billion allocated to the Plan) have been devoted to the cultural and creative sector. Of the 455 million devoted, 300 million will benefit the Cinecittà studios, and the remaining 155 will be used to support culture. Despite the state's budget, with less than 1% allocated to culture, the PNRR is nonetheless a boost for society. An effective management system and the preparation of streamlined procedures that can be implemented efficiently within a short period of time will certainly prove invaluable. The human capital and the specific skills of workers will therefore play a key role in the implementation of the PNRR, particularly their interpersonal skills (Ghia, 2022).

4.4 The UNESCO Culture 2030 Indicators

The Culture 2030 Indicators were prepared by UNESCO to measure and monitor progress on the contribution of culture to the implementation of the SDGs at both national and local levels. They can be applied voluntarily by different states, which are free to use them to verify the efficiency of their policies. Indicators involve the use of qualitative and quantitative data to obtain analytical results and to identify best practices that can be applied to achieve the desired results (UNESCO, 2019).

These indicators are considered successors to the Culture for Development Indicators Suite (CDIS), which was developed in 2009 by UNESCO with the support of the Spanish government. According to UNESCO's 1996 "Our Cultural Diversity Report" (UNESCO, 2019), the purpose of the report was to assess the contribution of culture to development as a component of the Millennium Development Goals (MDGs). Seventeen countries, including Italy, adopted the CDIS, which was based on an analysis of seven key dimensions: economy, education, governance, social, gender, communication, and legacy. A strength of these indicators was the need to incorporate into analysis data that were not normally included in national datasets. Through this approach, it was possible to study and investigate additional aspects that were generally not considered and to improve the quality of the evaluation (UNESCO, 2019; Cicerchia, 2016).

A revised set of indicators was developed by UNESCO following the endorsement of the 2030 Agenda and the identification of the Sustainable Development Goals (SDGs). In some cases, they are derived directly from CDIS, whereas in others, they are derived from scratch but benefit from past experience. During their preparation, the difficulties encountered in the application of the previous indicators were considered, and efforts were made to prevent them from recurring. Testing was scheduled to begin in January 2020 but did not take place as planned (UNESCO, 2019).

Twenty-two indicators were identified, and each one was defined, proposed, and calculated according to the guidelines. Indicators were developed to be applicable to all countries, regardless of their statistical capacity or data availability. The indicators are flexible and can be adapted based on the peculiarities of each country. Rather than comparing results between countries, the focus is on improving internal progress by self-assessing the objectives achieved by policies. Thus, the aim is more ambitious than normative. In addition, there is a desire to recognize opportunities for

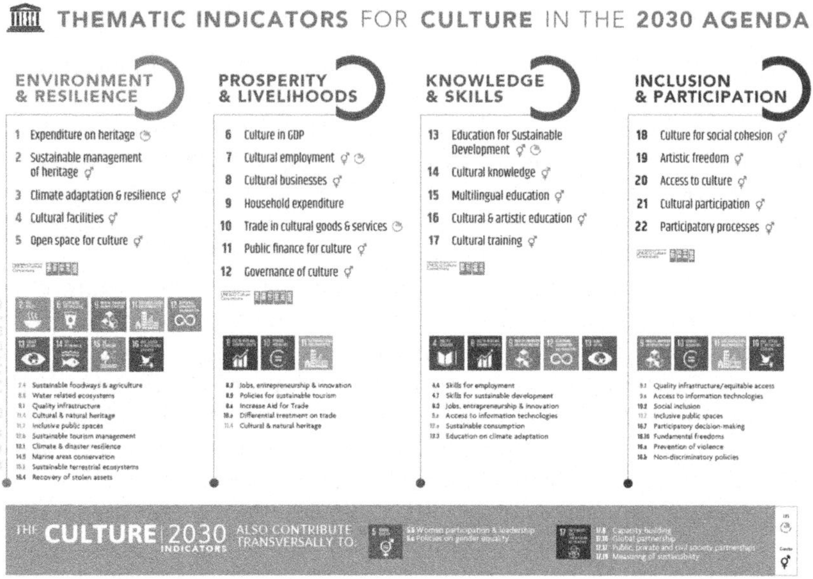

Fig. 4.1 Thematic indicators for culture in the 2030 Agenda. (Source: UNESCO, 2019, p. 2)

improvement rather than to focus on simply measuring achievements or failures in absolute terms (UNESCO, 2019).

The Culture 2030 Indicators have been divided into four thematic dimensions: Environment and Resilience, Prosperity and Livelihood, Knowledge and Skills, and Inclusion and Participation, which will now be analyzed (UNESCO, 2019).

Those indicators, together with the SDGs to which they refer, are summarized in Fig. 4.1.

A. *Environment & resilience*

This thematic dimension aims to assess the role and contribution of culture to sustainable development, focusing on cultural heritage, both tangible and intangible, and on natural heritage. The indicators, therefore, aim to measure the commitment of states to safeguarding heritage, which must demonstrate that they are adopting sustainable management and including culture in their planning. Specifically, the indexes of this dimension assess the contribution of culture to the pursuit of SDGs: 2. Zero hunger, 6. Clean water and sanitation, 9. Industry, innovation, and infrastructure, 11. Sustainable cities and communities, 12. Responsible consumption and production, 13. Climate action, 14. Life below water, 15. Life on land, and 16. Peace, justice, and strong institutions. There are five indicators belonging to this area, one of which is quantitative, and the remaining are qualitative. They will be described below (UNESCO, 2019):

1. Expenditure on heritage is the indicator which aims to illustrate whether the actions performed for safeguarding cultural and natural heritage by public authorities (also in partnership with the private sector and with civil society organizations) directly impact the sustainability of the cities where the heritage sites. It is the only quantitative indicator in the thematic area;
2. Sustainable management of heritage is a qualitative indicator consisting of a checklist aimed at investigating the role played by public action in protecting and promoting the sustainability of heritage. This is done by analyzing three groups of information: national and international registers containing lists of natural and cultural heritage assets; actions taken by authorities to safeguard and manage cultural heritage, which have an effect on all stakeholders and promote sustainability; and support offered by private individuals or associations in safeguarding and revitalizing heritage. The checklist contains some questions that need to be answered with numerical data and others with yes/no, and it analyzes both actions carried out at the national and at local levels;
3. Climate adaptation & resilience is an indicator that is intended to evaluate the measures taken to reduce climate change and increase resilience through the preservation and sustainable management of cultural and natural heritage. As a result, it measures the degree to which sustainable materials and techniques are employed in the country's construction practices. For historic cities, new construction should be aligned with the existing landscape without destroying it. Buildings that are visually harmonious with what is already present must also be environmentally friendly. For example, for this purpose, energy conservation measures such as solar panels can be installed. This checklist contains some questions that require numerical responses, while others require yes/no responses, and it is divided into two parts, one regarding resilience and climate

adaptation and the other concerning traditional knowledge and its role in increasing resilience;
4. Cultural facilities is an indicator that aims to assess the diversity of cultural facilities in a country and their distribution across the territory. It makes it possible to identify cultural areas and relate them to population, transport, administration, and economic centers. In particular, the index assesses how cultural facilities are integrated into the urban landscape and whether they provide a suitable environment for cultural events and the widespread presence of businesses and professionals. Facilities are evaluated based on their numerical presence in the considered area, their economic output, the public funding received, and the number of registered users, which are compared with reference values identified ex ante by UNESCO;
5. Open space for culture measures the number and size of open spaces available for cultural purposes, also assessing their nature and spread across the territory (UNESCO, 2019).

B. *Prosperity & livelihoods*

The second thematic dimension examines the contribution of culture to the increase in revenues and employment through the provision of cultural goods and services. These indicators analyze and demonstrate the contribution of culture to the achievement of SDG 8. Decent work and economic growth, 10. Reduce inequalities, and 11. Sustainable cities and communities. This thematic area comprises seven indicators, which will now be displayed with the same numbering used in the UNESCO document (UNESCO, 2019):

6. Culture in GDP, which assesses the percentage of gross domestic product attributable to the cultural sector. The criticality of this indicator is its inability to take into account the value of informal or nonpaying cultural activity;
7. Cultural employment, an index assessing the number of employees in the cultural and creative sector, as a percentage of total employment for the previous calendar year;
8. Cultural businesses, an indicator that looks at the number of businesses operating in the sector. However, it does not take into account the size of the enterprises, their productivity, or the number of their employees;

9. Household expenditure is an indicator that measures the percentage of household expenditures on cultural goods, services, or activities. It aims to identify the value that households recognize to culture by observing the transactions they decide to make in favor of cultural purchases and to assess the potential value of the local cultural market. It is important to note, however, that the index constructed in this manner does not capture all the value associated with the sector, as it excludes all the products that are not exchanged for money on the market from the calculation;
10. Trade in cultural goods & services, an index assessing the value of exports of cultural goods and services over the total exports. The data used are from the COMTRADE database for tangible goods and EBOPS (or equivalent for countries where it is not used) for services;
11. Public finance for culture is an indicator that shows the amount of public expenditure allocated to cultural and creative activities, including both disbursements and budget allocations. As part of this analysis, the amount set aside for each individual administrative unit, the type of planned expenditure (current or capital), the value of public expenditure per person, the sector of intervention, and the source (donations, taxes, central government allocations) are examined;
12. Governance of culture, an indicator that provides an overall view of the policies adopted by governments and the regulations in force relating to the activities of the cultural sector, must demonstrate that they are aimed at contributing to economic and social development and support for decision-making processes in the field of culture. The index is structured in the form of a checklist containing some questions to be answered with numerical data and others with yes/no (UNESCO, 2019).

C. *Knowledge & skills*

The third thematic dimension focuses on assessing the contribution of culture to the transmission of local cultural values, knowledge, skills, and a sense of responsibility, which can be achieved through processes, policies, and the dissemination of educational materials. The indicators aim to measure the level of commitment of authorities and institutions in the integration of cultural knowledge to enhance respect and appreciation of cultural diversity. There are five indicators, covering SDGs N. 4. Quality education, 8. Decent work and Economic Growth, 9. Industry, innovation and infrastructure, 12. Responsible consumption and production, and 13. Climate action. The indicators are the following (UNESCO, 2019):

13. Education for sustainable development, which aims to assess the extent to which global citizenship education, education for sustainable development, and cultural diversity education are incorporated into national education policies, curricula, teacher training, and student assessment;
14. Cultural knowledge examines how cultural knowledge influences sustainable development practices by focusing on cultural education and capacity-building programs. This checklist contains some questions that need to be answered with numerical data and others that need to be answered with yes/no responses;
15. Multilingual education, concerning the percentage of hours dedicated to multilingualism out of the total institutional hours dedicated to languages in primary and secondary education;
16. Cultural & artistic education, measuring the percentage of hours dedicated to cultural education during the first two years of secondary school compared to the total school hours;
17. Cultural training aims to measure the number of students enrolled in cultural and creative studies after secondary school by calculating their share of the total number of students enrolled in courses of study in the same grade (UNESCO, 2019).

D. *Inclusion & participation*

The last thematic dimension concerns measuring the contribution of culture in creating social cohesion, inclusion, and participation. It focuses on the possibilities of individuals to access cultural resources, participate in cultural life, and freely express their culture, including artistic and creative freedom. Its five indicators aim to assess the capacity of culture to stimulate the effective involvement of a country's population in public and community life and thus cover SDG N. 9. Industry, innovation, and infrastructure, 10. Reduce inequalities, 11. Sustainable cities and communities, and 16. Peace, justice, and strong institutions. Those indicators will be described below (UNESCO, 2019):

18. Culture for social cohesion, which evaluates intercultural tolerance (a measure of individuals who do not find it problematic having neighbors who are of a different cultural background), interpersonal trust (i.e., the percentage of individuals who claim to trust others), and perceptions of gender equality (evaluating whether the population believes there are gender differences in cultural, social, economic, and political opportunities between men and women in the country to which they belong);
19. Artistic freedom aims to measure the level of development of a sustainable environment for artists, focusing in particular on the regulatory point of view, employing a checklist containing some questions to be answered with numerical data and others with yes/no;
20. Access to culture measures the degree of accessibility of cultural facilities for those who could use them. The number of facilities of each type in each administrative district or province is then assessed, and the population living in that area is considered. The standard deviation of each facility is then calculated as an indicator of the measure of equity of distribution of facilities in the area;
21. Cultural participation, which aims to determine the number of visitors to cultural sites and facilities as well as analyze their trends. The aim is to identify the share of the population who participates in cultural events as well as the trend of this figure and to determine the extent to which people participate in cultural activities at home, as well as the role of online cultural activities;
22. Participatory processes, an indicator used to assess stakeholder participation in the development and implementation of cultural policies, programs, and initiatives. The calculation checklist includes some questions that require numerical data and others that require yes/no answers (UNESCO, 2019).

The Culture 2030 Indicators are designed to assist states in assessing the progress they have made in achieving sustainability goals on a national and local level. In light of this, institutions should not only observe individual data but also analyze their trend over time to determine whether the choices made have improved results and to ensure that culture continues to play a key role in the formulation of policies (UNESCO, 2019). Consequently, the indicators serve to provide an ex-post analysis of the contribution of culture to achieving the 2030 Agenda's goals. However, the figure is influenced by the particularities of each country, which must strive to limit how much of its culture may negatively affect the pursuit of sustainable development (Zheng et al., 2021).

Although it is generally agreed among states that there is a need for an instrument to measure the role of culture, some of them, for example, Estonia, are skeptical about its actual measurability; others, such as the Czech Republic or the Netherlands, believe that the application of UNESCO indicators in different ways in different nations may be a weak point of the framework and that, on the contrary, the harmonization of data is truly necessary, although they recognize that the demand for trade-offs is very costly from the point of view of coordination and homologation by national agencies in charge of measurement (Petti et al., 2020).

There are additional critical issues that can be noted regarding the Culture 2030 Indicators, such as the relationship between culture and sustainable development, as the question can be raised as to whether and how culture can contribute to sustainability. From these indicators, it is not possible, for example, to determine whether there are better working conditions or greater gender equality in the cultural sector, which would be expected to be more influenced by culture itself because it is closely related to it. Moreover, data collected for other purposes are often used for the assessment of sustainable development goals, which does not guarantee the same level of quality as that of data collected ad hoc. A proper measurement, in particular, that is carried out correctly, can increase the awareness of the role of culture in local sustainable development strategies and influence decision-making as well as the determination of the priority to be given to the various objectives to be pursued (Montalto et al., 2019). This is the only effective method for integrating the protection of cultural heritage with its economic and legal aspects (Inglese & Caragnano, 2022).

4.5 Accounting and Sustainability: Multiple Case Studies—The European and Italian Capital Cities of Culture

4.5.1 Overview

The idea of the establishment of a European City of Culture was born in 1985, thanks to the proposal of Melina Mercouri, Greek Culture Minister, who emphasized the relevance of culture, alongside the already recognized role of trade and economics, in the pursuit of the common goal of European integration (European Parliament et al., 2014). Her proposal was favorably accepted, and on June 13, 1985, the European Commission established that a European City of Culture would be named annually, with the aim of "highlighting the cultural wealth and diversity of the cities of Europe while emphasizing their shared cultural heritage and the vitality of the arts" (Council Resolution 85/C 153/02). The European City of Culture was subsequently renamed the European Capital of Culture by the Decision of the European Parliament and Council No. 1419/1999/EC of May 25, 1999, to highlight the richness, diversity, and common characteristics of European cultures. Every year since 2007, two European cities have been nominated as European Capitals of Culture (Aiello & Thurlow, 2006), and in 2014, an Italian city was selected: Matera, which was the European Capital of Culture 2019 along with Plovdiv, Bulgaria (Ministero della Cultura).

In Italy, based on the success of Matera's selection as the European Capital of Culture for 2019, it was suggested that it might be an excellent idea to propose the nomination of an Italian Capital of Culture. Specifically, it was established by the Decree of the Minister of Cultural Heritage and Activities and Tourism dated December 12, 2014, for the years 2016–2020, an initiative that was then proposed again for subsequent years. The objectives that the project set at the national level were offering support to the cultural sector—including through the granting of funding—to enhance cultural heritage; improving the cultural and tourist services offered; developing the cultural and creative industry; and spreading among the population the concept of culture as a factor that can ensure economic progress and greater social cohesion (Ministero della Cultura).

Being named the Italian Capital of Culture comes with strong responsibilities; it means pursuing public interest objectives, both locally and nationally. However, the first call for bids published for the awarding of the title of Italian Capital of Culture 2016 and 2017, which saw Mantua and Pistoia, respectively, as winners, did not include any request regarding the evaluation and measurement of the objectives achieved (Ministero dei Beni e delle Attività Culturali e del Turismo, 2015). In support of this, in the dossier prepared by Pistoia for its application, there is no reference to any performance measurement indicators (Comune di Pistoia, 2015).

An obligation has been placed on cities applying for the title of Italian Capital of Culture 2018: to mention in their candidacy dossier the goals they intend to achieve, both qualitatively and quantitatively, as well as the metrics they will use to measure the success of those goals (Ministero dei Beni e delle Attività Culturali e del Turismo, 2016). A performance measurement methodology, however, was not included in the criteria for awarding the title, as it was deemed necessary only for an ex-post evaluation. Additionally, no reference was made in the call to an obligation to use methods that were already available: those preparing the dossier may choose the method they deem most appropriate, even by building their own indicators (Ministero dei Beni e delle Attività Culturali e del Turismo, 2016).

The pursuit of sustainability as outlined in the UN 2030 Agenda for Sustainable Development was first included in the call for nominations for the Italian Capital of Culture 2021. Additionally, stated in that document was that the consistency of the proposed program with the SDGs was a criterion for selecting the city (Ministero per i Beni e le Attività Culturali e per il Turismo, 2019).

According to Article 183, paragraph 8, of Decree-Law No. 34 of 19 May 2020, there has been no nomination of an Italian Capital of Culture for 2021 as a result of the outbreak of the COVID-19 pandemic. Parma, which was awarded the title of Capital of Culture 2020, has retained the title for 2021 as well (Ministero per i Beni e le Attività Culturali e per il Turismo, 2020). The ongoing procedure for 2021 then decreed the winner for 2022: Procida, which was also the first to be evaluated based on its commitment to the pursuit of sustainability goals (Ministero della Cultura, 2021a). The reference to the initiative's necessary contribution to the achievement of the SDGs also remained present in subsequent calls (Ministero per i Beni e le Attività Culturali e per il Turismo, 2021). As a consequence, it is expected that candidacy dossiers filed after 2021 will also include references to SDG achievement as part of their ex-post assessment.

4.5.2 *Methodology*

The research included the analysis of the candidacy and, where present, evaluation dossiers of Matera (European Capital of Culture 2019) and of four Italian Capitals of Culture: Palermo (2018), Parma (2020+21), Procida (2022), and Bergamo and Brescia (2023). Those cities have been selected for this study because the call for the Capital of Culture 2018 nomination, won by Palermo, was the first to require performance indicators to be included in the candidacy dossier. It was therefore decided to start from the analysis of this city's performance and to continue with a longitudinal analysis of all the Capitals of Culture nominated in Italy after it, which have already made public at least their candidacy dossier (case of Bergamo and Brescia 2023). Although Pesaro has already been proclaimed as the Italian Capital of Culture 2024 (Ministero della Cultura, 2021b), its dossier has not yet been released.

Specifically, the study seeks to verify the existence of performance indicators in the considered reports, highlighting the presence of accounting indicators. Text analysis (Lacity & Janson, 1994) was used for this purpose.

Palermo was chosen as the Italian Capital of Culture before the Culture 2030 Indicators were published, and the initiative was evaluated in the year of their publication. In this regard, there were surely no plans to develop a system of performance measurement similar to the one used by UNESCO. Instead, UNESCO's recommendations were compared with the measures and targets proposed by the other Capitals of Culture.

In addition, a content analysis was implemented (Harwood & Garry, 2003), which focused on identifying, within the dossiers, the indicators proposed by the cities for measuring the cultural and sustainable performance of the activity they carried out (or will carry out) during the initiative.

Moreover, any similarities between the indicators set out in the dossiers and the Culture 2030 Indicators proposed by UNESCO were investigated, and a comparative analysis was carried out to highlight differences between the reports prepared by Matera, the European Capital of Culture, and the Italian Capitals of Culture.

Finally, *Sketch Engine* software was used to highlight the most important elements of the Capitals of Culture projects in terms of sustainable performance measurement. In this analysis, the following variables were considered: Palermo's performance in 2018, Matera's evaluation in 2019, Parma's relevant themes in 2020+21, Procida's strategic objectives in 2022, and Bergamo and Brescia's performance in 2023. By using the "*Frequencies*" function, the software created a table, from which prepositions, articles, conjunctions, adverbs, pronouns, and the names of the evaluated cities were removed to construct Table 4.14. Its results have been discussed to understand which concepts are, to date, most relevant for evaluating the sustainability of the "Capital of Culture" initiatives in Italy.

4.5.3 Results

Palermo—Italian Capital City of Culture 2018

As requested in the call for nominations, in the candidacy dossier prepared by the city of Palermo—nominated the Italian Capital of Culture 2018—there is a reference to the monitoring of the actions put in place for achieving the set objectives. However, measurement methods are not defined in the dossier: there is only a mention that useful indicators for monitoring were going to be defined later and that each action implemented will have a measuring indicator (Comune di Palermo, 2016). The ex-post evaluation of the effects of Palermo as the Italian Capital of Culture on the territory and stakeholders was carried out by the "Human Foundation Do&Think Tank for Social Innovation," commissioned by the "Sant'Elia Foundation," which was conferred by the City of Palermo the responsibility for the management and implementation of the project. For the evaluation, quantitative and qualitative data collected through questionnaires submitted to stakeholders or through focus groups were analyzed (Human Foundation, 2019).

In particular, the ROI (Return on Investment) index on the institutional communication of the initiative was calculated, and the results achieved in the interest of stakeholders were evaluated, focusing on the project partners. To this end, the following variables were analyzed: the types of organizations involved; the economic contribution offered by the partners; the evaluation of their contribution and the number of initiatives in which they were involved; the funding they accessed; their degree of collaboration and satisfaction; the channels used to promote the partners' initiatives; the increase in their visibility; the increase in relations between local cultural institutions and between them and the local government; the strengthening of the partners' network within the sector; and the evaluation of the integration, diversification, and increase in local cultural offerings (Human Foundation, 2019). The application of an accounting indicator for measuring cultural performance (ROI) must be highlighted.

Concerning the outputs related to territorial development in terms of tourism and considering the historical trend of the data collected, the following variables were evaluated: the number of accommodations available; the number of restaurant activities; the activities of travel agencies, tour operators and reservation services and related activities; the presence of creative, artistic, and entertainment activities; and the activities of libraries, archives, museums, and other cultural activities. Moreover, an analysis of data on tourists was performed (considering their age, education level, occupation, spending during the visit, and their opinions on the experience in Palermo) and on the local population, who were asked whether the initiative strengthened their sense of belonging to the area and their knowledge of the city's cultural value (Human Foundation, 2019).

Palermo's performance measurement does not directly consider the pillars of sustainability but instead focuses on the interests of stakeholders. Even though the evaluation was published after the approval of the 2030 Agenda, the latter did not have any effect on the initiative's goals or measurement of its outcomes. This is probably because it was not requested by the Ministry of Culture as well. The evaluation report can, however, be indirectly used for the purpose of analyzing the economic, social, and cultural sustainability of the initiative by performing a content analysis, as summarized in Tables 4.2 and 4.3. The absence of environmental indicators for the initiative must also be highlighted.

Matera—European Capital City of Culture 2019

The Matera European Capital of Culture 2019 candidacy dossier highlights that the program is based on two key projects: the Demo-Ethno-Anthropological Institute (I-DEA) and the Open Design School (ODS). The former aims to network (literally and metaphorically) Basilicata's innumerable archives to make unique, vast, and deep knowledge more accessible. The Open Design School, on the other hand, aspires to leave a rich legacy of knowledge, entrepreneurship, initiative, and the permanent inclusion of Matera in a broader European system of innovation-based institutions and networks. The initiative's "Open Future" slogan implies the opportunity to create an open culture in all its many forms: as "accessible to all," not obscurantist to thoughts and sensibilities, and "available for dialog" (Comitato Matera 2019, 2018).

The Committee of Matera 2019's approach to monitoring and evaluation is linked to the central goals shown in the dossier and the capacity-building strategy adopted. Its intention is to strengthen the research capacity of the cultural sector of the city and region, in collaboration with the University of Basilicata, by developing training courses on monitoring and evaluating cultural policies. Matera European Capital of Culture 2019 was expected to help in changing the attitudes and approaches toward evaluating the effects of cultural events in Matera, Basilicata, the *Mezzogiorno*, and the whole country (Comitato Matera 2019, 2018).

Table 4.2 Palermo 2018 sustainability indicators (pt.1)

Performance	*Measurement*	*Sustainability*
Access for partners to forms of fundings for PCC	Questionnaire (yes, source is specified/ no)	Economic sustainability
Collaboration among partners	Questionnaire (rating 1 to 5)	Economic sustainability
Good organization of PCC	Questionnaire (rating 1 to 5)	No reference, but it can assess economic sustainability
PCC's contribution to increasing the visibility of partners and their initiatives	Questionnaire (rating 1 to 5)	No reference, but it can assess economic sustainability
PCC's contribution to increasing available information about partners and their initiatives	Questionnaire (rating 1 to 5)	No reference, but it can assess economic sustainability
PCC's contribution to organizing relationships between different cultural institutions	Questionnaire (rating 1 to 5)	No reference, but it can assess social, cultural, and economic sustainability
PCC's contribution to organizing relations between cultural institutions and local government	Questionnaire (rating 1 to 5)	No reference, but it can assess social sustainability
Influence of participation in PCC on expanding the network of partner contacts	Questionnaire (rating 1 to 5)	No reference, but it can assess economic sustainability
Influence of participation in PCC on creating and/or participating in new opportunities to meet and collaborate with the cultural institutions involved	Questionnaire (rating 1 to 5)	No reference, but it can assess economic sustainability
Influence of participation in PCC on the creation of new formal partnerships with the cultural institutions involved	Questionnaire (rating 1 to 5)	No reference, but it can assess economic sustainability
PCC's contribution in making its institution and initiatives more deeply rooted in the local community	Questionnaire (rating 1 to 5)	No reference, but it can assess social and cultural sustainability
PCC's contribution in creating a sense of belonging to a common local cultural scene among the institutions/ organizations involved	Questionnaire (rating 1 to 5)	No reference, but it can assess social and cultural sustainability
Partners' awareness of the importance of networking	Questionnaire (rating 1 to 5)	No reference, but it can assess economic sustainability
Partners' intention to participate in future projects/initiatives based on PCC's partnership model	Questionnaire (rating 1 to 5)	No reference, but it can assess economic and cultural sustainability

Table 4.3 Palermo 2018 sustainability indicators (pt.2)

Performance	*Measurement*	*Sustainability*
Enhancement of local cultural offerings (integration, diversification, increase)	Questionnaire (rating 1 to 5)	No reference, but it can assess social and cultural sustainability
Presence of accommodation activities	Trend (2015–2018) of the number of available accommodations	No reference, but it can assess economic sustainability
Presence of food services	Trend (2015–2018) of the number of food service activities operating	No reference, but it can assess economic sustainability
Presence of activities related to tourist flows	Trend (2015–2018) of the number of travel agencies, tour operators and reservation services, and related activities	No reference, but it can assess economic sustainability
Presence of recreational and cultural activities	Trend (2015–2018) of the number of creative, artistic, and entertainment activities	No reference, but it can assess economic and cultural sustainability
	Trend (2015–2018) of the number of libraries, archives, museums, and other activities	No reference, but it can assess cultural sustainability
Direct expenditure incurred by tourists participating in PCC	Calculation of estimates of expenditure on overnight stays, meals, and transportation per visitor (information collected through questionnaires and focus groups)	No reference, but it can assess economic sustainability
The direct economic impact of PCC	= (New attendance recorded in 2018 × 0.25) × (Overnight spending + Meal spending + Transportation spending)	No reference, but it can assess economic sustainability
Propensity to spend for visitors residing in Palermo, in the Metropolitan City	Calculating estimates of expenditure on meals and transportation	No reference, but it can assess economic sustainability

(*continued*)

Table 4.3 (continued)

Performance	*Measurement*	*Sustainability*
Willingness to pay for cultural initiatives carried out free of charge	Questionnaire (indicated the amount people are willing to pay)	No reference, but it can assess economic sustainability
PCC's influence on increased knowledge of the cultural value of the city and/or its territory	Questionnaire submitted to tourists divided between tourists from other Sicilian provinces, other Italian provinces, EU countries, and non-EU countries (rating from 1 to 5)	No reference, but it can assess social and cultural sustainability
Satisfaction of tourists regarding the visiting experience	Questionnaire submitted to tourists divided among tourists from other municipalities in the Metropolitan City of Palermo, other Sicilian provinces, other Italian provinces, EU countries, and non-EU countries (rating from 1 to 5)	No reference, but it can assess economic sustainability
Increased knowledge of residents about the cultural value of the city and/or its territory	Questionnaire submitted to residents, divided between residents in Palermo and other municipalities of the Metropolitan City (rating from 1 to 5)	No reference, but it can assess social and cultural sustainability
Increased sense of belonging to the city and its territory	Questionnaire submitted to residents, divided between residents in Palermo and other municipalities in the Metropolitan City (rating from 1 to 5)	No reference, but it can assess social and cultural sustainability

Notes: PCC 2018 = Palermo Italian Capital of Culture 2018

The candidacy dossier explicitly states that it intends to assess the expected medium-long-term effects based on the dimensional themes outlined in the report "An international framework of good practices in research and delivery of the European Capital of Culture program" and the indicators associated with them:

1. Cultural vibrancy
2. Access to culture and participation
3. Cultural citizenship
4. Identity and image of the place
5. Philosophy and process management
6. European dimension
7. Economic impacts and processes

(a) Cultural tourism and its allied industries
(b) Employment and value creation by the cultural sector of creative industries in Matera and Basilicata
(c) Ability of the city and region to attract business and investments
(d) The city and region's ability to address the problem of brain drain.

Furthermore, considering the importance of tourism in Matera, surveys are also expected to be conducted to estimate the increase in tourist flows compatible with sustainable tourism for the city to prevent the massification of arrivals in locations that would not be able to cope with too high loads. Thus, the impacts of Matera 2019 on the length of stay of visitors from other parts of Italy and the world, as well as on the development of tourism infrastructure, will also be examined (Comitato Matera 2019, 2018).

According to the candidacy dossier, monitoring and evaluation activities would have to address additional dimensional issues closely related to the centrality of the cultural inhabitant, in particular:

1. Development of skills and social capital
2. Increase in active citizenship
3. Involvement of volunteers
4. Environmental sustainability of the project
5. Use and effects of social media
6. Impacts of the bid on urban renewal
7. Candidacy's impacts on schools and other educational activities

A clear objective of the initiative is to foster transparency and publicity, as it intends to make public not only financial management data but also all monitoring and evaluation data to facilitate dissemination and knowledge among all stakeholders and researchers (Comitato Matera 2019, 2018).

In the Candidacy Dossier, the objectives identified have been divided into several evaluative domains, for which one or more studies have been conducted to analyze in a structured and systematic manner the legacy of Matera 2019 in various dimensions. Each evaluative study was conducted by a different research team using a different evaluation methodology. In Tables 4.4 and 4.5, the Matera 2019 evaluation approach is summarized (Fondazione di partecipazione Matera-Basilicata 2019, 2021).

Table 4.4 Matera 2019 sustainability studies (pt. 1)

Evaluation scope	*Evaluation study*	*Methodology*
Impacts on the economy and tourism	The economic impact of Matera European Capital of Culture 2019. The 2014–2019 exploit, the risks after 2020: new challenges in Matera and Basilicata	The methodology used involves multipliers based on intersectoral tables of the economy to estimate the value of the economic impact generated by three channels identified ex-ante: spending by tourists, investment by the Matera-Basilicata 2019 Foundation, and private investment in the upgrading of accommodation, particularly in the renovation of accommodations for tourism purposes. The study also applies a comparative analysis, both at the European level—on the increase in tourism recorded in Matera and other European Capitals of Culture—and at the national level, comparing this event to what usually occurs in cities of art.
The cultural production in Matera. Effects and impacts on strengthening cultural and creative supply chains	The effects of Matera 2019 on the local skills system	The applied methodology involved a mixed approach based on qualitative and quantitative techniques and tools. Quantitative data collection took place through the distribution of an online questionnaire to a selection of actors identified on the intensity and significance of then involvement in cultural program activities. Qualitative data collection, aimed at validating information collected through the questionnaire, took place through a focus group attended by local cultural actors.
	The effect of original productions on the supply chains involved	The methodology adopted relies on quantitative analysis of the total economic volume generated by the Foundation and the Lucanian creative scene involved in the implementation of the cultural program, and of Excelsior-Unioncamere databases analyzed through the lens of ATECO codes. Information concerning the origin of cultural workers was also collected and analyzed.
	Project Leaders and Matera 2019—experience, entrepreneurial development, and social innovation	The study is a qualitative analysis developed through the case study approach, involving five project leaders identified as the object of investigation and in-depth study. Documentary research and in-depth interviews conducted with each of the project leaders, from September 2019 to March 2020, were used to develop the research.
	The Open Design School—living lab for the development of skills and entrepreneurship—is focused on supplier companies.	The analysis was developed according to an exploratory approach, employing qualitative research based on extensive documentary research and interviews with several key suppliers and professionals, who collaborated on the realization of some projects with the ODS and its manager.

Table 4.5 Matera 2019 sustainability studies (pt. 2)

Evaluation scope	*Evaluation study*	*Methodology*
Matera 2019 and access to culture	Audience survey: a study on the experience and the perceived benefits of Matera 2019	The study concerns an empirical analysis based on the quantitative analysis of two databases. The first includes information collected through the distribution of questionnaires to the public during three events in the concluding period of the Matera 2019 event. Audience segmentation was obtained through ACP (principal component analysis) and CA (cluster analysis). The second database analyzed was constructed using data collected during the survey "The experience of 2019 and the legacy of the European Capital of Culture—the point of view of tourists and residents" carried out by Datacontact srl. Based on the available information, the estimate of the benefits associated with the enjoyment of some specific events was obtained through DAP (willingness to pay) and VC (contingent valuation); the estimate of the benefits associated with the enjoyment of Matera 2019 as a whole was computed through TCM (travel cost method).
	Passport to Matera 2019. Analysis of purchasing and fruition behavior	This quantitative analysis studies the TicketOne database related to the ticketing management software (which the Matera-Basilicata 2019 Foundation used to manage the Passport to Matera 2019) to build a set of synthetic evaluation indicators. The Passport to Matera 2019 is then compared with five other similar tools proposed in Italy in previous years to encourage the integrated fruition of tourism and culture, to assess its scalability, level of integration with other services related to tourism or visiting art sites or transportation and potential value in terms of audience enlargement.

(*continued*)

Table 4.5 (continued)

Evaluation scope	*Evaluation study*	*Methodology*
The Matera 2019 model: co-creation and the active participation of citizens	Co-create in Matera	This study fits in the social research framework, from which the main quantitative and qualitative methodological tools used were taken: a closed questionnaire distributed on a regional scale, a semi-structured interview with a sample composed of key informants internal to the design/implementation of the event projects; and a focus group carried out with the participation of the ODS group. The research also involved the construction of some indicators, modeled on six dimensions identified after a preliminary literature review in the field of cultural impact assessment: active participation, co-creation, social relations, empowerment well-being, and resilience.
Matera 2019: The transformative impact on urban spaces	The event spaces and events in space	The study fielded a punctual and georeferenced mapping work capable of detecting and reconstructing the processes of the city, conducting an analysis starting from the study of the event venues, selecting more than 150 spaces from the mapping done in the "Venues of Matera" platform created by the ODS and deepening some aspects of spatial investigation relevant to urban analysis techniques.
Matera 2019 and its legacy	Role and future functions of the Matera-Basilicata 2019 Foundation	The study is based on a benchmarking analysis with other European Capitals of Culture and on an in-depth listening activity with 36 interviews aimed at stakeholders involved in various ways in the Matera 2019 project (representatives of the Foundation's component institutions; representatives of the project leaders and the Lucanian creative scene and civil society; citizens who have taken part in co-creation processes, artists, and observers of international caliber). It was precisely this wide range of voices, called upon to comment on what had happened during 2019, that enabled the evaluator to build an overview of the role played by the Foundation, highlighting the strengths and weaknesses that an entity such as the Foundation has encountered during its work, and at the same time to develop recommendations on the role and functions it could play after 2019.

The candidacy dossier did not explicitly mention sustainability goals (the term sustainability is not frequently mentioned in the text); however, the studies conducted can also highlight the event's economic, social, environmental, and cultural sustainability. Several indicators were calculated for each study, including accounting indicators.

Parma—Italian Capital City of Culture 2020+21
The candidacy dossier for Parma Italian Capital of Culture 2020 emphasizes the central role of investments in culture recognized by the city. The initiative is based on solid project lines, monitoring practices, and expectancies for a concrete return that leaves structures, methodologies, and cultural systems alive and capable of generating, communicating, and sustaining themselves. In particular, it is based on the principles of inclusion and sustainability (Comune di Parma, 2019).

Its goals are aligned with the previous statements. In fact, the four identified objectives are as follows:

1. Public–private: stabilize public–private collaboration aimed at cultural production, raising cultural consumption among young people, and entrenching the culture of creativity as a driver of growth in the entrepreneurial system;
2. Promoting creative-driven entrepreneurship: activating a broad and virtuous relationship between cultural action, market, and third sector to produce a quality rise in work time, configuring it as a time of well-being;
3. Making the cultural tourism system accessible: defining a set of services and technological tools that systematize the enhancement of resources, being aligned with the values of hospitality for all;
4. Promote international reflection on Culture and Democracy: establish a workshop for reflection on civil and constitutional values, aiming for an inclusive community that sees the cultural heritage of territories as a space for the rooting of democratic principles and values (Comune di Parma, 2019).

Parma faced additional challenges following the outbreak of the COVID-19 pandemic. As an example, it had to develop strong digital infrastructure during the lockdown period to maintain access to culture (Guerra, 2021).

The Parma 2020+21 program was designed to serve as a culturally based strategic plan for the development of the territory. The document, developed by a team of multidisciplinary professionals from the City of Parma and the Fondazione Promo PA, incorporates European guidelines for cultural transition and the 2030 Agenda for Sustainable Development into a proposal that aims to produce long-term effects. This is also reflected in the monitoring and evaluation system designed for Parma 2020+21, where the tool identified is a composite data collection system that seeks to assess the impact of cultural investments and activities against Sustainable Development Goals through two different checklists for all Program initiatives. Additionally, included are assessments of the performance of the years 2019–2022 and the creation and implementation of a database that can be used annually to align sector policies. Additionally, these data could be used to develop new projects for financing by national and European funds, as well as by the Italian PNRR, which increasingly rewards integrated approaches (Velani, 2021).

The methodology for monitoring, measuring, and reporting on the social, environmental, and governance impacts generated by the culture that Parma 2020+21 seeks to adopt is decidedly innovative and hopefully an example for other future cultural programs. The methodology adopted is based on three main inspirational frameworks:

1. Specific KPIs inspired by the UNESCO framework (Culture | 2030 Indicators) aimed at measuring and monitoring the contribution of culture to the national and local implementation of the SDGs of the 2030 Agenda, analyzing both the role of culture as a sector of activity and the crosscutting contribution that culture can make in different areas related to the SDGs. They, therefore, aim to look specifically at the impacts generated by the program and culture on the territory, the environment, and society;
2. The Guidelines for the Preparation of the Social Report of Third Sector Entities, adopted by Decree July 4, 2019, by the Ministry of Labor and Social Policy;
3. Where applicable, information is required following a selection of the GRI Sustainability Reporting Standards (GRI-referenced claims) published in 2016 by the Global Reporting Initiative (GRI), which allow for comparability of information with what other organizations of the same sector have published, or on a time scale (Brambilla & Ghilardi, 2021).

With the application of the Culture 2030 Indicators, Parma 2020+21 is considered a "pioneering" project in Italy for measuring and reporting the impacts of cultural programs. All of these indexes were analyzed, and only the ones that were most relevant to the reality of Parma Italian Capital of Culture were selected and applied. In many cases, the calculation methods and KPIs proposed by UNESCO were rethought, owing to the specificities of that cultural program, which had defined timeframes, and, consequently, different characteristics than the public and political contexts, which are the principal applications of the framework.

Compared to what was initially decided, the Impact Report indicates that the survey method has also been adopted for the 12 domains that comprise the observation panel of the BES project for the measurement of Equitable and Sustainable Well-being, which was formulated by ISTAT and published on December 27, 2010 (in its tenth edition in 2021) (Brambilla & Ghilardi, 2023).

This information includes not only the activities and initiatives carried out within the framework of the dossier but also those promoted by third parties with the coordination of the Committee for Parma 2020. Approximately 270 checklists were sent to those responsible for projects, including the City of Parma, with a response rate of 55% (Brambilla & Ghilardi, 2023).

The content to be reported was selected, as suggested by the GRI Standards Principles (GRI 3: 2021), based on the results of a materiality analysis conducted in a "desk mode" and shared with the organizers and key stakeholders of the program. This analysis allowed the identification of relevant aspects of Parma 2020+21 and its stakeholders, which were measured and reported and classified under the four pillars identified by the UNESCO framework (Brambilla & Ghilardi, 2023).

Tables 4.6, 4.7, 4.8, and 4.9 show the different thematic indicators defined by UNESCO and adopted by Parma 2020+21, for each of which the KPIs monitored and reported are illustrated. The data were collected through the checklists, except for the economic data, which were based on information taken from the Parma 2020 Budget Committee (Brambilla & Ghilardi, 2023).

Procida—Italian Capital City of Culture 2022

As evident from the Procida Italian Capital of Culture 2022 candidacy dossier, the project was influenced by the United Nations 2030 Agenda, as highlighted by the inclination of the missions to pursue the 17

Table 4.6 Parma 2020+21 sustainability indicators—environment and resilience

Pillar 1: Environment and resilience

Relevant theme	*Related SDGs*	*UNESCO indicator*	*Data collection*	*GRI indicators*	*BES domain*
Creating quality infrastructure	2, 6, 9, 11, 12, 13, 14, 15, 16	1. Expenditure on heritage	Checklist	GRI 203-2, a), b), GRI 205-3	Landscape, cultural heritage
Protection and enhancement of artistic and cultural heritage		2. Sustainable management of heritage	Checklist, desk analysis, periodic institutional surveys	GRI 205-3, GRI 403-7, a)	Landscape, cultural heritage
Environmental responsibility		3. Climate adaptation and resilience	Checklist	GRI 302-4, b), GRI 305-5, d), GRI 306-2, a)	Environment
Supporting sustainable tourism		4. Cultural facilities	Checklist	N/A	Landscape, cultural heritage
		5. Open space for culture	Desk analysis	N/A	Landscape, cultural heritage

Source: Translated from Brambilla and Ghilardi (2023, p. 58)

Sustainable Development Goals. The actions and events organized for the initiative, especially those aimed at the younger generation, are all sustainability-oriented, balancing the three dimensions of sustainable development indicated by the United Nations (environmental, social, and economic) while emphasizing gender equality and women's empowerment. The Plan for the Sustainable Management of Cultural Events makes direct reference to some of the SDGs that inspired the Organizing Committee when planning the event: 4. Quality Education, 6. Clear water and sanitation, 7. Affordable and clean energy, 11. Sustainable cities and communities, 12. Responsible consumption and production, and 14. Life below (Comune di Procida, 2021).

Furthermore, the project Committee has chosen to align it with some of the objectives of the South 2030 Plan—presented by the Minister for the South and Territorial Cohesion in Gioia Tauro on February 14, 2020—and intends to respond, through its actions, to the invitation of the

Table 4.7 Parma 2020+21 sustainability indicators—prosperity and livelihoods

Pillar 2: Prosperity and livelihoods					
Relevant theme	*Related SDGs*	*UNESCO indicator*	*Data collection*	*GRI indicators*	*RES domain*
Generation of direct, indirect, and induced economic impacts Promotion of local food and wine culture	8, 10, 11	6. Culture in GDP	Checklists, desk analysis, periodic institutional surveys	2-6 a), b) i, ii GRI 203-2 a); b)	Economic well-being
Job creation		7. Cultural employment	Checklist	GRI 2-7 a) GRI 2-8 a) GRI 405-1 a); i	Labor, work-life balance
		8. Cultural businesses	Not applicable due to the characteristics of the Parma 2020+21 Program and incomparability with previous periods or similar events		
Innovation and progress		9. Household expenditure	Not applicable due to the characteristics of the Parma 2020+21 Program and incomparability with previous periods or similar events		
		10. Trade in cultural goods & services	Not applicable due to the characteristics of the Parma 2020+21 Program and incomparability with previous periods or similar events		
		11. Public finance for culture	Desk analysis	N/A	Landscape, cultural heritage
		12. Governance of culture	Desk analysis	GRI 405-1 b); i	Policy and institutions

Source: Translated from Brambilla and Ghilardi (2023, p. 64)

Italian Government to cocreate a different future for the southern regions (Comune di Procida, 2021).

The Procida 2022 program wanted to emphasize the centrality of the "cultural citizenship" concept. The cultural program proposed was intended to trigger a self-generative flow of learning, involvement, and

Table 4.8 Parma 2020+21 sustainability indicators—knowledge and skills

Pillar 3: Knowledge and Skills					
Relevant theme	*Related SDGs*	*UNESCO indicator*	*Data collection*	*GRI indicators*	*BES domain*
Accessibility to culture and information	4, 8, 9, 12, 13	13. Education for sustainable development	Indicator still being developed by UNESCO		
		14. Cultural knowledge	Checklists, desk analysis	N/A	Innovation, research, creativity
		15. Multilingual education	Checklists, desk analysis	N/A	Social relations
Enhancement and development of human and cultural capital		16. Cultural & artistic education	Checklist	N/A	Education, learning
		17. Cultural training	Checklist	N/A	Education, learning

Source: Translated from Brambilla and Ghilardi (2023, p. 67)

Table 4.9 Parma 2020+21 sustainability indicators—inclusion and participation

Pillar 4: Inclusion and participation					
Relevant theme	*Related SDGs*	*UNESCO indicator*	*Data collection*	*GRI indicators*	*BES domain*
Social cohesion	9, 10, 11, 16	18. Culture for social cohesion	Desk analysis	GRI 406-1	Social relations
Promotion of expression freedom		19. Artistic freedom	Desk analysis	N/A	Personal well-being
Diversity, inclusion, and equal opportunities		20. Access to culture	Desk analysis	N/A	Quality of services
Development of partnerships and collaborations		21. Cultural participation	Checklists, desk analysis	N/A	Quality of services
		22. Participatory processes	Checklists, desk analysis	GRI 413-1	Social relations

Source: Translated from Brambilla and Ghilardi (2023, p. 70)

long-term skills development. The main tool of the application process was cocreation, which is considered a capacity-building process for the community (Comune di Procida, 2021).

For the ex-post evaluation of the results achieved by the program, a monitoring and evaluation group was specifically established outside the working group to ensure the impartiality and independence of the evaluation function. The group will be composed of researchers and professors from the Department of Economics of the University of Campania "Luigi Vanvitelli," the Department of Social Sciences and the Department of Architecture of the University of Naples Federico II (Comune di Procida, 2021).

The evaluation process of Procida 2022 will include a set of observation and monitoring activities through a combination of methods to assess the ability to achieve the stated strategic objectives in the medium and long term, as well as to measure the sociocultural, economic, and environmental impact of the event from an integrated sustainability perspective. From the community-based perspective, the dominant orientation of the evaluation and monitoring process of the initiative sets specific objectives of a sociocultural nature that will have to be appropriately measured with a qualitative–quantitative approach: the community's sense of belonging, social cohesion, civic pride, strengthening of ties, development of skills, cultural participation, and acquisition of new skills by young people (Comune di Procida, 2021).

To measure the effects and impacts of the event, a multidimensional model that employs a set of variables that can provide information of different natures from different sources of information will be adopted. The multistakeholder perspective of the event calls for an evaluation approach that embraces different areas of impact. For this reason, the Monitoring and Evaluation Group decided to adopt the triple bottom line (TBL) method, appropriately adapted and complemented by tools for evaluating the social impact of a cultural event: Generic Social Outcomes (GSO); Generic Learning Outcomes (GLO); Social Return on Investment (SROI) (Comune di Procida, 2021).

The TBL approach is described in detail in the candidacy dossier by distinguishing the impacts expected to result from the event, which can be related to the following areas:

- Economic impacts related to the consequences in terms of money flows introduced into the destination and the direction of these

flows, taking into account, in particular, the direct and indirect contributions to the total value added or revenue generated by the event, the expenditure made by visitors and tourists, and the employment created or increased by the event (the number of employees increased or created by the event);
- Tourism impacts related to visitor flows (walkers and tourists), average stay times, consumption behavior, and perceptions regarding destinations;
- Social impacts of changes in resident quality of life and skill acquisition;
- Environmental impacts concerning the consequences on the ecosystem generated by event-related activities, based on average values of consumption, production, or recycling, which will be used to determine if the event has a greater or lesser impact on the environment than average (Comune di Procida, 2021).

According to the reporting methodology, which has already been identified by the Monitoring and Evaluation Group and explained in the candidacy dossier, there is no intention of adopting the Culture 2030 Indicators proposed by UNESCO, even though there is an explicit reference to the SDGs of the 2030 Agenda. However, the two performance measurement models have several issues in common: the need to allocate more space for the conduct of cultural activities, the goal of increasing artistic freedom and the employment of artists, increasing access to culture by younger people, verifying and increasing public participation in cultural initiatives, and measuring the number of cultural enterprises operating.

For each of the missions identified in Procida 2022's candidacy dossier, there is a table that identifies the strategic objectives that correspond to them and the indicators that will be used to measure their performance. Moreover, the last column of the tables lists the targets, which are the quantitative results corresponding to the performance that the initiative seeks to achieve (Comune di Procida, 2021). From Tables 4.10 and 4.11, it is evident that all missions are inspired by the three pillars upon which the initiative claims to be based: economic, social, and environmental sustainability.

Bergamo e Brescia—Italian Capital Cities of Culture 2023

In the candidacy dossier of Bergamo and Brescia Capitals of Culture 2023, the indicators are crosscutting and do not only consider the economic

Table 4.10 Procida 2022 sustainability indicators (pt.1)

Mission/route	*Strategic objective*	*Performance indicator*	*Target*
1. Procida Invents | projects that plan processes and events that are property artistic: exhibitions, cinema, performances, and site-specific works.	**OS1** | Renovate/ regenerate cultural places in Procida	**IP1** | Number of places and spaces to be permanently dedicated to cultural activities in Procida	≥ 3
	OS2 | Attract artists and creative businesses to encourage exchange and sharing processes	**IP2** | Number of artists and businesses invoked in the project	≥ 100
		IP3 | Number of partnerships between local artists and businesses and non-local artists and businesses within the project	≥ 10
		IP4 | Number of workshops targeting young residents of Procida (≤ 25 years old)	≥ 5
2. Procida Inspires | Projects that describe the island as a source of inspiration, both as a real place and as a space of imagination.	**OS3** | Experimenting with innovative forms of sustainable tourism/ ecotourism slow tourism	**IP5** | Perception of visitors who consider Procida as a suitable destination for sustainable tourism	10% increase over the result in 2020
		IP6 | Perception of visitors who choose Procida as a cultural tourism destination	20% increase over the result in 2020
		IP7 | Overall degree of satisfaction of visitors who chose Procida as a tourist destination for cultural and environmental reasons	An average rating above 4 on a scale of 1–5
		IP7 | Mentions of Procida as a sustainable island in media	20% increase over the result in 2020
	OS4 | Lower the risks of over-tourism and environmental pressure on fragile destinations through event-based strategies for seasonal adjustment	**IP8** | Share of projects implemented in low season months in the total (high season = July, August)	≥ 60%
		IP9 | Seasonality index (landings)	20% improvement
		IP10 | Seasonality index (attendance)	20% improvement

Source: Translated from Comune di Procida (2021, pp. 56–57)

Table 4.11 Procida 2022 sustainability indicators (pt.2)

Mission/route	*Strategic objective*	*Performance indicator*	*Target*
3. Procida Includes | It concerns social inclusion projects, which use the languages of art as tools of expression of the individual, who has relations with the community.	**OS5** | Building a supportive community that recognizes itself in cultural legacies and beauty	**IP11** | Share of participation of residents out of total residents in events	≥ 30%.
		IP12 | Share of participation of young residents (max 25 years old) in the total of young residents	≥ 50%
		IP14 | Cultural consumption in residents	Increase 10% yearly
	OS6 | Place people's rights at the center of public interest, regardless of the census, ethnic, religious, and cultural backgrounds, sexual orientations, and gender affiliation	**IP15** | Number of workshops open to fragile individuals	≥ 5
		IP16 | Share of projects out of total with involvement of fragile subjects in the organization	≥ 80%
		IP17 | Share of projects in the total with guaranteed access to people with disabilities	100%
4. Procida Innoves | Projects that promote the relationship between culture and innovation, fostering moments of confrontation between the national community of innovators and the local community, in a process of strategic rethinking of its cultural heritage.	**OS7** | Reinterpreting history and disseminating culture through new digital technologies	**IP18** | Number of projects using digital technologies	≥ 10
		IP19 | Number of workshops open to young residents for learning digital technologies	≥ 5
	OS8 | Encouraging the development of new cultural entrepreneurship as a cure for fragile ecosystems at risk of abandonment	**IP20** | Number of new cultural enterprises with registered offices in Procida	Increase 15%
		IP21 | Number of new cultural enterprise and tourism supply chain projects followed in the year	≥ 25

(*continued*)

Table 4.11 (continued)

Mission/route	*Strategic objective*	*Performance indicator*	*Target*
5. Procida Learns | Projects that promote the strengthening of an educational community through the creation of open alliances that aim to involve all territorial actors from the public to the private social sector.	**OS9** | Fostering informal learning processes and learning by doing for residents and temporary citizens	**IP22** | Share of events with the participation of residents involved in the organization	≥ 50%
		IP23 | Share of resident participation in total workshop participants	≥ 60%
		IP24 | Share of young residents of Procida (≤ 25 years old) in total participants in workshops	≥ 40%
	OS10 | Disseminate good practices for environmental sustainability and energy transition in small islands	**IP25** | Number of good practices introduced in Procida to improve energy transition	≥ 4

Source: Translated from Comune di Procida (2021, pp. 56–57)

aspect or what is directly related to culture. The dossier states that the indicators were identified by using as a reference the framework prepared by the European Commission for the ex-post evaluation of the performance of European Capitals of Culture (European Commission, 2018), readjusted to the national request. As part of the evaluation and monitoring system for Bergamo and Brescia 2023, they will examine the economic, employment, and communication impacts that will result from the implementation of the initiative, as well as the social, environmental, and educational dimensions. All of them are considered relevant objectives of the initiative (Comuni di Bergamo e Brescia, 2022). This evaluation will focus on the following four design areas, for which different monitoring methods have been identified:

- Culture as care: observation of coordination tables for the management of cultural interventions within care systems and for the implementation of innovative cultural welfare projects; surveys of citizens (e.g., a local sample will be considered and used for some parts of the ISTAT survey on aspects of daily life, or online surveys will be conducted) and visitors; involvement of citizens, students, and volunteers, also to assess the increase in the sense of belonging and civic pride;

- The Nature City: observation of institutional mechanisms, particularly to strengthen governance in the preparation of Climate Transition Strategies and identifying effective indicators for their evaluation; analysis of environmental data; a collection of data related to slow tourism and sustainability;
- City of Hidden Treasures: observation of coordination tables for area promotion and destination management; observation of cultural programming over time; interviews with experts and users from various disciplines; preparation of experience diaries; a collection of data on artistic collaborations and original productions; satisfaction questionnaires and interviews on audience perceptions; collecting and evaluating data on library system usage and museum pass purchases; recording data on attendance, arrivals and departures, receptivity, and economic impact; collecting data on media coverage, social presence, and web sentiment;
- The city that invents: Observation of the education and training systems; observation of the spread of urban cultural productions, particularly in the peripheral areas of the two provinces; collection of documentation about business culture, which incorporates scientific, technological, and humanistic aspects; collection of data on productions and events (Comuni di Bergamo e Brescia, 2022).

It is easy to identify the sustainability goals of the initiative in the indicators proposed by Bergamo and Brescia, even if there are not always direct references. In this instance, the indicators are constructed by considering the pillars of sustainability: they are concerned with the economic, social, and environmental aspects of the initiative. Bergamo and Brescia's indicators emphasize their collective interest.

There is no reference to the Culture 2030 Indicators proposed by UNESCO, which could also have served as a basis for developing the performance indicators. However, the dossier does identify some objectives in common with the framework. Occasionally, both are designed to measure the same variable. Similarities are noted with the measurement objects of the following UNESCO indicators: 3. Climate adaptation and resilience; 4. Cultural facilities; 12. Governance of culture; 18. Culture for social cohesion; 20. Access to culture; 21. Cultural participation.

The analysis of the dossier, however, provides only the foundation for future evaluation: it would be necessary to consult the evaluation document to verify the effectiveness of the measurement and to understand which indicators have been truly used and how they were constructed, but this document has not yet been prepared.

Tables 4.12 and 4.13, which show what indicators will be used to evaluate each initiative following the Bergamo and Brescia 2023 Italian Capital of Culture initiative, present a summary of how sustainable cultural performance will be measured. We have also attempted to make explicit, where possible, the presence of variables related to one or more of the four pillars of sustainability: economic, social, environmental, and cultural.

4.5.4 *Discussion*

The sustainable cultural performance evaluation methods adopted by the different Italian Capital of Culture committees are very different. While Parma 2020+21 decided to apply UNESCO indicators, the others preferred to draw different indicators that could better account for the results achieved by the initiatives. Those dissimilarities make it complex to compare them and to try to identify the best evaluation methodology. Accounting was used as a tool by all measurement and evaluation groups, especially to identify the economic results achieved by the initiative.

Sustainability goals, except for Palermo 2018, are highlighted in all the candidacy dossiers and are included as performance targets to be pursued. Their reporting shows the cities' interest in pursuing them and their alignment with what is needed, at the national level, in the calls for applications for the title of Italian Capital of Culture.

The case of Matera 2019 is an outlier: its evaluation involved many working groups, which analyzed multiple aspects in a more detailed way. The reporting work required by the city was also accompanied by an audit by the European Commission, which judged the initiative from the points of view of relevance with the request coming from the European Union, efficiency, and effectiveness. It took into consideration the evaluations carried out at the local level and expanded them to obtain a more general picture of what had taken place. The audit focused primarily on the added value that the Capital of Culture would bring to the European Union as well as on its consistency and complementarity with the other European Capitals of Culture. In fact, the Commission aimed to obtain information

Table 4.12 Bergamo and Brescia 2023 sustainability indicators (pt.1)

Performance	*Measurement*	*Sustainability*
Establishment of a coordination table to manage cultural interventions in and out of care systems and joint implementation of innovative cultural welfare protects	Observation of coordination tables	No reference, but it can assess social and cultural sustainability
Perception of cities as inclusive and supportive cities by city residents, province residents, visitors	Surveys on citizens (e.g.: local sample for some parts of ISTAT survey on Aspects of Dairy Life; online surveys, etc.) and visitors	No reference, but it can assess social and cultural sustainability
Increased sense of belonging/civic pride	Involving citizens, students, volunteers	No reference, but it can assess social sustainability
Strengthening of institutional structures for governance of climate transition strategies, the linkage between the structures in charge of this purpose in the two cities, and increased integration between entities involved and their capacities to interact with partners, stakeholders, and citizens and to manage in a coordinated way the actions of STC—Climate Transition Strategies (internal organization)	Observation of institutional mechanisms	No reference, but it can assess environmental sustainability
Urban transformation for environmental sustainability and climate transition	STC indicators	No reference, but it can assess environmental sustainability
Sustainable mobility in cities	Environmental data	No reference, but it can assess environmental sustainability
Promotion of slow and sustainable tourism in cities and territory	Data on slow tourism and sustainability	Environmental, economic, and cultural sustainability
Coordination table for territorial promotion and destination management	Observation of coordination tables	No reference, but it can assess economic and environmental sustainability
Creation of systematic and lasting forms of collaboration between cultural institutions and festivals in the two cities	Observation of cultural programming over time	No reference, but it can assess economic, social, and cultural sustainability
Shared enabling infrastructures	Interviews with experts and users from various disciplines	No reference, but it can assess social and cultural sustainability

Table 4.13 Bergamo and Brescia 2023 sustainability indicators (pt.2)

Performance	*Measurement*	*Sustainability*
Greater diversity in cultural production	Journals of experience, data on artistic collaborations, original productions	No reference, but it can assess cultural sustainability
Enlargement of audiences: involvement of groups that for different reasons do not access cultural activities	Awareness questionnaires, interviews on perceptions: data on library system usage, museum passes, etc.	No reference, but it can assess cultural and social sustainability
Professionalization of tourism supply	Data on utilization of library systems, museum passes, etc.	No reference, but it can assess cultural and social sustainability
Economic inducement of events	Data on attendance, arrivals and departures, accommodation, and economic impact	No reference, but it can assess cultural and economic sustainability
Growth prestige and international attractiveness	Data on media coverage, social presence, web sentiment, etc.	No reference, but it can assess economic sustainability
Strengthening of the educational system of the two territories aimed at innovation and new technologies for manufacturing (universities, research centers, ITS, companies)	Observation of the educational system and training systems	No reference, but it can assess cultural and social sustainability
Initiation of a design process aimed at implementing a system of enabling technologies for the dissemination of urban cultural productions in the more peripheral locations of the two provinces	Observation of the dissemination of urban cultural productions	No reference, but it can assess economic and social sustainability
Creation of a system of support for the integration of scientific and technological culture in the humanities to create a model of widespread and permanent training and experimentation (new enterprise)	Documentation on enterprise culture	No reference, but it can assess economic and social sustainability
Between business representations, universities, and research centers present in the territories for the promotion of an ecosystem devoted to innovation, particularly in manufacturing	Documentation on business culture	No reference, but it can assess economic, social, and environmental sustainability
The increased presence of contemporary art in cultural offerings	Data on productions and events	No reference, but it can assess economic and cultural sustainability

that could improve the program's efficiency in the future (European Commission et al., 2020).

In Italy, there is no provision for this double control by the authority, even if, in 2022, the General Secretariat of the Ministry of Culture decided to start a reflection along these lines and involved the "Fondazione Scuola Beni Attività Culturali" to work on a study, the aim of which is to offer a critical analysis on models for ex-post and in progress monitoring and evaluation of the Italian Capitals of Culture initiative and, more generally, of cultural activities, as well as to offer guidelines to the following Italian Capitals of Culture and those working in the sector (Fondazione Scuola Beni Attività Culturali, 2022).

The Culture 2030 Indicators prepared by UNESCO have been adopted by only one of the Italian Capitals of Culture: Parma 2020+21. For the other initiatives, however, some common evaluation themes can be highlighted. What emerges is that tendentially, the Capitals of Culture carry out measurements aimed at emphasizing the changes that have occurred in the area of cultural performance and sustainability due to the impact of the initiative, while the UNESCO indicators tend to pay more attention to assessing the degree to which sustainability goals are being pursued in a given place at a given time. This is probably why they are not chosen by the Cities as an evaluation framework, considering that they are not even required by the European Union to evaluate future European Capitals of Culture (European Commission, 2014).

Table 4.14 presents the most frequent measurement objects accounted for in the Capitals of Culture analyzed in this chapter.

The results of the analysis, therefore, show that the evaluation focuses on the cultural project's stakeholders: residents (12), cities (11), enterprises (8), partners (8), institutions (6), visitors (5), and youth (5) are among the most frequent terms. It is also particularly significant for the evaluation, however, of how the initiative was structured (organization—6), what the cultural offerings were (projects—6, activities—5, initiatives—5, events—5, workshops—5), and their local (8) impact (participation—8) from the perspectives of tourism (7), sustainability (sustainable—5), innovation (4), technologies (4), territory (4), transition (4), development (4), integration (3) and from an economic perspective (4).

Table 4.14 Frequency of terms used as the object of sustainable cultural performance measurement in Capital of Culture projects

Item	*Frequency*	*Item*	*Frequency*	*Item*	*Frequency*
Cultural	25	Visitors	5	Greater	4
Residents	12	Initiatives	5	Development	4
Cities	11	Events	5	Climate	3
Number	10	Youth	5	Perception	3
Enterprises	8	Sustainable	5	Experience	3
Local	8	Workshops	5	Offer	3
Participation	8	Presence	4	Participants	3
Partners	8	Increase	4	Collaboration	3
Involved	7	Culture	4	Membership	3
Tourism	7	Influence	4	Artists	3
Organization	6	Innovation	4	Impact	3
Projects	6	Technologies	4	Sense	3
Contribution	6	Territory	4	Creating	3
Institutions	6	Economic	4	Integration	3
Activities	5	Transition	4	Territories	3
Promotion	5	System	4	Destination	3
Creation	5				

4.6 Final Remarks

In this study, the relationship between culture and sustainability was examined to highlight the contribution that culture can make to achieving international goals. Despite the absence of a Sustainable Development Goal pertaining to culture, the literature review indicates that there is a significant relationship between the two concepts, which is now universally recognized. It is true that culture can at the same time be viewed as both an integral part of sustainability and as a functional component of it (Dessein et al., 2015).

However, the topic of measuring cultural performance remains highly articulated and under development. Since there is no universally accepted measurement framework at the international level, this study examined a number of possible alternatives. It focused in particular on a critical analysis of the Culture 2030 Indicators, a recent proposal that has received little attention. It is nevertheless important to note that the role that this framework is intended to play is indeed relevant, as it fills a gap in a context that has gaps.

Consequently, a method for measuring sustainable cultural performance has not yet been universally adopted, even at the national level. Consequently, further investigation is necessary to identify a possible, agreeable solution to achieve this evaluation goal. More specific guidelines on performance measurement by institutions would certainly accelerate this process. As an example, the assessment of the impact of cultural capabilities is completely left to the city, which constructs the indicators based on its own knowledge and reporting needs.

To achieve this goal, it would be necessary to focus on the culture of measurement, which is still modest today but which, given its relevance, must be expanded (Folan & Browne, 2005). As a result of accounting, it is possible to report what has been accomplished, which is essential for understanding the effectiveness of the actions implemented, as well as the progress made in achieving objectives, highlighting the difficulties encountered and laying the foundation for understanding where improvements should be made. In fact, the results of the reporting activity can be used to develop more effective policies and to enhance the legitimacy of the promoters of the initiatives.

Figure 4.2 illustrates a conceptual model of how sustainable cultural performance is, at the moment, measured in Italy based on the Italian Capitals of Culture.

Fig. 4.2 Sustainable cultural performance measurement

The constructed model indicates that the analyzed reports are consistent with the four pillars of sustainability: economic, social, environmental, and cultural. However, it would also be beneficial to study the measurement methods adopted by other countries to assess the performance of European Capitals of Culture. By comparing numerous cases, the different reporting methods could be more accurately compared, and thus, best practices could be identified. This would allow for the development of more efficient and effective sustainable cultural performance measurement tools, even in Italy, thus accelerating the pursuit of sustainability goals.

References

Aiello, G., & Thurlow, C. (2006). Symbolic capitals: Visual discourse and intercultural exchange in the European Capital of Culture scheme. *Language and Intercultural Communication, 6*(2), 148–162.

Behn, R. D. (2003). Why measure performance? Different purposes require different measures. *Public Administration Review, 63*(5), 586–606.

Blake, J. (2000). On defining the cultural heritage. *International & Comparative Law Quarterly, 49*(1), 61–85.

Brambilla, V., & Ghilardi, R. (2021). Misurare la cultura. In Comitato per Parma 2020 (Ed.), *Il progetto Parma Capitale Italiana della Cultura 2020+21* (pp. 83–89). Electa.

Brambilla, V., & Ghilardi, R. (2023). Impact report Parma Capitale Italiana della Cultura 2020+2021. In Deloitte & Promo PA Fondazione (Eds.), *Impact report Parma Capitale Italiana della Cultura 2020+2021 | Il valore di un programma* (pp. 18–85).

Carpentier, C. L., & Braun, H. (2020). Agenda 2030 for sustainable development: A powerful global framework. *Journal of the International Council for Small Business, 1*(1), 14–23.

Cerreta, M., & Giovene di Girasole, E. (2020). Towards heritage community assessment: Indicators proposal for the self-evaluation in Faro convention network process. *Sustainability, 12*(23), 9862.

Cicerchia, A. (2016). Culture and development. The global quest for indicators. *Economia della Cultura, 26*(2), 249–260.

Comitato Matera 2019. (2018). Matera città candidata capitale europea della cultura 2019. https://www.matera-basilicata2019.it/it/matera-2019/dossier.html

Comune di Palermo. (2016). Palermo Capitale Italiana della Cultura 2018 | Dossier di candidatura 30 giugno 2016. https://www.comune.palermo.it/js/server/uploads/_31012017161757.pdf

Comune di Parma. (2019). Parma Capitale Italiana della Cultura 2020 | Programma ufficiale 18.04.2019. https://assets.loescher.it/Risorse/LOE/Public/O_3891/3891/Risorse_online/Dossier_Parma2020.pdf

Comune di Pistoia. (2015). Pistoia città candidata Capitale Italiana della Cultura 2016/2017 | Dossier II fase. http://www.fondazionecrpt.it/wp-content/uploads/2016/05/Allegato-A-Dossier-Pistoia-Capitale-Cultura-2017.pdf

Comune di Procida. (2021). Procida Capitale Italiana della Cultura | Città candidata. https://www.procida2022.com/la-cultura-non-isola

Comuni di Bergamo e Brescia. (2022). "LA CITTÀ ILLUMINATA" Dossier di programmazione. https://www.comune.bergamo.it/sites/default/files/allegatinews/BGBS2023.pdf

Council of Europe. (2005). Council of Europe Framework Convention on the value of cultural heritage for society (CETS No. 199). https://rm.coe.int/1680083746

Council of Europe. (2017). Recommendation of the Committee of Ministers to member States on the European Cultural Heritage Strategy for the 21st century. https://rm.coe.int/16806f6a03

Culture 2030 Goal Campaign. (2019). Culture in the implementation of the 2030 Agenda. https://asvis.it/public/asvis2/files/Approfondimenti/Report_campagna_cultura2030goal.pdf

Dessein, J., Soini, K., Fairclough, G., & Horlings, L. (Eds.). (2015). *Culture in, for and as sustainable development. Conclusions from the COST Action IS1007 investigating cultural sustainability*. University of Jyväskylä, Finland.

Di Capua, V. (2021). La Convenzione di Faro. Verso la valorizzazione del patrimonio culturale come bene comune. *Aedon*, (3), 9–18.

European Commission. (2014). European Capitals of Culture 2020 to 2033 | A guide for cities preparing to bid. https://culture.ec.europa.eu/sites/default/files/capitals-culture-candidates-guide_en_vdec17.pdf

European Commission. (2018). European Capitals of Culture (ECoC) 2020–2033 | Guidelines for the cities' own evaluations of the results of their ECOC. https://culture.ec.europa.eu/sites/default/files/2021-04/ecoc-guidelines-for-cities-own-evaluations-2020-2033.pdf

European Commission. (2020). A new European agenda for culture—SWD(2018) 267 final. https://culture.ec.europa.eu/document/new-european-agenda-culture-swd2018-267-final

European Commission, Directorate-General for Budget. (2021). *The EU's 2021–2027 long-term budget and NextGenerationEU: Facts and figures*. Publications Office of the European Union. https://data.europa.eu/doi/10.2761/808559

European Commission, Directorate-General for Education, Youth, Sport and Culture. (2019). *Quadro d'azione europeo sul patrimonio culturale*. Publications Office. https://data.europa.eu/doi/10.2766/622226

European Commission, Directorate-General for Education, Youth, Sport and Culture, Pavlova, A., Mobilio, L., & Goffredo, S. (2020). *Ex-post evaluation of the 2019 European capitals of: Executive summary* (A. Pavlova, L. Mobilio, S. Goffredo, & T. Fox, Eds.). Publications Office. https://data.europa.eu/doi/10.2766/7912

European Parliament, Directorate-General for Internal Policies of the Union, Garcia, B., & Cox, T. (2014). *European capitals of culture: Success strategies and long-term effects.* Publications Office. https://data.europa.eu/doi/10.2861/44227

Fitri, I., Ahmad, Y., & Ahmad, F. (2015). Conservation of tangible cultural heritage in Indonesia: A review current national criteria for assessing heritage value. *Procedia-Social and Behavioral Sciences, 184*, 71–78.

Folan, P., & Browne, J. (2005). A review of performance measurement: Towards performance management. *Computers in Industry, 56*(7), 663–680.

Fondazione di partecipazione Matera-Basilicata 2019. (2021). Guida alle valutazioni di Matera 2019. https://www.matera-basilicata2019.it/it/report-2019/studi-valutativi-su-matera-2019/guida-alle-valutazioni.html

Fondazione Scuola Beni Attività Culturali. (2022). Capitale italiana della Cultura | Riflessioni metodologiche e consultazioni pubbliche per la definizione di un modello di valutazione. https://www.fondazionescuolapatrimonio.it/capitale-italiana-della-cultura-valutazione/

Ghia, G. (2022). *Vademecum per i mecenati della cultura: art bonus, sponsorizzazioni e metodi di raccolte fondi per valorizzare conservando.* Gangemi Editore spa.

Governo Italiano. (2021). Piano Nazionale di Ripresa e Resilienza. https://www.governo.it/sites/governo.it/files/PNRR.pdf

Guerra, M. (2021). Il modello culturale e la sfida post-pandemica. In Comitato per Parma 2020 (Ed.), *Il progetto Parma Capitale Italiana della Cultura 2020+21* (pp. 29–35). Electa.

Harwood, T. G., & Garry, T. (2003). An overview of content analysis. *The Marketing Review, 3*(4), 479–498.

Human Foundation. (2019). Valutazione di Palermo Capitale Italiana della Cultura 2018 | Gli effetti dell'iniziativa sul territorio, sul partenariato istituzionale e sul sentiment di Palermo. https://www.comune.palermo.it/js/server/uploads/_16122019185032.pdf

Inglese, I. D., & Caragnano, R. (2022). Work and employment for the heritage: System analysis of an economic asset for an innovative welfare model. *Athens Journal of Law, 8*, 9.

Ippolito, M. (2021). Il Patrimonio Digitale della Cultura: un'opportunità di fruizione dei beni culturali "senza barriere". *PA Persona e Amministrazione, 9*(2), 751–772.

Lacity, M. C., & Janson, M. A. (1994). Understanding qualitative data: A framework of text analysis methods. *Journal of Management Information Systems, 11*(2), 137–155.

Ministero dei Beni e delle Attività Culturali e del Turismo. (2015). Bando per il titolo: Capitale Italiana della Cultura 2016 e 2017. https://www.beniculturali.it/mibac/multimedia/MiBAC/documents/feed/pdf/Bando%20capitale%20cultura%20italiana%202016%202017-imported-49193.pdf

Ministero dei Beni e delle Attività Culturali e del Turismo. (2016). Bando per il conferimento del titolo "Capitale Italiana della Cultura 2018". https://storico.beniculturali.it/mibac/multimedia/MiBAC/documents/1459433701961_BANDO_PER_IL_TITOLO_CAPITALE_CULTURA_2018.pdf

Ministero della Cultura. (2021a). Procida Capitale Italiana della Cultura per il 2022. https://www.beniculturali.it/procida2022

Ministero della Cultura. (2021b). Pesaro è la Capitale Italiana della Cultura 2024. https://www.beniculturali.it/capitaleitalianadellacultura

Ministero della Cultura. Capitali e città europee della cultura. https://capitalidellacultura.cultura.gov.it/capitali-e-citta-europee-della-cultura/

Ministero per i beni e le attività culturali e per il turismo. (2019). Bando per il conferimento del titolo di «Capitale italiana della cultura» per l'anno 2021. https://www.beniculturali.it/mibac/multimedia/MiBAC/documents/1574095368113_Bando_Capitale_italiana_2021_decr._rep._n._382-signed.pdf

Ministero per i beni e le attività culturali e per il turismo. (2020). Ulteriore modifica del bando per il conferimento del titolo di «Capitale italiana della cultura» per l'anno 2021: riferimento della procedura di selezione all'anno 2022 e modifica dei termini. https://www.beniculturali.it/mibac/multimedia/MiBAC/documents/1590067116961_Decreto_SG_21.05.2020_rep._n._300-signed.pdf

Ministero per i beni e le attività culturali e per il turismo. (2021). Bando per il conferimento del titolo di «Capitale italiana della cultura» per l'anno 2024. https://media.beniculturali.it/mibac/files/boards/388a5474724a15af0ace7a40ab3301de/file_pdf/Decreto%20SG%20461_16.06.2021_CIC%202024_%20bando-signed.pdf

Montalto, V., Moura, C. J. T., Langedijk, S., & Saisana, M. (2019). Culture counts: An empirical approach to measure the cultural and creative vitality of European cities. *Cities, 89*, 167–185.

Montella, M., Petraroia, P., Manacorda, D., & di Maccco, M. (2016). La Convenzione di Faro e la tradizione culturale italiana/The Faro Convention and the Italian cultural tradition. *IL CAPITALE CULTURALE. Studies on the Value of Cultural Heritage*, 13–36. https://doi.org/10.13138/2039-2362/1551

Nocca, F. (2017). The role of cultural heritage in sustainable development: Multidimensional indicators as decision-making tool. *Sustainability, 9*(10), 1882.

Petti, L., Trillo, C., & Makore, B. N. (2020). Cultural heritage and sustainable development targets: A possible harmonisation? Insights from the European perspective. *Sustainability, 12*(3), 926.

Prott, L. V., & O'Keefe, P. J. (1992). 'Cultural heritage' or 'cultural property'? *International Journal of Cultural Property, 1*(2), 307–320.

Sciacchitano, E. (2015). L'evoluzione delle politiche sul patrimonio culturale in Europa dopo Faro. In *Citizens of Europe* (pp. 45–62). Edizioni Ca' Foscari.

Soini, K., & Dessein, J. (2016). Culture-sustainability relation: Towards a conceptual framework. *Sustainability, 8*(2), 167.

UNESCO. (2019). Culture | 2030 Indicators. https://uis.unesco.org/sites/default/files/documents/publication_culture_2020_indicators_en.pdf

United Nations. (2015). Transforming our world: The 2030 Agenda for sustainable development | A/Res/70/1. https://sdgs.un.org/sites/default/files/publications/21252030%20Agenda%20for%20Sustainable%20Development%20web.pdf

Velani, F. (2021). Un programma di sviluppo territoriale a base culturale. Obiettivi, attuazione, legacy. In Comitato per Parma 2020 (Ed.), *Il progetto Parma Capitale Italiana della Cultura 2020+21* (pp. 57–65). Electa.

Wiktor-Mach, D. (2020). What role for culture in the age of sustainable development? UNESCO's advocacy in the 2030 Agenda negotiations. *International Journal of Cultural Policy, 26*(3), 312–327.

Zagato, L. (2015). The notion of "Heritage Community" in the Council of Europe's Faro Convention. Its impact on the European legal framework. Markus Tauschek (Eds.), *Between Imagined Communities and Communities of Practice*, 141–168.

Zheng, X., Wang, R., Hoekstra, A. Y., Krol, M. S., Zhang, Y., Guo, K., Sanwal, M., Sun, Z., Zhu, J., Zhang, J., Lounsbury, A., Pan, X., Guan, D., Hertwich, E. G., & Wang, C. (2021). Consideration of culture is vital if we are to achieve the Sustainable Development Goals. *One Earth, 4*(2), 307–319.

CHAPTER 5

The Resilience in Cultural Heritage Management: Which Role for Accounting?

Abstract Defining "resilience" is not an easy task. There are different interpretations of the concept in the literature. Even more challenging is the measurement of resilience and the identification of an organization that possesses this characteristic from one that does not. Globally, the spread of COVID-19 impacted a number of organizations, including cultural organizations both public and private, causing buildings to be inaccessible to visitors. This chapter attempts to understand, in particular, how Italian University Museums and Italian Corporate Museums responded to the COVID-19 pandemic emergency during the lockdown. Did they prove to be resilient? In which ways has accounting for organizational resilience played a role?

Keywords Cultural heritage • Resilience • Accounting • Museums • Technology

Michela Magliacani is author of Paragraphs 5.3., 5.3.1., and 5.4.
Valentina Toscano is author of Paragraphs 5.1., 5.2., and 5.3.2.

M. Magliacani, V. Toscano, *Accounting for Cultural Heritage Management*, https://doi.org/10.1007/978-3-031-38257-4_5

5.1 Introduction

Resilience is a difficult concept to define, with different scholars approaching it over time and coming up with very different definitions. As an example, it was initially identified as the means and time an organization needs to overcome economic, environmental, or social stress (D'Arpino & Mancini, 2015).

The term was further defined by Zolli and Healy as the ability of a system, firm, or individual to maintain its integrity and fundamental purpose even in the face of a drastic change in circumstances (Zolli & Healy, 2012). According to these authors, a system can be considered resilient either in the case where due to a necessity originating from the occurrence of a critical situation, it can reorganize itself dynamically to achieve its goals, demonstrating that it has capabilities that are not used daily but that resurface when the shock occurs, proving indispensable to overcome it, or where the system can "deidentify" or "decouple" itself from the context in which it operates and the resources it uses to reinvent itself and reduce its dependency relationships. Being resilient does not mean being infallible, however, as sometimes a system that seems stable turns out to be more unstable. In contrast, a system that is continually subjected to shocks and forced to reinvent itself may prove more capable of overcoming difficulties. Resilience is chaotic, imperfect, and inefficient, yet it survives (Zolli & Healy, 2012).

Consequently, this chapter will discuss resilience in the context of economics and organizations. A review of the managerial literature on the notion of resilience will be presented, followed by the development and analysis of several theoretical models of resilient organizations, to identify what characteristics and structures are typical of an enterprise that can be described in this manner, according to different authors. Furthermore, we discuss the issue of measuring resilience, which is still subject to debate and is difficult to apply, citing some of the models that have been proposed in the literature.

After that, we will discuss the role of technology as a resilience tool, looking at Italian universities' museums and Corporate Museums and Archives during the COVID-19 pandemic, to understand how this has affected the continuity of cultural activities conducted by these organizations. Finally, we will investigate the role played by accounting in achieving the resilience goals of these Italian cultural organizations.

5.2 The Notion of Resilience in Management Studies

Since the 1980s, the concept of resilience has been formally discussed in the economic literature, primarily in relation to business management and organization. Staw et al. published the first study on this topic in 1981, while Meyer published the second in 1982, with opposing content (Linnenluecke, 2017). According to Staw et al. (1981), a good structure of an organization, based on existing and routinely applied knowledge, can immediately assist it in overcoming a difficult situation. It is important to note that threat-rigidity effects—derived from the assumption that a specific threat can lead to rigidity in the handling of a given issue—are not always negative for the company. In contrast, they may prove to be an important factor in recovering from shocks (Staw et al., 1981). The authors do not directly mention the term resilience in their text, which is instead found in Meyer's (1982) article. The author states that organizations are characterized by their ideas, values, and knowledge, which enable them to differentiate themselves from other companies operating in the same industry. These characteristics allow an organization to respond with resilience or retention during times of difficulty. When an organization is in the first situation, it can absorb the negative effects of the damage, while in the second case, it can find a new equilibrium, adapt, and identify new behaviors to survive (Meyer, 1982). Meyer suggests that resilience is influenced by corporate strategy, whereas retention is influenced by organizational structure and ideologies (Linnenluecke, 2017).

Over the years, there has been much debate in the literature regarding the meaning of the term "resilience," but no universally accepted definition has been reached. Even the same author may have formulated different definitions depending on the context. Hallegatte (2014), for example, suggests that macroeconomic resilience and microeconomic resilience should be distinguished. According to the first view, it refers to the ability of the economic system to combine "instantaneous resilience" (the ability to immediately reduce the impact of losses) with "dynamic resilience" (the ability to rebuild and recover rapidly after losses). On the other hand, microeconomic resilience considers the impact and distribution of losses across individuals, the ability to meet basic needs, to contain shocks, and to assist people in recovering through social security systems (Hallegatte, 2014).

Economic resilience can also be defined as a firm's ability to efficiently adapt to possible difficulties it may encounter so that it can cope with them, thanks to its resourcefulness, and overcome them, strengthening itself (Vogus & Sutcliffe, 2007). It is therefore regarded as a positive, preferable characteristic for a company since it enables it to handle and overcome a variety of adversities in its business activities (Linnenluecke, 2017).

An organization must be able to continuously reinvent and update its strategies to continue operating after an external event that is difficult to predict occurs. The ability to survive a crisis cannot, therefore, be summed up as the definition of resilience. However, it is imperative that the company is able to anticipate the evolution of economic trends and modify its core business in advance so that it can make the necessary renovations before irreversible damages occur and changes become the only viable solution to enable it to overcome the crisis (Hamel & Valikangas, 2004).

It follows that the concept of resilience has been superseded to emphasize the importance of durable adaptive capacity in the context of overcoming difficulties over the concept of resilience based on the ability to survive a shock and return to equilibrium after the shock has occurred (Coppola, 2016).

A further classification that has been used in the literature is the division into "inherent" and "adaptive" resilience. The first refers to the simple ability of a system to recover after a shock, such as the ability to replace a factor of production that is no longer available due to the extraordinary event that has occurred with another that is still available. "Adaptive" resilience is instead the ability to overcome a moment of difficulty thanks to inventiveness, ingenuity, and additional efforts, for example, the readiness to invent a new factor of production, with different characteristics compared to those previously used but capable of satisfying the same need (Rose, 2004).

Therefore, it is necessary to understand how organizations can succeed in being resilient. Approaches aimed at studying the possible development of resilience systems have focused on reducing uncertainties, risks, and vulnerabilities (Winnard et al., 2014). A risk is a future event that is thought to occur in any system but whose probability cannot be calculated (Burnard & Bhamra, 2011; Ivanov et al., 2021), whereas uncertainty refers to events that could occur in the future but whose probability cannot be calculated. While they are derived from uncertainties, they can be identified, analyzed, controlled, and regulated, unlike the latter (Ivanov et al., 2021). Finally, vulnerabilities are defined as exposure to potential losses (Cutter, 1996).

To minimize the negative effects caused by possible future events, the organization must prepare a strategy that is based on analytical data but is also feasible and efficient at the same time. There must also be variables in the data that relate to future trends, even though it is rationally impossible to predict all possible scenarios that have not yet occurred (Pugh & Bourgeois, 2011).

Being resilient, moreover, is not to be regarded as a characteristic that can be learned by studying and analyzing the experiences and behaviors of others; it is not a written formula that can be applied indiscriminately and successfully by all organizations (Engemann & Henderson, 2014). Instead, it must result from the efforts of the single organization. It must have an internal structure that is prepared to adapt to changes because a shock has already been anticipated (Gover & Duxbury, 2018). The ability to build a resilient structure, therefore, requires time and studies on a single case, and the process, being so singular, is very difficult in its structuring and application (Palumbo & Manna, 2019).

According to some studies, for an organization to be resilient, it is important that the manager has a resilient mindset, is innovative, and has great intellectual capabilities (Bernard & Dubard Barbosa, 2016). The study conducted by Korber and Mcnaughton (2017), based on a literature review on the relationship between management and resilience, identifies six types of relationships:

1. ancestors of entrepreneurial resilience, according to which resilience is an ex ante present condition, which enables the manager to handle potential crises or difficult times with more awareness;
2. resilience as a determinant of entrepreneurial intentions, according to which only a manager who feels resilient and self-confident will decide to embark on starting a business;
3. entrepreneurial behavior as a determinant of organizational resilience, whereby it is argued that the manager's thinking and peculiarities influence business resilience. In particular, it can be observed in times of difficulty. It is relevant to analyze how the manager behaves when confronted with a moment of crisis. This is done by focusing on the transformations he decides to apply and how creative and adaptive these prove to be;

4. entrepreneurship fosters macroeconomic resilience, a relationship demonstrated through statistical studies based on the relationships between managerial activity and some economic indicators calculated following periods of difficulty. It has been found that, in general, the two factors are positively correlated;
5. entrepreneurs who exhibit resilience are more likely to continue their businesses even after a failure because of their resilience. However, the literature does not explain how this can happen or whether this is convenient for the manager;
6. adaptive resilience is a process of recovery and transformation whereby managers, to be resilient, must continuously innovate and be updated on the environment around them (Korber & Mcnaughton, 2017).

To be considered resilient, it is therefore necessary for an organization to have an adequate internal structure to fulfill this role, which considers the possibility of risks occurring and is designed based on the peculiarities of the individual organization (Pugh & Bourgeois, 2011; Engemann & Henderson, 2014; Gover & Duxbury, 2018; Palumbo & Manna, 2019). What the characteristics of a resilient internal organizational structure are, however, is an issue that is still debated. The literature on the topic is vast, and several effective resilience models have been devised. They are very different from each other, but by analyzing them, it is possible to identify some factors they have in common.

According to Mallak (1998), resilience is based on the capabilities of individuals operating within an organization. Their adaptive behaviors are indispensable, as well as their ability to learn from mistakes and situations and their ability to practice bricolage. Furthermore, the role of managers is considered key, as they are not only responsible for organizing the activities efficiently but also for incentivizing and supporting workers. His model, therefore, considers staff as the sole factor of resilience (Mallak, 1998), but this position is not well supported in the literature, where the concept of resilience based on structure and organizational climate prevails (Home & Horr, 1997).

In Lengnick-Hall and Beck's (2005) resilience model, on the other hand, the role of human capital and the knowledge it has acquired is limited. It is part of only one of the three components of resilience: context resilience. It is flanked by cognitive resilience (i.e., the ability to identify behaviors to adopt to overcome difficulties) and behavioral resilience (i.e., the ability to access information about the context in which one operates and to have different plans of action that can be used if necessary). Resilience in this model thus depends on the routines the organization has developed from the information obtained and its skills (Lengnick-Hall & Beck, 2005). In the later model of Lengnick-Hall et al. (2011), however, the role of human capital takes over and becomes the central factor of the organizational resilience model. Human resources have the knowledge, skills, and competencies that enable the development of the routines necessary for the organization to survive when exceptional events occur. Human capital, therefore, plays a predominant role, as it does in Mallak's model (1998), but it is placed in a broader context, where additional factors are considered for resilience.

According to McManus et al. (2007), resilience is regarded as an organizational function that consists of context awareness, adaptive capacity, and the ability to identify and manage vulnerabilities. According to Mallak (1998), leadership plays an important role in making decisions and acquiring information and knowledge. Moreover, McManus et al. (2007) recommend developing strategies to be implemented when vulnerabilities occur, which must be structured and tested through simulation exercises. However, the organization must be aware that it cannot overcome difficulties on its own, which is why it is essential to engage in a network with which it can cooperate (McManus et al., 2007). This model differs from previous ones by paying greater attention to external risks and their management. Furthermore, it emphasizes the role of top management rather than that of employees. As a result of the model, an organization is not viewed as a single entity but rather as a part of the environment in which it operates, where it must cooperate with other organizations and companies to survive (McManus et al., 2007).

Gulati (2010) identifies customer centricity as the main resilience variable, thus defining resilient organizations as those that aim to meet customer needs, offer better goods or services than competitors and have an elastic structure that can be adapted in case of changes in buyers' needs. Therefore, market studies, research, innovation, and partnerships with external parties are fundamental because it is not possible to produce everything in-house. The company is particularly required to focus on five levers of resilience: coordination, cooperation, power, capabilities, and relationships (Gulati, 2010). In the present model, the importance of relationships with external stakeholders that already exist in the model of McManus et al. (2007) and the role of employees and their skills emphasized by Mallak (1998) and Lengnick-Hall et al. (2011) are complemented by the need for excellent coordination within the organization and the use of power, divided among the individuals heading the units, to support the efficient functioning of the mechanisms at the core of the organization (Gulati, 2010).

According to Johnsen (2010), resilience must be included in business planning through the preparation of a model that sets out the life cycle of the business, constructed by considering the seven principles of resilience that he has identified. It is indispensable, as McManus et al. (2008) stated, to identify, through preliminary analysis, the risks that are expected so that proper actions can be planned to limit their occurrence or consequent damage. Redundancy is relevant for the author when it does not make the company excessively vulnerable (Johnsen, 2010).

Kantur and Işeri-Say (2012) propose that resilience and organizational evolution have a consequential relationship based on their resilience model. Employees, particularly those who develop the strategic capability necessary for decision-making in times of difficulty and whose positive perception fosters corporate resilience, play an important but not predominant role, as in Mallak (1998) and Lengnick-Hall et al. (2011). Moreover, their involvement and proactive attitude are crucial when adversity occurs. However, the strategic capability must be accompanied by strategic actions, which need to be planned, but at the same time be flexible and innovative, as also envisaged by Johnsen (2010) and McManus et al. (2007).

Last, the resilience model according to the BSI emphasizes the ability to prepare and implement best practices. In other words, it is a business model based on offering products and services that are innovative and competitive, produced through innovative and flexible processes, employing workers who, according to Kantur and Işeri-Say (2012), share the same corporate values and are aware of the importance of customer loyalty. According to Mallak (1998) and McManus et al. (2007), leadership must be capable of preparing strategic plans and applying a forward-looking perspective to decision-making (Kerr, 2016).

It should be noted, however, that conformity to a model in the literature does not mean that an organization is resilient. Numerous qualitative and quantitative models are available in the literature for the measurement of an organization's resilience. Among the qualitative ones, the Resilience Architecture Framework (RAF) provides the possibility, based on the assessment of some characteristics of an organization, to place it in a quadrant of the graph prepared by the authors and to assess its resilience in this way (Limnios et al., 2014). Somers (2009), on the other hand, developed a quantitative measurement model by constructing a visual scale of values (VAS) based on six variables, referring, in particular, to the employees' activities, which are regarded as central to corporate resilience. The author assessed the following variables: targeted solutions to achieve a given objective; risk avoidance; understanding of critical situations; ability of team members to play multiple roles; degree of reliability of information sources; and access to resources.

A more comprehensive model that takes more variables into account is Venzin and Perotti's (2014) self-assessment analysis of resilience and their VOLARE (Volatility and ROE) indicator, which considers the company's performance over the past ten years and requires both qualitative and quantitative variables to be weighed to determine it. According to the authors, this model was needed because it was still possible to assess resilience using economic-financial analysis, but it was no longer considered suitable for obtaining reliable results (Venzin & Perotti, 2014).

In addition to the role played by managers, the contributions of governments, which have designed and implemented programs to support them, and of the private sector are also important in achieving resilience goals. To assist organizations in becoming more resilient, the latter has offered commercial service support to them. This is the case, for example, for 4warPRO, which has built its business on corporate resilience, offering its 30 years' experience to all companies wishing to improve their internal organization. It offers a specialized consultancy service, tailored to the individual organization, based upon the sector in which it operates, its skills, and technology used (4ward srl).

After the COVID-19 pandemic, public companies also needed to develop resilience strategies to ensure that their service offerings would be continuous. As an example, universities had to convert their established face-to-face teaching methods into distance learning lectures and examinations; university museums found that they were only able to provide their services via digital means. The technologies they adopted, however, permitted them to maintain firm contact with visitors, who had the possibility of living virtual experiences, participating in video conferences or creative workshops, or having access to resources such as video narratives, which were made available later, in an asynchronous manner (Magliacani & Sorrentino, 2022).

A detailed analysis of the cultural sector's response to the pandemic, particularly the museum sector, is the focus of the present research, which examines how one of the drivers of resilience, technology, influences museums and cultural organizations, both public and private, in achieving the resilience goal.

5.3 Digital Technologies for Resilience

The conceptual framework of value cocreation acknowledges the centrality of processes and practices of interaction and exchange within the relationships between suppliers and consumers (Payne et al., 2008). Suppliers must be able to stimulate the latter, activating forms of engagement in the various stages of the process if consumers' ability to cocreate is dependent upon the information, skills, and operational resources they can access and use. Both public and private organizations utilize those interactions and transactions that facilitate resource, skill, and practice exchanges as antecedents to the process of value cocreation. The value of a product or service can be determined by its use (*value-in-use*) and its price (*value-in-exchange*), according to Lusch and Vargo (2006). A special emphasis is placed on this dual aspect of value in public management studies, which are increasingly conceiving cocreation as a new approach to value formation in the community (Osborne et al., 2016; Osborne, 2018). In fact, the New Public Governance paradigm views cocreation as a strategy to address governmental austerity and trust issues (Cepiku et al., 2016, Steccolini et al., 2020). According to Alves (2013, p. 677), the process of value cocreation is initiated by value in use, mediated and monitored by exchange value. As a result of this reasoning, cocreation occurs with the community and not for the community, generating significant social consensus toward local government. The value propositions companies make to their customers depend on the process through which the latter make the service their own (*service appropriation*). By engaging in cocreation, companies can explicitly articulate the desired benefits (well-being, satisfaction, utility, pleasure, etc.) (Mifsud et al., 2015, p. 707).

Service appropriation is a cognitive approach to the service (i.e., knowledge of the service, awareness of the service, creation of the service and control of the same) according to which consumers can manage it, with digital technology deemed most appropriate (Mifsud et al., 2015, p. 719). From this perspective, ICT allows consumers to transform and personalize the value of the services they use. Digital technologies have transformed supplier-consumer interactions and into value cocreation (Garrido-Moreno et al., 2020).

Several studies have highlighted the importance of social media in stimulating customer engagement (Rubalcaba et al., 2012). They are not viewed so much as social innovation in itself but rather as a driver of innovation in the services themselves. According to the theory of service-dominant logic (S-D), it is the output of a process of integration of resources contributed by different actors in various ways in the context of the cocreation of value. Recent surveys have highlighted how creativity derives from curiosity and continuous learning, which lead companies to create and use relevant insights. Considering the worldwide diffusion of digital applications, technological knowledge offers the potential to generate ideas for innovation and to transform these ideas into innovative services, with a positive impact on organizational performance (Tsai & Huang, 2020).

The transformative power of digital technologies in creating new ways of interaction and collaboration deserves to be further investigated from the perspective of organizations, considering that most of the studies have dealt with ICT mainly assuming the point of view of consumers (Kunz & Walsh, 2020). Technological knowledge (skills, methods, systems, and equipment) affects, in fact, the ability of an organization to create social impact and multilevel well-being (Aksoy et al., 2019). From this point of view, digital technology represents social, process, and/or product innovation, which encourages corporate behavior aimed at achieving short- and medium- to long-term objectives through stakeholder engagement (Periac et al., 2018, p. 21).

This study is therefore motivated by the study of digital technology's transformative power in service companies, including cultural organizations (Díaz-Méndez & Gummesson, 2012). The value created by them, as is known, is given by the experience lived by the user of the artistic goods managed by them (Prahalad & Ramaswamy, 2004). More specifically, the creation of value arises from the alignment between the design intention of cultural organizations (i.e., the planned experience) and the actual experience of the users (i.e., the realized experience) (Ponsignon et al., 2017).

Digital technology is mainly explored from the user's point of view with the aim of verifying its effectiveness in increasing the experiential impact of the use of collections. There are also contributions on the effects of digital use on cultural content, on its mediation between cultural organizations and users and on its use as an audience development tool (Agostino et al., 2020; Kunz & Walsh, 2020; Saunila et al., 2018).

However, what appears to be of particular interest for research is the analysis of the preconditions that allow the adoption of digital technology as a driver of social innovation (Toivonen & Tuominen, 2009). Assuming the managerial viewpoint, this chapter will focus on the micro level, that is, technology as a social innovation by a cultural organization, with particular regard to public museums (i.e., university museums) and private ones (i.e., Corporate Museums and Archives), leaving developments for future research on the meso (cultural networks) and macro (cultural ecosystem) levels. In addition to the gap in cultural heritage management, the health emergency of the COVID-19 pandemic added further relevance to this research topic by grafting it into the field of corporate resilience.

5.3.1 *The Lessons from the Italian Universities' Museums During the COVID-19 Pandemic*

Overview

The objective of this study, conducted during the first wave of coronavirus (February–June 2020), was to contribute to the doctrinal debate regarding the resilience of cultural organizations, particularly Italian University Museums. In particular, the research aimed to verify their ability to restore or recover equilibrium during the implementation of precautionary measures taken against the spread of the virus.

Italian University Museums were selected for the following reasons:

1. as a result of the pandemic, cultural organizations in the public sector, such as universities, have faced numerous critical issues (i.e., remote teaching, "smart" working) (Watermeyer et al., 2021);
2. the relevance of university collections in the context of university outreach, which is assuming increasing importance, as well as for the purposes of evaluating the quality of the Italian academic system by ANVUR (National Agency for University Evaluation and Research) but has been poorly explored in the management literature (Mozzoni et al., 2018);
3. the rapid spread of coronavirus in Italy, the country most affected by it immediately following China (Agostino et al., 2020).

Therefore, this study has attempted to answer the following research questions: *how did Italian University Museums react to the COVID-19 pandemic emergency during the lockdown? What has been the role of accounting for organizational resilience?*

Methodology

A survey based on primary sources was conducted to answer the previous research questions. Using a questionnaire, the entire population of Italian University Museums was surveyed, and the data are available on the Ministry of University and Research website (http://dati.ustat.miur.it/dataset/metadati). There are 78 universities listed in this source, of which 58 are public and 20 are private.

An analysis of Italian public universities that manage collections in museums or museum systems was conducted. Thirty-eight Italian University Museums were included in the analysis. An initial version of the questionnaire was prepared and sent to a random sample of university museums (9.8% of the population) to collect the information necessary to answer the research questions. This made it possible to verify whether the questions had been asked clearly and whether further alternatives had to be included in the multiple-choice answers. The final version of the questionnaire consists of ten questions divided into four sections: section I requires data from university museums (e.g., organizational model, size, opening hours, ticketing); sections II and III concern, respectively, the activities—including accounting—that these museums used to carry out before the lockdown and that they carried out during the lockdown itself; and section IV includes a final question on the role of accounting during museum management at the time of the pandemic (Table 5.1).

In its final form, the questionnaire was sent via a digital platform to the President, Director, and Curator of any Italian University Museum. The survey was conducted between May and June 2020, with a 91% return rate.

Responses were coded as binary variables and treated as quantitative data, except for the last open response. This approach is based on the interpretation of the data as a social construction (Englund et al., 2011; Giddens, 1981). An analysis of the background of the museums considered was conducted to compare their activities prior to and during the pandemic (Yin, 2018).

Results

According to the analysis of the data (34 respondents out of a total of 38 respondents), the identity of Italian University Museums was determined (Table 5.2). The majority of the samples examined are located in Southern

Table 5.1 The questionnaire structure used for the survey

Questionnaire Structure	*Contents*	*Objectives*
Section I	1. The organizational position of the compilers of the questionnaire 2. The organizational model 3. The number of staff 4. The opening hours 5. Ticketing	To define the identikit of the University Museum(s)
Section II	6. The pre-lockdown activities	To understand the value creation processes
	7. The activities carried out during the first lockdown	To check the University Museum's capabilities to react to the pandemic
Section III	8. ICT investment	To explore the efforts done in ICT context
	9. The contribution of accounting in managing University Museums during the Covid-19 pandemic	To verify the contribution of accounting to the museum management in times of pandemic
Section IV	10. The role of culture for society during the Covid-19 pandemic	To understand the level of awareness of the museum managers to create value for the society at first of lockdown against the Covid-19 pandemic

Italy (47%) and represent a cost center for the university (50%). A total of 23.5% of the sample is part of the general management of the university. In 41% of museums, there are fewer than three human resources, but in the same number, there are more than ten. For 50% of the sample, access to the collections is possible during office hours. University collections are managed with a value for money approach based on a balance between economy and sociality, and paid tickets are provided even if targeted (61.8%).

Information on value creation processes carried out before and during the lockdown was collected from Sections II and III of the questionnaires. Based on the degree of organizational and financial autonomy of the institutions to which they belong, we considered it necessary to divide the sample into three clusters (C1–C2–C3). It is true that the ability to create value is not only a function of the number and specific skills of the personnel devoted to the collections but also of the combination of autonomy

Table 5.2 Identikit of the Italian University Museum

Variable	*Category*	*Number*	*Percentage*
Location	North	8	23.5
	Centre	10	29.4
	South	16	47.1
Organizational model	Cost centre	17	50
	Service centre	4	11.8
	Foundation	1	2.9
	Central administration unit	8	23.5
	Department unit	4	11.8
Size (staff units no.)	≤ 3	14	41.2
	4–6	4	11.8
	7–10	2	5.9
	10–20	7	20.6
	≥20	7	20.6
Opening hours	Always	7	20.6
	2 days/week	1	2.9
	Office hours	17	50
	By appointment	5	14.5
	Flexible	4	11.8
Accessibility	Free access	4	11.8
	Fee entrance	9	26.5
	Diversified fee entrance	21	61.8

and responsibility, namely, the capacity to decide on cultural initiatives and related expenses, taking into account the administrative and legal ties with the university of origin. In this regard, a university museum that is organized as a service center will have greater financial capacity and operational dynamism than one organized as a cost center. On the basis of this lens, the following clusters were identified:

(a) Cluster 1 (C1) represented by museums that have spending autonomy (cost centers), with a collection manager;
(b) Cluster 2 (C2) consisted of collections managed directly by the management or departmental structure of the university (without any autonomy of its own);
(c) Cluster 3 (C3) consisted of museums that have independent spending but also a specific organizational structure within that of the university to which they belong (service centers) or managed by another entity in which the university participates (e.g., foundation).

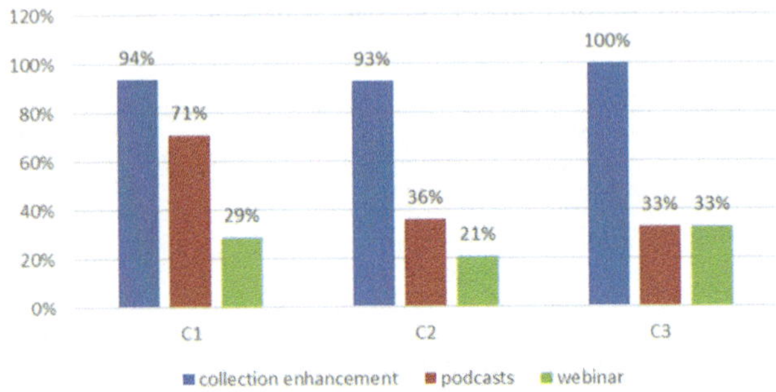

Fig. 5.1 Value creation processes in the Italian University Museums during the first lockdown

The value creation processes in which Italian University Museums were engaged before the pandemic concerned the care, conservation, and enhancement of the collections (Fig. 5.1).

As part of their main "core" creation processes, these museums emphasize collection enhancement, guided tours, exhibitions, and educational workshops to promote the development of public engagement, which is necessary for outreach. As a result of the lockdown, only the C1 cluster was able to guarantee cultural content by using podcasts to inform the public about the collections (71%). On the other hand, other clusters drastically reduced their operations, which included the organization of conferences in addition to previous activity at a distance.

It has been difficult for educational laboratories, for example, to work with schools owing to the pandemic's distancing, even though some museums, such as C3, have managed to work with schools by simply using a remote mode (Fig. 5.2).

To disseminate digital content about collections, the management of social media, as a cultural support process (Giannini & Bowen, 2019), has been of crucial importance. With the exception of C2, which recorded a slight decrease during the pandemic, the use of digital communication has increased significantly. It is evident, however, that the use of digital technology for communication with users has more than doubled in museums in C3 (Fig. 5.3).

Aside from other cultural support processes, there is also control of the number of visitors as a managerial accountability practice, which was maintained even during the pandemic (Fig. 5.4).

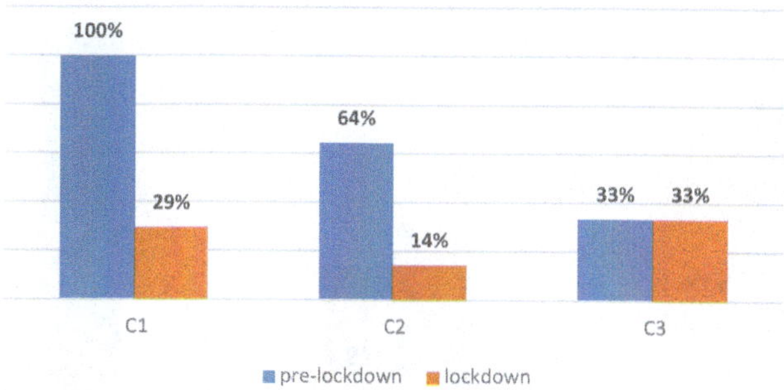

Fig. 5.2 Edutainment labs in Italian University Museums before and during the first lockdown

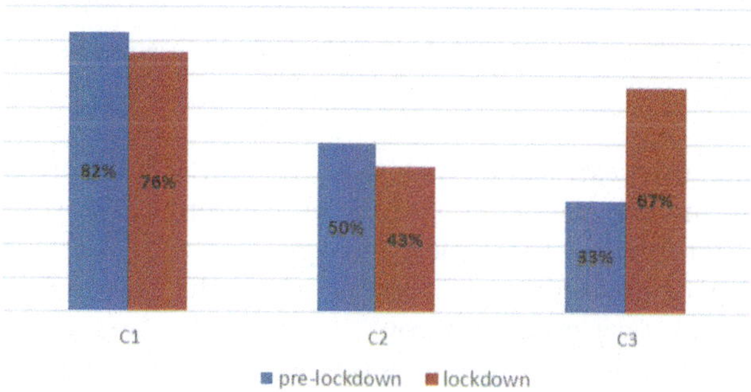

Fig. 5.3 Social media management in Italian University Museums before and during the first lockdown

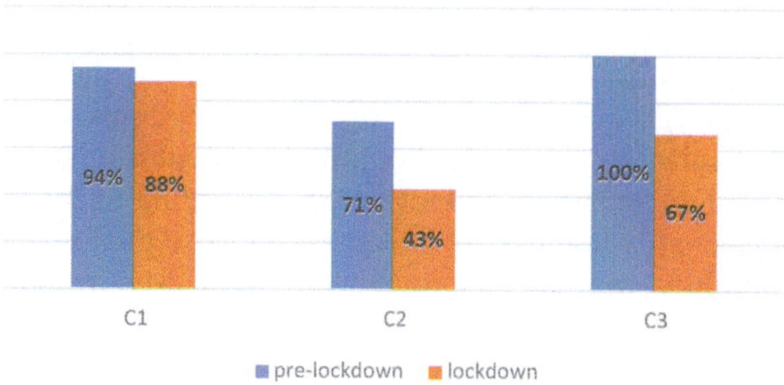

Fig. 5.4 Visitors' accounting in Italian University Museums before and during the first lockdown

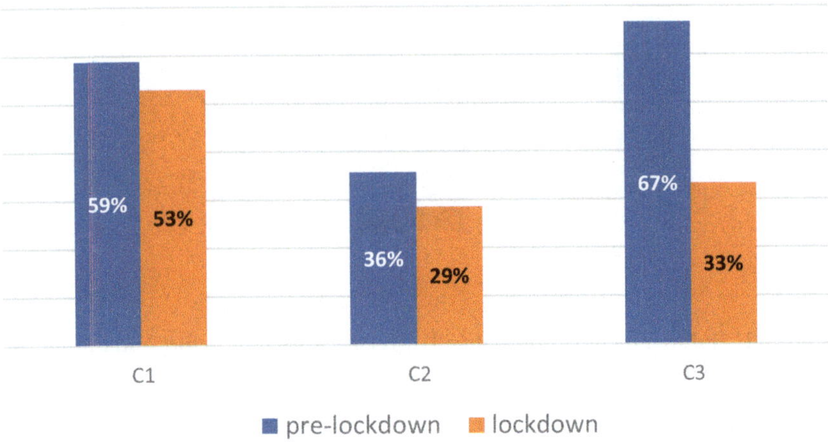

Fig. 5.5 Visitors' satisfaction with Italian University Museums before and during the first lockdown

From the user satisfaction analysis, C1 and C3 reported a drastic decrease during the pandemic (Fig. 5.5). Therefore, C2 shows a slight reduction, considering the typical management of collections from the point of view of university departments, where the function of study and research prevails over public fruition.

As part of the value creation processes, accountability reporting regarding university museum staff activities (Fig. 5.6) was also included. It is not surprising that the rapid and widespread use of smart working (Fig. 5.7), never experienced by Italian University Museums in the past, has increased within Italian University Museums (Busco et al., 2007; Magliacani & Sorrentino, 2022).

According to cultural heritage management theory, the questionnaire addressed a specific question to the university museums that were analyzed. In particular, we asked whether public awareness of the importance of cultural heritage in society had increased. According to the information gathered, university museums are effectively aware of the impact they have on the community: they are able to generate value even from a distance.[1]

[1] Having established a list of museums coded with a number in accordance with the return timing of the relevant questionnaire, we have ensured that the right to privacy provided for in the questionnaire sent via the web is protected. Therefore, the acronym MU31 refers to the university museum whose questionnaire was completed after the first 30 days.

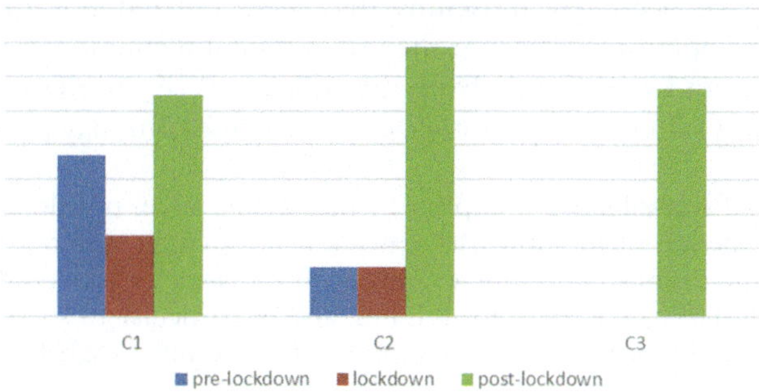

Fig. 5.6 Accountability reporting in Italian University Museums before, during, and after the first lockdown

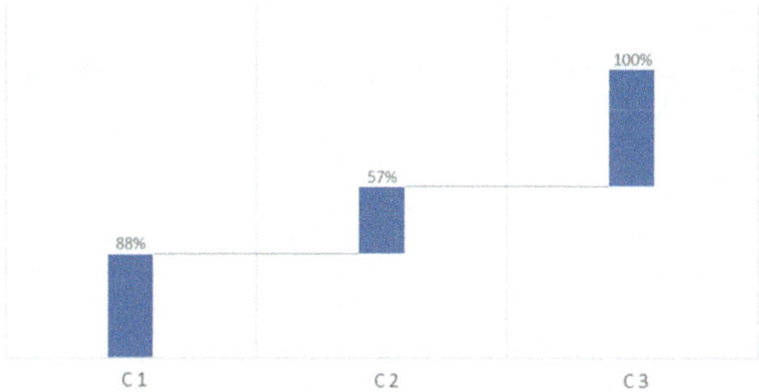

Fig. 5.7 Smart working in Italian University Museums during the first lockdown

In general, the viewpoints of the university museums are summarized in the following answers:

> Art and culture have, in my opinion, provided not only a means of escape but also a means for personal and collective growth due to the availability of time. (MU#31)

> The cultural assets of a community certainly represent a refuge during times of crisis, as they represent a community's reassuring identity. As a result of pandemic isolation, content and values have been emphasized, too often taken for granted, and above all the irreplaceability of face-to-face interaction. As a result, smart solutions are needed so that the virtual is more integrated with the needs that have emerged rather than merely being an end in itself. (MU#8)

There have been few museums that have utilized this question to express their opinions regarding the use of digital technologies to transfer the contents and values underlying the collections. From this perspective, the following statement by another university museum may prove useful:

> The digital accessibility put in place by the various places of culture during the long period of lockdown have made it possible to explore, discover, deepen the various opportunities present in the area, as evidenced by the very high index of accesses to websites, and in particular to social media, museums and other cultural organizations of the country. (MU#2)

Another particularly relevant finding collected by this section concerns the role attributed to digital technology in the cocreation of value, which is certainly strategic when direct access to collections is prevented. As was well expressed by the previous museum:

> Digital visits are a prelude, in most cases, to the *in situ* visit and represent its preparation. (MU#2)

Discussion

The evidence obtained suggests that Italian University Museums are characterized by dynamism due to their organizational characteristics and their degree of autonomy from their owner institution (Bozeman, 2019; Bozeman & Johnson, 2015).

However, the COVID-19 pandemic has put these cultural organizations in crisis by altering their normal operating conditions. In all three clusters examined, digital technology was widely used to share cultural content, specifically via social media. This technology has enabled the transfer of value that is normally cocreated during visits to collections or in situ edutainment activities into virtual reality. However, the difficulty in detecting the degree of interaction with the public and the inability to reach a wider audience due to the digital gap encountered in society during the pandemic has certainly compromised the process of cocreating value in the activities core of the museum (Magliacani & Sorrentino, 2022).

Returning to the research questions, Italian University Museums have demonstrated their ability to respond to external shock by using digital technology to restore a sense of normality during the lockdown (Agostino et al., 2020). To avoid worse repercussions, they have maintained their usual activities within the limits set by the provisions imposed by the ministry on the management of the health emergency. Despite the closing of places of culture and the digital gap that exists in society, they were able to restore the pre-pandemic balance within a short period of time through their creativity and the use of digital technology.

The evidence highlights the "reactive" approach adopted by Italian University Museums to restore a preexisting condition of normality (*precursor resilience*) and to ensure the transfer of material and immaterial cultural heritage of the collections to the public, albeit remotely. As part of this evolutionary framework, performance measurement activities have been maintained, although with regard to the number of users (rather than in situ visitors) of digital content.

5.3.2 The Experience of the Italian Association of Corporate Archives and Museums

Overview

Museimpresa (the Associazione Italiana Archivi e Musei d'Impresa) brings together approximately 100 museums and archives of large, medium, and small Italian companies. Founded in Milan in 2001 on the initiative of Assolombarda and Confindustria, it is the most comprehensive network at the European level. It is committed to bringing together new players in business culture, influencing training processes, safeguarding the memory of Italian industries, and enhancing the testimonies of an extraordinary manufacturing capacity that is the engine of sustainable development and the cornerstone of a widespread economic, social, and civil culture (Museimpresa, a).

The mission of this Association is to promote enterprises' cultural policies through the dissemination of quality standards. This will encourage the exchange and dissemination of knowledge and experiences among the museum community, enterprises, cultural institutions, and the general public. In addition, it aims to carry out research, training, development, and in-depth studies in the field of museology and business archives, as well as to increase the relationship and interaction between businesses and archives operating nationally and internationally, with a view to joint enhancement projects. Finally, it aims to stimulate different institutional actors to invest in business culture to prevent the dispersion of significant entrepreneurial heritages (Museimpresa, a).

Through these museums, enterprises do not intend to sell goods and services but rather to tell something about themselves to transform their experiences into collective memories (Gonizzi, 2019), thereby enhancing and preserving Italian industrial culture (Montemaggi, 2008).

According to the website of the Association, 99 museums or archives are affiliated, sharing the same goals and contributing to the development of its programmatic lines (Museimpresa, b).

Following the outbreak of the COVID-19 pandemic and the implementation of distancing and lockdown measures, these organizations were forced to suspend the provision of in-person services. For this reason, it was considered worthwhile to analyze how they responded to this situation since the dissemination of culture was a primary objective of theirs. Corporate Museums and Archives were chosen as the subject of analysis since they were unable to fulfill their corporate purpose as usual and established. Moreover, they constitute unique cases in that they are private museums run by enterprises, pursuing corporate objectives. Furthermore, they are Italian, thus being from the first country heavily affected by the pandemic after China (Agostino et al., 2020).

Reorganization and technology are two of the main drivers of resilience, so it was decided to focus on one of the possible modes of adaptation most popular during the pandemic: the use of technology to accomplish corporate objectives (Dindarian, 2019).

Thus, the study aims to answer the following research question: *how have Corporate Museums and Archives responded to the COVID-19 pandemic? What lessons have they learned? Did accounting play a relevant role in the pursuit of resilience goals?*

Methodology

To answer the research questions, the study involved the analysis of primary sources through the preparation of a survey (Jamsen & Corley, 2007). We first mapped Corporate Museums and Archives from the association's website (Museimpresa, b). Of the association's 99 members, 50 (50% of the total population) were randomly selected and sent a questionnaire. We received 32 responses (64% response rate). However, five of them were from Archives that affirmed they had kept their services the same after the pandemic outbreak or from organizations that stated that, because of their small size, they could not be considered Corporate Archives capable of providing meaningful data for our study. Nevertheless, 54% of the surveyed organizations provided relevant information for our investigation.

The questionnaire sent included 12 questions divided into five sections, as shown in Table 5.3.

Table 5.3 Questionnaire structure

Questionnaire Structure	*Contents*	*Objectives*
Section I	1. Role of technology before COVID-19	To analyze the baseline situation in the use of technologies (pre-pandemic)
	2. Types of technologies adopted by corporate museums before COVID-19	
Section II	3. Variations in technology use after the pandemic outbreak 4. Types of variation 5. Influence of technology on continuity of service offered	To verify whether and how the corporate museum responded to the pandemic by adopting solutions in terms of technology
Section III	6. Maintenance of improvements after the pandemic 7. Perception of service improvement to users due to changes made during the pandemic	Effects of change
Section IV	8. Perception of technology as a tool for resilience 9. Influence of organizational change on business resilience 10. Key elements of resilience	To check museums' perceptions of the relevance of technology's role in resilience
Section V	11. Perception of the need to make changes in the performance measurement system 12. Reporting changes	Changes in terms of accounting and reporting

Questions N. 3, 5, 6, 9, and 10 were coded as binary variables and then treated as quantitative data. Questions N. 1, 7, and 8 involved answers given on a scale of 1 to 5 and were also treated as quantitative data. Instead, the remaining answers required the indication of adopted instruments: they were analyzed using a qualitative approach based on the interpretation of the data as a social construction (Englund et al., 2011; Giddens, 1981). A comparison with pre-pandemic conditions was made, as was done in the case of university museums, to identify what changes took place following the outbreak of the pandemic (Yin, 2018).

Results

A summary of the identity of the Corporate Museums and Archives analyzed is provided in Table 5.4. A majority of the association members who responded to the questionnaire were located in northern Italy (70.3%) and were museums (59.26%). The sector to which they belong is mainly Food (29.63%), followed by Banking and Insurance (11.11%), Energy (11.11%), and Manufacturing (11.11%). Most are open to the public (only one is not), and access is usually free, but booking is required (55.56%).

In section I of the questionnaire, it appears that technology plays a medium to high role in Corporate Museums and Archives, as 26 out of 27 museums gave it a significance of three or higher (Fig. 5.8).

A notable observation is that Corporate Museums and Archives primarily used technology for public outreach before the outbreak of the pandemic: they updated their websites (74.07%) and actively managed their social networking profiles (55.56%). Only a few had already introduced interactive totems (25.93%) or activated the possibility of conducting virtual tours (18.52%) (Fig. 5.9).

Table 5.4 Identikit of the Corporate Museums and Archives

Variable	*Category*	*Number*	*Percentage*
Archive/Museum	Archive	7	25.93
	Museum	16	59.26
	Museum and archive	4	14.81
Location	Centre	5	18.52
	North	19	70.37
	South	3	11.11
Sector of production	Food	8	29.63
	Automotive	2	7.41
	Banking and insurance	3	11.11
	Design	2	7.41
	Publishing	1	3.70
	Energy	3	11.11
	Manufacturing of paper and paper products	2	7.41
	Industrial	1	3.70
	Manufacturing	3	11.11
	Textiles and clothing	2	7.41
Accessibility	Free admission upon request	15	55.56
	Diversified fee entrance	7	25.93
	Fee entrance	3	11.11
	N/A	1	3.70
	Not accessible	1	3.70

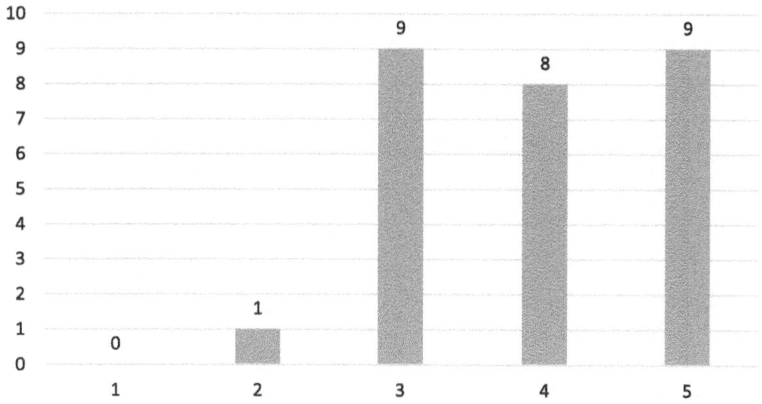

Fig. 5.8 Relevance of the use of technology in the organization

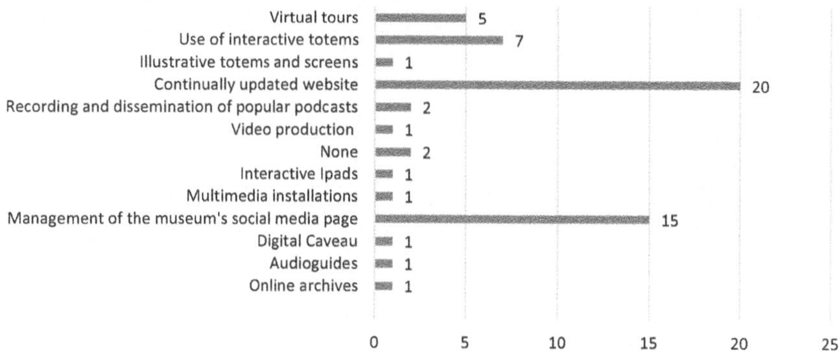

Fig. 5.9 Technologies adopted by corporate museums before the pandemic

Following the pandemic outbreak, changes in the use of technological tools took place in 81.5% of museums and archives (22 out of 27) (Fig. 5.10).

Changes were primarily focused on improving the use of existing technologies (improvement of the website—13 museums/archives, purchase of new technological tools—11 museums/archives) as well as the implementation of new technology-based applications, such as recording and disseminating popular podcasts, arranging guided tours, or opening museum/archive pages on social media (Fig. 5.11).

Fig. 5.10 Existence of changes in the use of technology

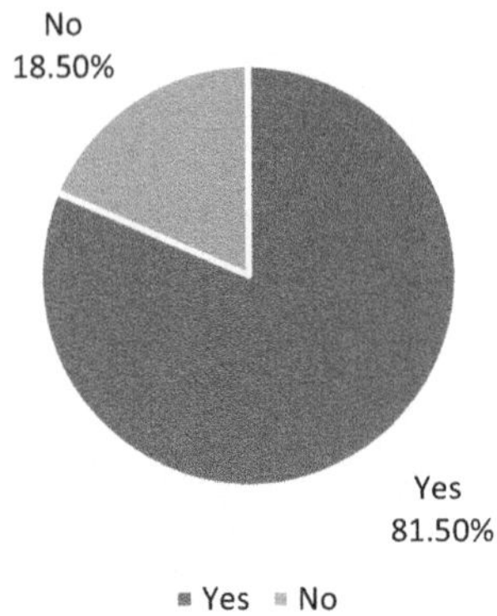

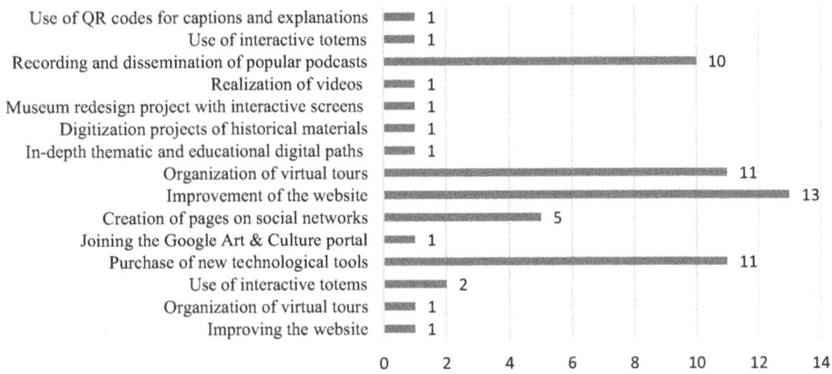

Fig. 5.11 Types of changes in the use of technology

The survey found that 74.1% of respondents believe that technology has been instrumental in enabling the Corporate Museum and Archives to continue providing services, ensuring continuity in terms of access to culture for visitors despite the pandemic (Fig. 5.12).

It is important to note that in 80% of cases, these new technological applications were maintained after the pandemic emergency period (Fig. 5.13), as they recognized their importance and the improvement they had on their activities, particularly on their accessibility to the public. In fact, 17 out of 27 museums/archives considered technology relevant or reasonably relevant to improving accessibility (Fig. 5.14).

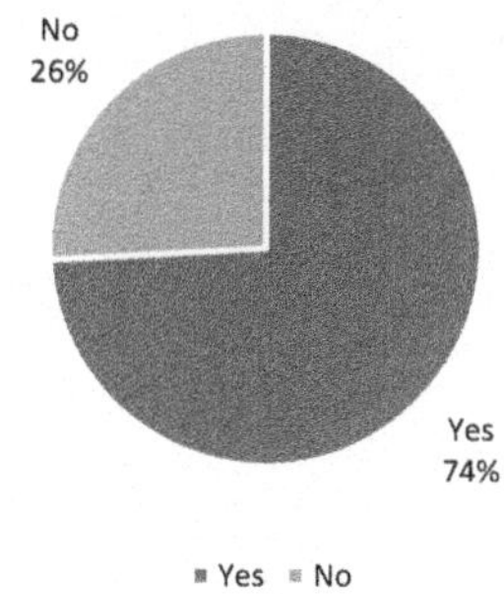

Fig. 5.12 Influence of technology on continuity during the pandemic

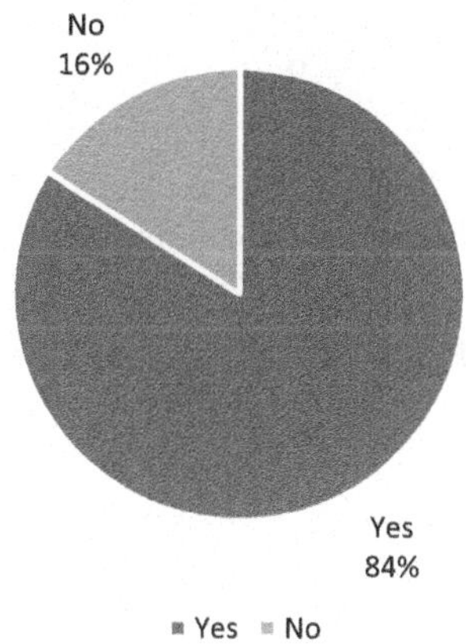

Fig. 5.13 Maintaining new uses of technology after the pandemic

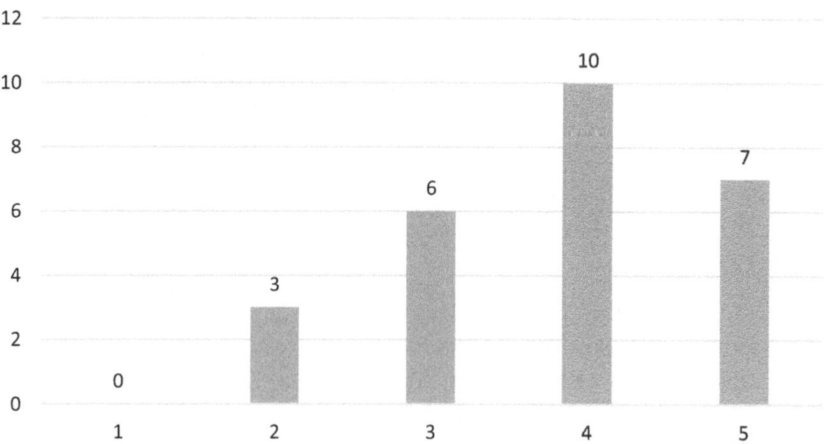

Fig. 5.14 Improved museum accessibility through technology

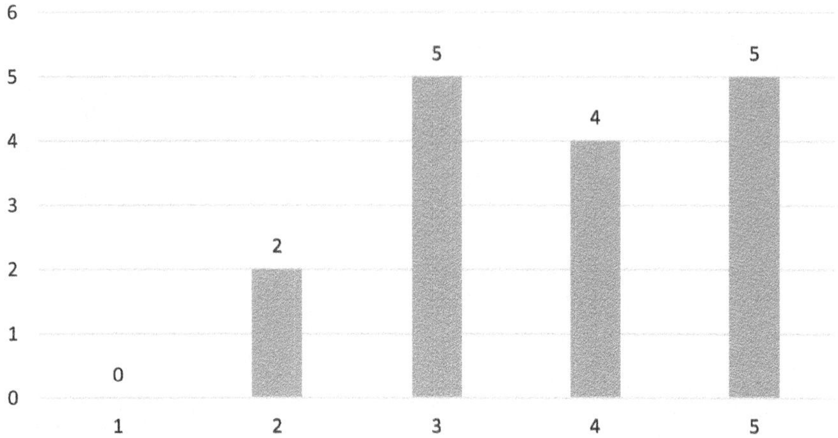

Fig. 5.15 Defining their museum as resilient

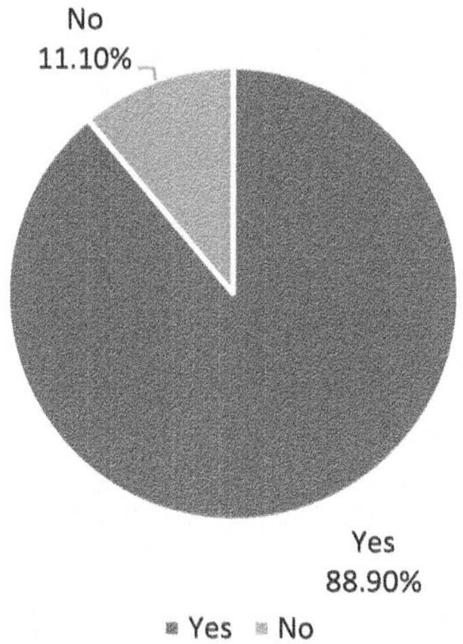

Fig. 5.16 Technology as a driver of resilience

The majority of museums and archives believe that they have handled the pandemic efficiently and describe themselves as resilient (25.9%) or reasonably resilient (48.1%) (Fig. 5.15). A total of 88.9% of them also believe that technology has played an important role in achieving their resilience objectives (Fig. 5.16).

In addition, museums and archives were asked to indicate what they believed were three key drivers of resilience in the environment of Corporate Museums and Archives. Using *Wordcoud.com* software, a Word Cloud was generated using their responses, as shown in Fig. 5.17. Based on the picture, it is shown that, according to the Corporate Museums and Archives, it is necessary to have the ability to innovate, modify the business, anticipate changes, and be ready to react—even through the use of technology—to be resilient.

The changes in technology after the pandemic did not necessitate any variation in the accounting practices of Corporate Museums and Archives in most cases (69.2%) (Fig. 5.18).

Among those who made changes (8 museums/archives), these mainly concerned the publication of information on their website (7 museums/archives) and the preparation of nonfinancial reporting (4 museums/

Fig. 5.17 Word Cloud: drivers of resilience

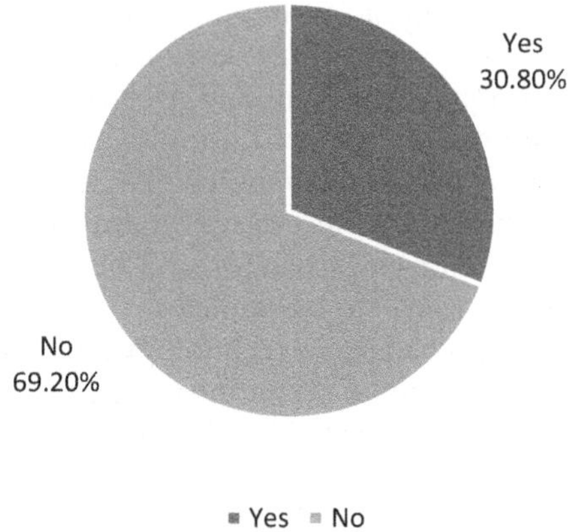

Fig. 5.18 Reporting changes after the pandemic

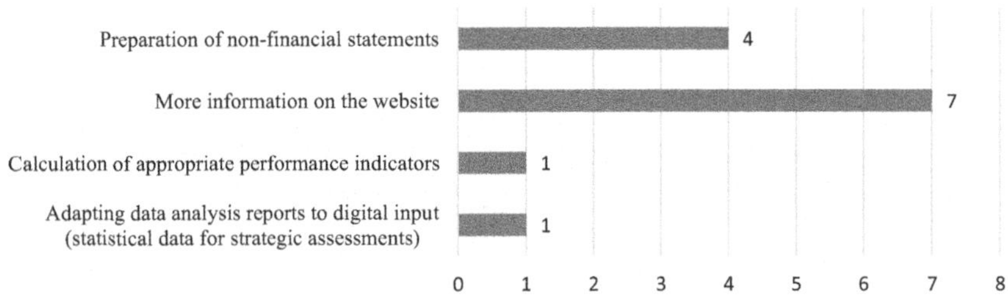

Fig. 5.19 Type of reporting changes after the pandemic

archives). To calculate performance indicators, the Museo della Liquirizia "Giorgio Amarelli" has opted to utilize measures related to staff training and further education, management innovation, and community strengthening. The Museo Storico Reale Mutua, on the other hand, decided to adapt data analysis reports to digital input: statistical data were calculated for a strategic evaluation of the changes made (Fig. 5.19).

Discussion

The current study on Corporate Museums and Archives is designed to be exploratory and provide an initial understanding of how these particular cultural organizations are organized and managed, even during times of crisis. A number of changes have been made as a result of the pandemic to ensure continuity of services provided, as seen by comparing the endowment and use of technological tools during the precrisis and postcrisis periods. Strong support from technology has been provided to museums and archives in this regard, enabling them to continue to disseminate culture using new tools while maintaining their value creation processes. Visually, through virtual visits, as well as auditorily, through the distribution of podcasts, this has been accomplished.

To continue to reach the public and provide their services, most of the museums and archives analyzed have reorganized their activities through the use of technology. As a result, they were able to cope with the crisis and overcome it. Furthermore, they maintained the changes made even after the state of emergency, sometimes improving the services offered, demonstrating their resiliency (Vogus & Sutcliffe, 2007; Linnenluecke, 2017).

According to the analysis of these case studies, little emphasis was placed on the use of reporting tools to verify the effectiveness and efficiency of the changes made. Only 30.8% of museums and archives participating in the study felt that they had to make changes to their reporting. They did not consider that accounting can potentially play a crucial role in crises, providing support for decision-making and verifying ex-post the efficiency of the choices made.

5.4 Final Remarks

Digitization represents a phenomenon studied in different fields and under various aspects. It represents a social innovation in the context of service management studies focused on the cocreation of value, considering its contribution to the virtual interaction between supplier and consumer (Rubalcaba et al., 2012).

As an organizational competence, digital technology can also facilitate dialog with stakeholders to enhance their participation in the various phases of value creation, from conception through evaluation (Alves, 2013). This competence has recently been analyzed in the context of studies focused on resilience, especially in relation to the COVID-19 pandemic. Moreover, the role of digital technology in facing the pandemic has also been investigated in the context of cultural organizations, with particular regard to museums (Agostino et al., 2020).

Due to the closure imposed during the first lockdown and the following lockdown, which forced cultural organizations to operate differently, the debate on the use of technology has certainly widened.

The conceptual model that emerged from the surveys highlights technological knowledge as a prerequisite that has favored a rapid return to normality, albeit conditioned by the restrictions induced by the regulatory decrees concerning the management of the pandemic. The closure of places of culture has accelerated the use of digital technology in the "core" processes of value creation (podcasts, online educational laboratories, virtual tours) and, in the case of university museums, in collateral processes (webinars) and in supporting ones (performance measurement and accountability reporting), as well as in the *modus operandi* of the museums' personnel (smart working).

In terms of cocreation of value, the opinions expressed by the employees who completed both questionnaires were illuminating. This was indeed an essential condition for responding to the pandemic, since it allowed scientific-cultural content to be disseminated to a wide audience equipped with synchronous and asynchronous technological devices. Moreover, digital technology should not be considered a sufficient condition for guaranteeing the cocreation of value in university museums, especially when considering the public, which is not equipped with a digital device.

Considering the theoretical models assumed on resilience (Conz & Magnani, 2020), the museums investigated—both public and private—have shown that they can deal with the health emergency by giving continuity to some "core" activities through "smart" management of knowledge and cultural heritage. It is therefore an example of *precursor resilience* based on technology as a driver of this capacity (Fig. 5.8). In this way, museums have been able to respond to changes in the environment in a timely, reactive manner consistent with the concept of homeostasis between the organization and its environment (Fig. 5.20).

It is hoped that the proposed conceptual model will provide operators with a means of comparing what has been accomplished by Italian University Museums and Corporate Museums and Archives when facing an external shock, such as a pandemic, which threatens their daily lives. Thus, what has been the precondition for such resilient behavior? Museums are evaluated not only on the basis of their ability to utilize digital technologies but also on the basis of their organizational cultures in relation to digital technology. Whether the Italian museums were autonomous or not, their resilience was sparked by organizational values such as dedication to work, trust, sharing, and awareness of their high mission to society.

Fig. 5.20 Digital technology as a driver of cultural organizations' resilience

The study thus provides valuable insight into how the power of transformation is not exclusively the property of digital technology but that of cultural goods, so long as their fruition is accompanied by a narrative voice that makes a visit enjoyable and instructive for anyone interested in learning about a community's cultural heritage (i.e., the history of the university or the history of "Made in Italy"). According to recent studies on museum management, the direct fruition of collections remains an essential condition for the cocreation of value through service appropriation by users of culture (Samaroudi et al., 2020; Agostino et al., 2020; Magliacani & Sorrentino, 2022).

References

Agostino, D., Arnaboldi, M., & Lampis, A. (2020). Italian state museums during the COVID-19 crisis: From onsite closure to online openness. *Museum Management and Curatorship, 35*(4), 362–372.

Aksoy, Y., Basso, H. S., Smith, R. P., & Grasl, T. (2019). Demographic structure and macroeconomic trends. *American Economic Journal: Macroeconomics, 11*(1), 193–222.

Alves, H. (2013). Co-creation and innovation in public services. *The Service Industries Journal, 33*(7–8), 671–682.

Bernard, M. J., & Dubard Barbosa, S. (2016). Resilience and entrepreneurship: A dynamic and biographical approach to the entrepreneurial act. *M@ n@gement, 19*(2), 89–123.

Bozeman, B. (2019). Public values: Citizens' perspective. *Public Management Review, 21*(6), 817–838.

Bozeman, B., & Johnson, J. (2015). The political economy of public values: A case for the public sphere and progressive opportunity. *The American Review of Public Administration, 45*(1), 61–85.

Burnard, K., & Bhamra, R. (2011). Organisational resilience: Development of a conceptual framework for organisational responses. *International Journal of Production Research, 49*(18), 5581–5599.

Busco, C., Quattrone, P., & Riccaboni, A. (2007). Management accounting: Issues in interpreting its nature and change. *Management Accounting Research, 18*(2), 125–149.

Cepiku, D., Mussari, R., & Giordano, F. (2016). Local governments managing austerity: Approaches, determinants and impact. *Public Administration, 94*(1), 223–243.

Conz, E., & Magnani, G. (2020). A dynamic perspective on the resilience of firms: A systematic literature review and a framework for future research. *European Management Journal, 38*(3), 400–412.

Coppola, A. (2016). Cambiamento climatico, resilienza e politiche urbane. *Italiani europei, 4.*

Cutter, S. L. (1996). Vulnerability to environmental hazards. *Progress in Human Geography, 20*(4), 529–539.

D'Arpino, F. & Mancini, M. (2015). La resilienza economica e sociale. In *La Magia della Resilienza.* .

Díaz-Méndez, M., & Gummesson, E. (2012). Value co-creation and university teaching quality: Consequences for the European higher education area (EHEA). *Journal of Service Management, 23*, 571–592.

Dindarian, K. (2019). *Exploring enterprise resilience through the theoretical lens of complexity: A case study situated in the high value-manufacturing sector.* The University of Manchester (United Kingdom).

Engemann, K. J., & Henderson, D. M. (2014). *Business continuity and risk management: Essentials of organizational resilience.* Rothstein Publishing.

Englund, H., Gerdin, J., & Burns, J. (2011). 25 years of Giddens in accounting research: Achievements, limitations and the future. *Accounting, Organizations and Society, 36*(8), 494–513.

Garrido-Moreno, A., García-Morales, V., King, S., & Lockett, N. (2020). Social Media use and value creation in the digital landscape: A dynamic-capabilities perspective. *Journal of Service Management, 31*(3), 313–343.

Giannini, T., & Bowen, J. P. (2019). *Museums and digital culture: New perspectives and research.* Springer.

Giddens, A. (1981). *A contemporary critique of historical materialism* (Vol. 1). University of California Press.

Gonizzi, G. (2019). La rete di Museimpresa. Il museo d'impresa come modello contemporaneo. *Economia della Cultura, 29*(1), 43–48.

Gover, L., & Duxbury, L. (2018). Inside the onion: Understanding what enhances and inhibits organizational resilience. *The Journal of Applied Behavioral Science, 54*(4), 477–501.

Gulati, R. (2010). *Reorganize for resilience: Putting customers at the center of your business.* Harvard Business Press.

Hallegatte, S. (2014). Economic resilience: Definition and measurement. *World Bank Policy Research Working Paper* (6852).

Hamel, G., & Valikangas, L. (2004). The quest for resilience. *icade. Revista de la Facultad de Derecho, 62*, 355–358.

Home, J. F., III, & Orr, J. E. (1997). Assessing behaviors that create resilient organizations. *Employment Relations Today, 24*(4), 29–39.

Ivanov, D., Tsipoulanidis, A., & Schönberger, J. (2021). Supply chain risk management and resilience. In D. Ivanov, A. Tsipoulanidis, & J. Schönberger (Eds.), *Global supply chain and operations management: A decision-oriented introduction to the creation of value* (pp. 485–520). Springer International Publishing.

Jamsen, J., & Corley, K. (2007). E-survey methodology. In *Handbook of research on electronic surveys and measurements* (pp. 1–8). IGI Global.

Johnsen, S. (2010). Resilience in risk analysis and risk assessment. In *Critical infrastructure protection IV: Fourth annual IFIP WG 11.10 International Conference on Critical Infrastructure Protection, ICCIP 2010, Washington, DC, USA, March 15–17, 2010, Revised Selected Papers 4* (pp. 215–227). Springer .

Kantur, D., & İşeri-Say, A. (2012). Organizational resilience: A conceptual integrative framework. *Journal of Management & Organization, 18*(6), 762–773.

Kerr, H. (2016). Organizational Resilience: Sfruttare l'esperienza per cogliere le opportunità. https://www.bsigroup.com/globalassets/localfiles/it-it/organizational-resilience/

Korber, S., & McNaughton, R. B. (2017). Resilience and entrepreneurship: A systematic literature review. *International Journal of Entrepreneurial Behavior & Research, 24*(7), 1129–1154.

Kunz, W. H., & Walsh, G. (2020). After the revolution–new chances for service research in a digital world. *Journal of Service Management, 31*(3), 597–607.

Lengnick-Hall, C. A., & Beck, T. E. (2005). Adaptive fit versus robust transformation: How organizations respond to environmental change. *Journal of Management, 31*(5), 738–757.

Lengnick-Hall, C. A., Beck, T. E., & Lengnick-Hall, M. L. (2011). Developing a capacity for organizational resilience through strategic human resource management. *Human Resource Management Review, 21*(3), 243–255.

Limnios, E. A. M., Mazzarol, T., Ghadouani, A., & Schilizzi, S. G. (2014). The resilience architecture framework: Four organizational archetypes. *European Management Journal, 32*(1), 104–116.

Linnenluecke, M. K. (2017). Resilience in business and management research: A review of influential publications and a research agenda. *International Journal of Management Reviews, 19*(1), 4–30.

Lusch, R. F., & Vargo, S. L. (2006). Service-dominant logic: Reactions, reflections and refinements. *Marketing theory, 6*(3), 281–288.

Magliacani, M., & Sorrentino, D. (2022). Reinterpreting museums' intended experience during the COVID-19 pandemic: Insights from Italian University Museums. *Museum Management and Curatorship, 37*(4), 353–367.

Mallak, L. (1998). Putting organizational resilience to work. *INDUSTRIAL MANAGEMENT-CHICAGO THEN ATLANTA-*, 8–13.

McManus, S., Seville, E., Brunsdon, D., & Vargo, J. (2007). *Resilience management: A framework for assessing and improving the resilience of organisations* (p. 79). Resilient Organisations Research Group University of Canterbury. Department of Accounting and Information Systems.

Meyer, A. D. (1982). Adapting to environmental jolts. *Administrative Science Quarterly, 27*(4), 515–537.

Mifsud, M., Cases, A. S., & N'Goala, G. (2015). Service appropriation: How do customers make the service their own? *Journal of Service Management, 26*(5), 706–725.

Montemaggi, M. (2008). I musei d'impresa: un'opportunità per il Paese. *Economia della Cultura, 18*(4), 479–488.

Mozzoni, I., Fanelli, S., & Donelli, C. C. (2018). Italian university collections: Managing the artistic heritage of the university's ivory tower. *Journal of Cultural Management and Policy, 8*(1), 2224–2554.

Museimpresa (a). (n.d.). L'impresa è cultura. https://museimpresa.com/chi-siamo/

Museimpresa (b). (n.d.). Musei e archivi associati. https://museimpresa.com/associati/

Osborne, S. P. (2018). From public service-dominant logic to public service logic: Are public service organizations capable of coproduction and value co-creation? *Public Management Review, 20*(2), 225–231.

Osborne, S. P., Radnor, Z., & Strokosch, K. (2016). Coproduction and the co-creation of value in public services: A suitable case for treatment? *Public Management Review, 18*(5), 639–653.

Palumbo, R., & Manna, R. (2019). Un inquadramento concettuale della resilienza organizzativa. Verso la formulazione di una ricetta per rendere un'organizzazione "resiliente.". *IMPRESA PROGETTO, 2*, 1–22.

Payne, A. F., Storbacka, K., & Frow, P. (2008). Managing the co-creation of value. *Journal of the Academy of Marketing Science, 36*, 83–96.

Periac, F., David, A., & Roberson, Q. (2018). Clarifying the interplay between social innovation and sustainable development: A conceptual framework rooted in paradox management. *European Management Review, 15*(1), 19–35.

Ponsignon, F., Durrieu, F., & Bouzdine-Chameeva, T. (2017). Customer experience design: A case study in the cultural sector. *Journal of Service Management, 28*(4), 763–787.

Prahalad, C. K., & Ramaswamy, V. (2004). Co-creating unique value with customers. *Strategy & leadership, 32*(3), 4–9.

Pugh, J., & Bourgeois, L. J., III. (2011). "Doing" strategy. *Journal of Strategy and Management, 4*(2), 172–179.

Rose, A. (2004). Defining and measuring economic resilience to disasters. *Disaster Prevention and Management: An International Journal, 13*(4), 307–314.

Rubalcaba, L., Michel, S., Sundbo, J., Brown, S. W., & Reynoso, J. (2012). Shaping, organizing, and rethinking service innovation: A multidimensional framework. *Journal of Service Management, 23*(5), 696–715.

Samaroudi, M., Echavarria, K. R., & Perry, L. (2020). Heritage in lockdown: Digital provision of memory institutions in the UK and US of America during the COVID-19 pandemic. *Museum Management and Curatorship, 35*(4), 337–361.

Saunila, M., Ukko, J., & Rantala, T. (2018). Value co-creation through digital service capabilities. The role of human factors. *Information Technology & People, 32*(3), 627–645.

Somers, S. (2009). Measuring resilience potential: An adaptive strategy for organizational crisis planning. *Journal of Contingencies and Crisis Management, 17*(1), 12–23.

Staw, B. M., Sandelands, L. E., & Dutton, J. E. (1981). Threat rigidity effects in organizational behavior: A multilevel analysis. *Administrative Science Quarterly, 26*, 501–524.

Steccolini, I., Saliterer, I., & Guthrie, J. (2020). The role (s) of accounting and performance measurement systems in contemporary public administration. *Public Administration, 98*(1), 3–13.

Toivonen, M., & Tuominen, T. (2009). Emergence of innovations in services. *The Service Industries Journal, 29*(7), 887–902.

Tsai, K. H., & Huang, S. C. T. (2020). Service creativity reinforcement and firm performance: The roles of innovation intensity and contexts. *Journal of Service Management, 31*(1), 1–23.

Venzin, M., & Perotti, G. B. (2014). *Resilience: i sette principi per una gestione aziendale sana e prudente.* EGEA spa.

Vogus, T. J., & Sutcliffe, K. M. (2007, October). Organizational resilience: Towards a theory and research agenda. In *2007 IEEE international conference on systems, man and cybernetics* (pp. 3418–3422). IEEE.

Watermeyer, R., Crick, T., Knight, C., & Goodall, J. (2021). COVID-19 and digital disruption in UK universities: Afflictions and affordances of emergency online migration. *Higher Education, 81*, 623–641.

Winnard, J., Adcroft, A., Lee, J., & Skipp, D. (2014). Surviving or flourishing? Integrating business resilience and sustainability. *Journal of Strategy and Management, 7*(3), 303–315.

Yin, R. K. (2018). *Case study research and applications.* Sage.

Zolli, A., & Healy, A. M. (2012). *Resilience: Why things bounce back.* Hachette.

CHAPTER 6

Resilience, Sustainability, and Accountability: Conceptual Propositions

Abstract What steps can cultural organizations take to achieve resilience? What about sustainability? To achieve these objectives, what role do accounting and accountability play? The first objective of this chapter is to address these research questions. Additionally, it proposes a conceptual model that can serve as a link between the concepts of accountability and management of cultural organizations and those of resilience and sustainability.

Keywords Cultural heritage • Accounting • Accountability • Resilience • Sustainability

6.1 Introduction

Cultural organizations are constantly faced with challenges. Along with the going-concern objective, they have to pursue additional goals that are intrinsic and typical of their nature, characterized by the need to transmit and disseminate cultural heritage. Therefore, because of the social role they play, they are even more pushed to pursue the goals of resilience and sustainability. However, as highlighted in the previous chapters, they need appropriate tools to achieve these goals.

M. Magliacani, V. Toscano, *Accounting for Cultural Heritage Management*, https://doi.org/10.1007/978-3-031-38257-4_6

This chapter first highlights the relationship between cultural heritage and resilience. It will focus on the categories of resilience that need to be considered by organizations in the cultural heritage sector to achieve the resilience goal. Next, the links between cultural heritage management and the pursuit of the SDGs of Agenda 2030 will be analyzed. In addition, the need for efficient reporting to facilitate the pursuit of these goals will be raised. Finally, the topic of the role of accounting and accountability in cultural heritage management will be discussed to highlight the supporting function they could play if effectively adopted.

Accounting is a crosscutting theme in this chapter, which intends to highlight its relevance to pursuing all these objectives: efficient management, resilience, and sustainability.

Finally, a conceptual model that summarizes the overall findings of this research will be presented.

6.2 Cultural Heritage and Resilience

There are several factors that contribute to an organization's resilience, according to the management literature. Specifically, Dindarian (2019) identified ten categories of resilience, also divided into subcategories, and he pointed out the resilience drivers that can characterize and influence them based on the literature (Fig. 6.1). Regarding the categories, Leadership refers only to issues internal to the organization, which are the responsibility of managers, whereas the other nine—Technology, People, Supply Chain, Organization, Operations, Environment, Processes, Information, and Uncertainty—pertain to both internal and external issues (Dindarian, 2019).

In particular, technology must have an innovation component to positively influence business resilience (Adger, 2000). However, it must be combined with other competencies—particularly organizational competencies—such as adaptive response, efficient communication, ability to cope with change, manage complexity, uncertainty, emergence, ability to learn from the past, networking, resourcefulness, cognitive flexibility, the capacity of the system to tolerate change and not immediately collapse upon the occurrence of a threat, and effective performance measurement (Dindarian, 2019).

As an organizational competence, digital technology can facilitate dialog with stakeholders to increase their participation in the various stages of value creation, from conception to implementation and evaluation (Alves,

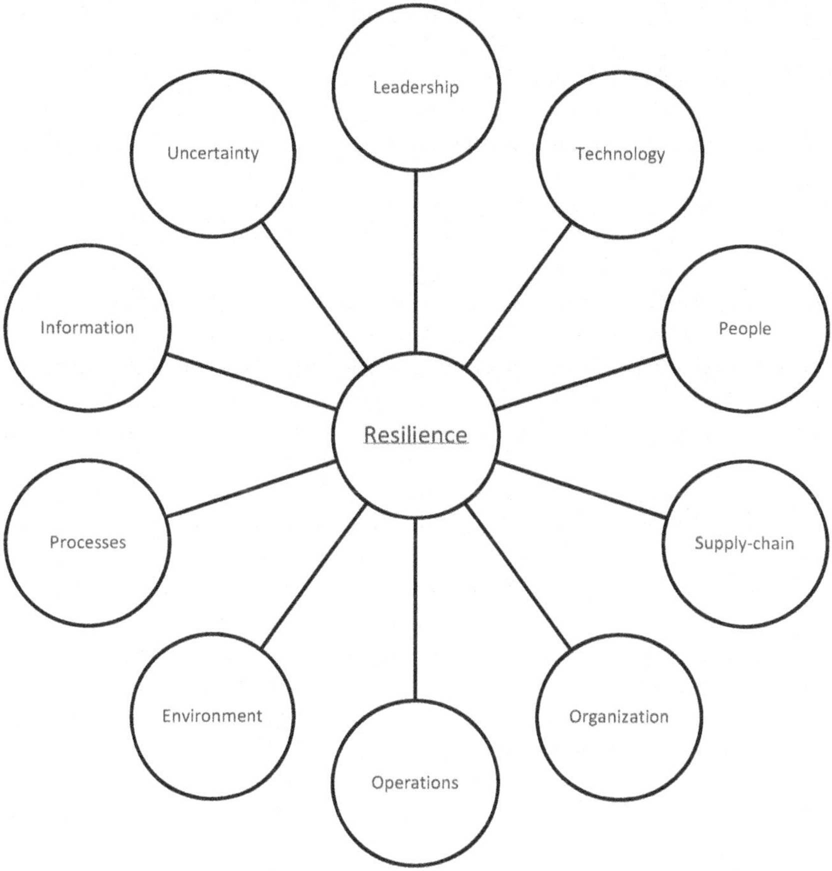

Fig. 6.1 Categories of resilience. (Source: Adaptation from Dindarian, 2019)

2013). It has recently been examined, especially since the COVID-19 pandemic, in the context of organizations involved in the management and transmission of cultural heritage, especially museums (Agostino et al., 2020).

By considering both public and private museums, it was noted that the strategy adopted to pursue the goal of business continuity was overall the same: it involved the reorganization of activities through implementing technology. The investigation set out in this research proposed a model in which technological knowledge was a prerequisite for organizations. In particular, it allowed a rapid return to normalcy, although it was conditioned by the restrictions imposed by regulatory decrees regarding management during the pandemic. The closure of cultural spaces accelerated the use of digital technology in the "core" processes of value creation (video-telling, online educational workshops, virtual tours) and for the collateral ones (online conferencing in the form of webinars and support, social media management, user monitoring, activity reporting).

This responsive behavior was also fostered by the museums' starting condition, present before the outbreak of the pandemic: the valid organizational culture. In fact, university museums have demonstrated that they are grounded in values such as dedication to work, trust, sharing, and the awareness of performing a high mission for the institution and society. As a result, they have been able to continue their value creation process, which has also contributed to the creation of human value (Catturi, 2003). Regarding the Corporate Museums and Archives, their goal of profit has been accompanied by the recognition that the functions for which they were established are still relevant: image, legitimacy, and social and cultural significance. In particular, they recognize the fact that they have different functions: display function (the museum serves as a means to present the company), historical-institutional function (the museum serves as a place to preserve and construct the company's history), digestive function (the museum serves as a tool to reuse the company's heritage), and identifying function (the museum serves as a symbol of the brand's institutional, cultural, and territorial identity). However, the functions that serve the company's purposes the most immediately are the display and digestive functions, since both relate to preserving and relocating its heritage within the company's communication flow and to its effective presentation (Montemaggi, 2008).

The organization's resilience is heavily dependent on its own management, which must be efficient and aware of the risks and difficulties it may encounter, regardless of the sector in which it operates. A government or the European Union may provide financial assistance when severe shocks occur to an organization by covering some of its costs or seeking funding, but the organization must accompany these resources with a proper strategy to avoid succumbing.

It has been widely debated in the literature as to which strategies or types of organizations are most efficient. In addition, the method of measuring the degree of resilience of an organization is still under investigation. Moreover, there are a number of limitations associated with the resilience models developed by scholars. To simplify and improve resilience assessments, it would be useful to identify a single model that is capable of considering all resilience drivers. However, the construction of such a model would be a complex process.

In times of crisis, such as those caused by the COVID-19 pandemic, resilience becomes even more important. A resilient organization is not only a characteristic that is positive but also one of its essential components, without which it would be unable to survive. The purpose of this chapter is to raise awareness and train managers and decision-makers on this topic so that they may understand that although this might appear to be an unprofitable investment, it can make a significant difference in certain situations.

The literature analysis and case studies, however, indicate that while accounting has been identified as an important tool in assessing an organization's resilience (Dindarian, 2019), it continues to play a marginal role in the construction of resilient business models and resilience measurement models. As a result, it appears to be of limited relevance from the perspective of corporate museums, as few of them have decided to report the changes they have made in their technologies or to modify their reporting procedure so that it is more effective. As stated by Venzin and Perotti (2014), accounting metrics can highlight the effects of resilience from a financial performance perspective. If resilience is measured through organizational variables, the effects of resilience are noted through economic-financial analysis, which is seen as the "steamroller" of resilience. Hence, the need to include economic-financial variables and accounting in future resilience measurement models could also help in the evaluation and monitoring of actions taken, to make management more effective and to be able to implement corrective actions for the pursuit of the goal of business continuity and resilience.

Figure 6.2 illustrates the contribution of this study: for cultural organizations to achieve resilience, they must implement the tools recommended in the literature (i.e., resilience categories), in addition to implementing a comprehensive and efficient accounting system.

6.3 Cultural Heritage and Sustainability

The literature review illustrates the expanding recognition of the relationship between cultural heritage, culture, and sustainability. The 2030 Agenda emphasizes the role that culture can play in achieving the

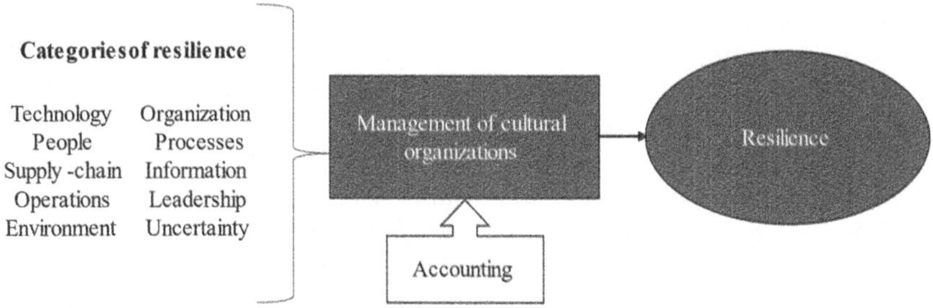

Fig. 6.2 Cultural heritage and resilience

Sustainable Development Goals. Efficient management of cultural heritage can play a crucial role in the achievement of SDG #11: "Make cities and human settlements inclusive, safe, resilient, and sustainable" (Magliacani, 2022).

Considering this relevance and influence, it is essential to measure the performance of the cultural sector, particularly to assess whether policies and actions undertaken have been effective, efficient, and sustainable. Additionally, if this has not been the case, accurate measurement and reporting would provide the necessary information to identify potential corrective measures.

Measurement of sustainable cultural performance is, however, a complex issue that is still in its infancy. First and foremost, the definition of culture represents one of the primary stumbling blocks encountered in measurement: based on the limitations placed on this concept, different, more specific, and appropriate evaluation methods can be identified. Cultural economies, traditional economies, and cultural diversity have many aspects in common, but they differ in some facets, which may have different impacts on sustainability. As an example, if all traditional aspects of culture were considered positive and functional in pursuit of sustainability goals, the results obtained would be distorted since more traditions would not equate to greater sustainability. Therefore, it would be necessary to first define the scope of measurement and then develop a valuable framework for assessing performance.

As there is no standard measurement framework imposed by governments or international organizations, this study examined some of the possible alternatives to determine which might be most appropriate. Therefore, the choice was to critically analyze the Culture 2030 Indicators prepared by UNESCO, the most recent proposal, but still poorly applied internationally.

It is intended that these indicators measure cultural performance in relation to achieving sustainability goals: two variables that are normally measured separately. For instance, in Italy, the Statistics Office of the Ministry of Culture prepares some indicators to assess how the cultural sector is performing (Sistan, a), while Istat's Annual Report on the Sustainable Development Goals examines the progress made in achieving sustainability goals (Istat, 2021b). The two documents coexist, but they remain separate reports, ignoring the connections between the topics they cover.

Therefore, the role that the UNESCO framework is intended to play is certainly important, as it fits into a context where there is a gap and attempts to fill it. In contrast, the critical issues noted are different: retrieval of data is difficult, flexibility is strong, and representation at the national level is not significant. Although this framework is a good starting point, further refinements and studies are required before it can prove effective. An alternative proposal would be to apply these indicators to a small-scale measurement—for example, on a city, as in the case of Parma Italian Capital of Culture 2020+21—to encourage their use. It is critical to emphasize that measurement should not only be undertaken to demonstrate that one is outperforming others (whether states, cities, or organizations) but also to assess one's own policies. To achieve the sustainable performance goals it has set, the organization must first improve itself.

Currently, no method for measuring sustainable cultural performance has proven to be effective and adequate: no tool can be disseminated and implemented efficiently. As a result, it would be necessary to investigate further to identify a feasible, acceptable solution to achieve this evaluation objective. A measurement obligation introduced by the institutions would undoubtedly accelerate this process, and they might also prepare more specific guidelines on how to measure performance. Actually, just as in the case of the impact assessment of the Capitals of Culture, the evaluation process is left to the city involved, which structures the indicators based on its own knowledge and reporting requirements.

A big data archive related to the culture model as a pillar of sustainability would be an additional useful tool that could be implemented for this purpose. This archive, compiled at least on a national level, could assist in monitoring the progress of sustainability goals through cultural heritage (Hoppe & Coenen, 2011). It is possible to enrich the descriptive statistics (number of visitors, the number of exhibited and preserved works, ticketing, etc.) already collected on a regular basis with measures that allow quantifying the contribution of culture to the realization of the 2030 Agenda in the Italian context and territories. In this way, it would be easier to disseminate positive practices, which can be a boost to the improvement of the performance of individual cultural contexts, both nationally and internationally (Ferreira, 2018).

Active participation, to this end, is required first and foremost for cultural organizations, which are the first to be called upon to contribute to the creation of sustainable value. This value will increase and facilitate the social, cultural, economic, and environmental development of the local, and subsequently global, community. However, to achieve this, specific skills are needed. These skills may already be present in the organization, as they are acquired during personnel selection or gained later through the continuing education of workers. In the first case, the tacit knowledge of individuals (human capital) will be transformed through a process of socialization and internal interaction into explicit knowledge (organizational capital), thus helping to determine the knowledge assets of the cultural enterprise (Catturi, 2003). In the second scenario, on the other hand, if "key" competencies (i.e., those deemed essential for the formulation and execution of strategies related to the institutional purpose) are not present within the organization, they can be acquired from the external environment or developed through a capacity-building-based learning process.

As a first step, it would be necessary to develop a culture of measurement, which is still modest in today's world but which must be expanded given its relevance (Folan & Browne, 2005). It appears from this perspective, as well as from the empirical analysis conducted, that the measurement of sustainable cultural performance requires accounting and managerial expertise, which is the subject of capacity building. In Italy, the National Recovery and Resilience Plan recognizes the need to invest in this area and shows that institutions are interested in it.

In this regard, the establishment of a task force at the national level made up of experts in accounting, statistics, and management could act as support during the decision-making and evaluation phases of the actions put in place and could be an improvement in training in this area to disseminate knowledge to all those who play an active role in the planning, management, monitoring, and evaluation of organizations or initiatives in the field of cultural heritage management. Figure 6.3 illustrates this concept in a simple manner.

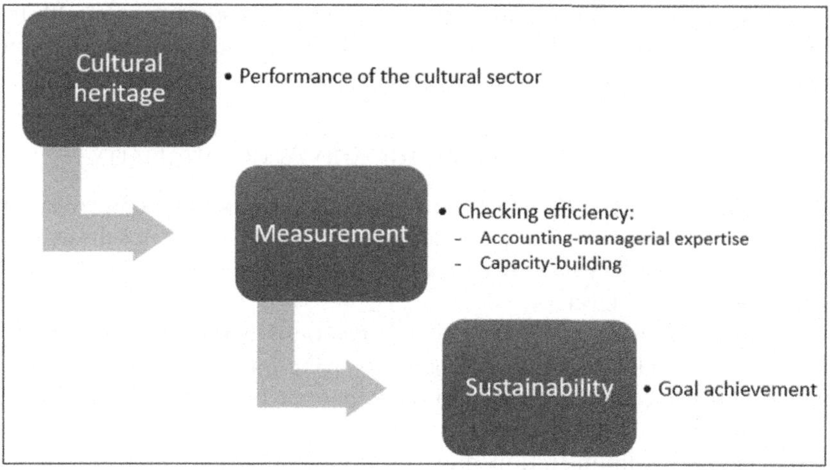

Fig. 6.3 Cultural heritage and sustainability

Considering this research from a theoretical perspective, it could be replicated in contexts other than the Capitals of Culture to promote a critical discussion about the validity of the cultural sustainability model. It also provides insights into the appropriateness of the measurement indicators proposed in the UNESCO framework for the various case studies. This would also imply studying the management of cultural heritage and the measurement of its performance from a sustainability perspective in other countries, European or non-European, to highlight existing differences and the level of advancement of practices at the global level and to identify adoptable best practices that are functional in the pursuit of sustainability goals.

Additionally, the use of more efficient and complete accounting techniques could play a significant role in promoting transparency and accountability, which are fundamental principles for sustainable development. Accounting can contribute to the development of trust and promote responsible behavior by providing accurate and timely information about an organization's sustainability performance (Magliacani, 2022).

Research conducted in this study lends itself to an interdisciplinary approach, as both culture and sustainability are crosscutting issues requiring expertise from different fields. The importance of this aspect cannot be overstated, not only from the perspective of maintaining the cultural heritage in a sustainable manner but also from the perspective of establishing educational paths that develop critical thinking skills and *forma mentis* capable of dealing with any change proactively.

6.4 Cultural Heritage and Accountability

Reporting on cultural heritage management's value is still a controversial topic in the literature. Italy, the country examined most closely in this study, has adopted a range of approaches, both at the national level and at the organizational level.

It is the Ministry of Culture that is responsible for reporting at the national level. He has a responsibility to make public a variety of data, which, however, relate primarily to the economic performance and accessibility of cultural organizations.

Every State administration must include an Office of Statistics in its organizational chart in accordance with Legislative Decree No. 322 of Sept. 6, 1989. Therefore, SISTAN (Sistema Statistico Nazionale) was also established in 1992 for the Ministry of Culture. This office carries out research, statistical analysis, publications, and internal statistical coordination (Ministero della Cultura, a). All statistical surveys of national interest entrusted to SISTAN, with their intended purposes, are included in the National Statistical Program (NSP) (Sistan, b), in which, as far as the Bureau of Statistics of the Ministry of Culture is concerned, the following surveys are requested (Ministero della Cultura, b):

1. Visitors and Introits of State Museums, Monuments, and Archaeological Areas, the number of which is calculated—in the case of fee-paying institutions—using the number of tickets issued, and in the case of free facilities through the calculation of attendance entered in the appropriate register or the use of a "people-counter" device. More specifically, eight tables are prepared and published, in which data are aggregated and reported using different logics. The tables are: Historical Data by Type of Museum Institute (Museums, Monuments, Archaeological Areas, Museum Circuits); Data by Province and Region; Data by Province, Region, and Type of Museum Institute; Monthly Data by Type of Museum Institute; Regional Data by Month: Total Visitors, Total Gross Receipts (Euro); Regional Data: Comparison with the previous year; Data by Individual Museum Institute; The Most Visited Museum Institutes (Top 30) (Ufficio di Statistica, b);

2. Additional services provided at State Museums, Monuments, and Archaeological Areas, as well as receipts issued and recorded in the areas of bookshops and gadgets, cafeterias and catering, guided tours, audio guides, and entrance ticket reservations. There are five tables, specifically: Historical Data by Type of Additional Service; Regional Data by Type of Additional Service; Historical Data by Museum Institute (Museums, Monuments, and Archaeological Areas, Museum Circuits) and Type of Additional Service; Dates of Activation of Additional Services by Museum Institute; Additional Services of State Museums, Monuments, and Archaeological Areas by Type of Service—Previous Year Comparison (Ufficio di Statistica, b);
3. Information about the 101 State Archives, the 33 sections that depend on them, and the Central State Archives. For this survey, the area of the premises, the stock of material, utilities, promotional activities, technical services, hardware and computer equipment, personnel, and operating expenses are considered. In detail, data are displayed in eight tables: Premises, shelving, material, personnel, study room attendance, research, and operating expenses; Premises by type; Material stored by type; Users: attendance and research by type; Promotional activities; Technical services, Archival School, and copying activities by type; Personnel by functional aggregation; Equipment by type (Ufficio di Statistica, b);
4. State Public Libraries, the data for which concern bibliographic material holdings, consultations, loans, staffing, and operating expenses as of 1999, relate to the 46 Public Libraries designated by Presidential Decree No. 417 of July 5, 1995, as amended by the Ministerial Decree of June 12, 2000. In this case, there are five tables provided: Consistency of material, consultations, loans, and personnel (Data by Province); Consistency of material, consultations, loans, and personnel; Shelving and material; Consistency of miscellaneous material and consultation activities; Loans, personnel, and operating expenses (Ufficio di Statistica, b);
5. Archival Superintendencies, the subject of which are the 19 regional Archival Superintendencies that have a supervisory role over public and private archives. These archives are assigned historical interest by the relevant territorial superintendency. The nine required tables must display data on the surface area of the premises. These data are broken down into different types, inspection visits, restricted mate-

rial, and consultation requests, and finally, the staff are divided into various areas. Data on promotional activities, technical services, and technical and computer equipment shall also be reported. The tables provided are the following: Premises, Inspection Visits, Restricted Material, Personnel, Consultation Requests, Holdings of Library Material, Operating Expenses; Premises by Type; Supervisory Activities at Local Authorities; Supervisory Activities at Other Authorities; Consultation Requests; Promotional Activities; Technical Services; Staff Holdings; Equipment by Type (Ufficio di Statistica, b).

On the other hand, concerning measuring the pursuit of the sustainability goals outlined in the 2030 Agenda, in Italy, ISTAT prepares the SDGs Report annually. This provides a representation of the scenario at the national level. In 2021, its fourth version was published, which included 354 statistical measures for 135 UN-IAEG indicators. In it, there is also a first mapping of the identifiable correlations between the SDGs and the Missions of the PNRR: within the same document, therefore, an attempt is also made to assess the progress of the implementation of the PNRR (Istat, 2021a). Considering the absence of an SDG concerning culture, no indicator in the SDG Report can measure the contribution of culture to the pursuit of the Sustainable Development Goals (Istat, 2021b).

The effectiveness and efficiency of the actions taken can be measured and controlled at the organizational level, as discussed in Chap. 3. Cultural organizations can also complement sustainable reporting (Aras & Crowther, 2008; Manes-Rossi et al., 2018), which legitimizes their development and emergence, not only toward supranational bodies (CETS—UNESCO) and territorial publics (Ministries, Regions, Municipalities) but also toward local communities, which are able to reap the benefits of the "sustainable" value generated by their value creation processes. Consequently, accountability is an important component of ensuring pragmatic legitimacy for cultural enterprises that create value, respect the principles of sustainability (moral legitimacy), follow their mission, and deliberate and implement strategies (cognitive legitimacy) (Thomas & Lamm, 2012).

The reporting process is a means of circulating the content object of legitimacy. The local community must be consulted for the report to be considered valid. It is important that the strategies and actions of the cultural organization are shared with and accepted by the public. It is

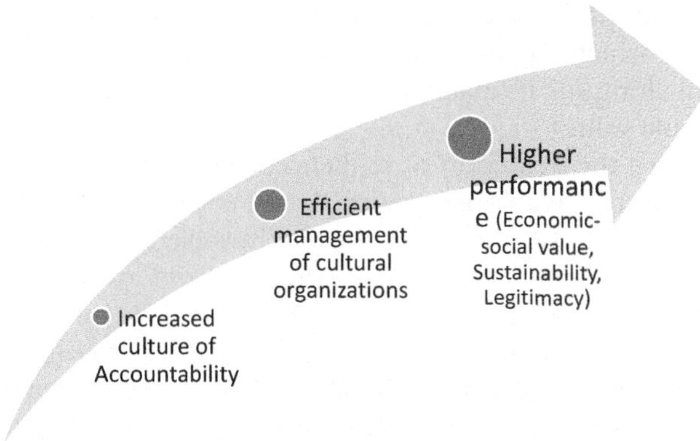

Fig. 6.4 Cultural heritage and accountability

essential that the community, both within and outside of the organizational perimeter, be involved in this process of sharing. A broader consensus is achieved with greater social participation. Every enhancement project relies on the economic dimension of sustainable development. Without this dimension, any project idea for local community development, regardless of its social and cultural values, is delegitimized. The challenge posed by sustainability to cultural practitioners is to operate within a value-based framework.

Based on the case studies analyzed, it has been observed that there is not always an adequate diffusion of the culture of accountability since the benefits and potential of proper accounting practices are not always recognized. As a matter of fact, accounting and accountability provide clear advantages to organizations, including greater legitimacy and empowerment of the decision-makers, enabling them to be more responsible and efficient managers and to achieve better results. To maximize the potential benefits of a managerial accounting system, it should be embedded and internalized into the corporate culture and organizational structure of the company. Figure 6.4 illustrates this concept.

6.5 Final Remarks: A Conceptual Model

This research aims to enlarge knowledge about the role of accounting in cultural organizations' management for the preservation and dissemination of cultural heritage. In particular, it focused on understanding the role that accounting could play in pursuing the goals of resilience and sustainability, which underlie the management of an organization and complement alongside its main objective: the creation of economic, social, and sustainable value.

According to the definition of resilience most widely used in the management literature, for an organization, being resilient does not necessarily mean being sustainable. Being sustainable, however, means being able to survive in the long run to continue operating from an ongoing concern perspective. For this reason, taking efficient management choices, being responsible for them, and being accountable can allow resilience and sustainability to coexist. Thus, management, accounting, resilience, and sustainability are closely interrelated, despite seeming distant.

A summary of this interrelation can be found in Fig. 6.5., the construction of which is supported by both theoretical and empirical findings.

Cultural organizations must report their management through accounting, which allows analysis of the effectiveness of the actions taken and, at the same time, holds decision-makers accountable. By making future decisions based on the results outlined in the reports, management is able to ensure that these decisions are tailored more appropriately to the organizational goals that have been established, as well as allowing management to monitor the organization's performance and to modify the strategies

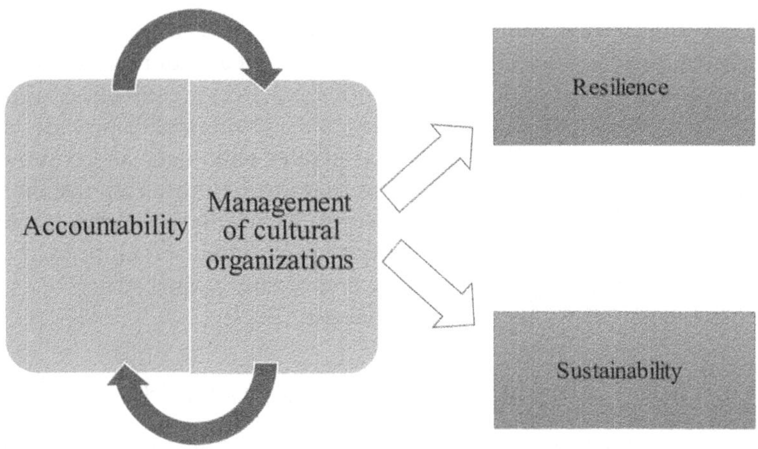

Fig. 6.5 Accountability, resilience, and sustainability in cultural organizations: a conceptual model

and policies adopted if they do not seem more effective. It is also important to recognize that cultural organizations' goals also include resilience and sustainability, and adequate reporting in these terms could also provide support in these directions. As a result, poor reporting culture is evident in this sector at this point. To improve performance in managing cultural heritage and its value, this needs to be rectified. The benefit would not only be for the organization in terms of its performance and legitimacy but also for the community in terms of knowledge and sustainability.

References

Adger, W. N. (2000). Social and ecological resilience: Are they related? *Progress in Human Geography, 24*(3), 347–364.

Agostino, D., Arnaboldi, M., & Lampis, A. (2020). Italian state museums during the COVID-19 crisis: From onsite closure to online openness. *Museum Management and Curatorship, 35*(4), 362–372.

Alves, H. (2013). Co-creation and innovation in public services. *The Service Industries Journal, 33*(7–8), 671–682.

Aras, G., & Crowther, D. (2008). Evaluating sustainability: A need for standards. *Issues in Social and Environmental Accounting, 2*(1), 19–35.

Catturi, G. (2003). *Principi di economia aziendale: l'azienda universale: l'idea forza, la morfologia e la fisiologia*. Cedam.

Dindarian, K. (2019). *Exploring enterprise resilience through the theoretical lens of complexity: A case study situated in the high value-manufacturing sector*. The University of Manchester (United Kingdom).

Ferreira, T. C. (2018). Bridging planned conservation and community empowerment: Portuguese case studies. *Journal of Cultural Heritage Management and Sustainable Development, 8*(1). https://doi.org/10.1108/JCHMSD-05-2017-0029

Folan, P., & Browne, J. (2005). Development of an extended enterprise performance measurement system. *Production Planning & Control, 16*(6), 531–544.

Hoppe, T., & Coenen, F. (2011). Creating an analytical framework for local sustainability performance: A Dutch case study. *Local Environment, 16*(3), 229–250.

Istat. (2021a). *Nota stampa sul Rapporto SDGs 2021 Informazioni statistiche per l'Agenda 2030 in Italia*. https://www.istat.it/it/files//2021/08/NOTA-STAMPA-RAPPORTO-SDGs_2021_PC.pdf

Istat. (2021b). *Rapporto SDGs 2021. Informazioni Statistiche per l'Agenda 2030 in Italia*. https://www.istat.it/storage/rapporti-tematici/sdgs/2021/Rapporto-SDGs-2021.pdf

Magliacani, M. (2022). How the sustainable development goals challenge public management. Action research on the cultural heritage of an Italian smart city. *Journal of Management and Governance*, 1–29.

Manes-Rossi, F., Tiron-Tudor, A., Nicolò, G., & Zanellato, G. (2018). Ensuring more sustainable reporting in Europe using non-financial disclosure—De facto and de jure evidence. *Sustainability, 10*(4), 1162.

Ministero della Cultura (a). (n.d.). Ufficio di statistica | La cultura nell'Informazione statistica. http://www.statistica.beniculturali.it/Sistan_e_ufficio.htm

Ministero della Cultura (b). (n.d.). Ufficio di statistica | La cultura nell'Informazione statistica | Rilevazioni e dati statistici. http://www.statistica.beniculturali.it/Rilevazioni.htm

Montemaggi, M. (2008). I musei d'impresa: un'opportunità per il Paese. *Economia della Cultura, 18*(4), 479–488.

Sistan (a). (n.d.). Attività in ambito statistico. https://www.sistan.it/index.php?id=197&tx_wfqbe_pi1%5Bsoggetto%5D=27

Sistan (b). (n.d.). Il Programma Statistico Nazionale (PSN). https://www.sistan.it/?id=52

Thomas, T. E., & Lamm, E. (2012). Legitimacy and organizational sustainability. *Journal of business ethics, 110*, 191–203.

Venzin, M., & Perotti, G. B. (2014). *Resilience: i sette principi per una gestione aziendale sana e prudente.* EGEA spa.

CHAPTER 7

Conclusions

Abstract The theoretical and empirical contributions proposed in this study have shown how cultural organizations need accounting knowledge to make rational and responsible decisions and, consequently, to operate in compliance with the principles of economic, social, and environmental sustainability. This requires capacity-building processes concerning not only strategic thinking and planning, management control, based on cost accounting and performance indicators but also community engagement and networking. The technicality must not be an end in itself, but it aims to provide useful information for managing cultural heritage by sustainable, resilient, accountable organizations, regardless of their public or private institutional form.

Keywords Accounting knowledge • Capacity building • Sustainability • Community engagement • Networking

This study has provided a contribution, both theoretical and practical, to the interdisciplinary debate on the role of accounting culture in cultural heritage management. In particular, cultural institutes can be the driving force behind the cultural and creative production ecosystem, provided they are aware of the importance of acting as organizations and

M. Magliacani, V. Toscano, *Accounting for Cultural Heritage Management*, https://doi.org/10.1007/978-3-031-38257-4_7

developing managerial skills that are geared toward addressing, with values, all the challenges posed by environmental changes. Furthermore, this is particularly relevant in light of the conditions under which cultural organizations have had to operate, even recently, in response to the pandemic emergency caused by COVID-19 (Agostino et al., 2020). In the wake of this shock, their operations have become critical, always characterized by the precariousness of both human and financial resources.

In this context, the study has attempted to inductively deduce how some cultural organizations are struggling with their mission when faced with crisis. This occurred thanks to their awareness of playing a significant role in the economy and society and consequently to their ability to acquire not only digital competences but also logic and accounting and managerial tools. Accordingly, capacity building, first at an individual level and then at an organizational and environmental level, is fundamental for every challenge that cultural organizations must face.

People who work within these organizations should be trained in the skills that allow them to understand the logic and functionality of the ex ante (planning) and ex post (measuring and evaluating results) results control tools. In addition to preparing projects cultural activities intended to obtain funding from fund providers, their adoption is also crucial for managing daily life and stimulating community engagement, which are sources of legitimacy for the activities conducted and the investments made with public resources in the eyes of internal and external stakeholders. Donato and Lohrasbi (2017) argue that capacity building requires the willingness of personnel to participate in learning processes as well as the commitment of the governing bodies.

The managerial literature has highlighted how, despite the success of some cultural projects, they have not stimulated innovative paths of knowledge creation, since they have been interpreted as a goal in themselves, rather than to increase one's intellectual heritage (Lusiani & Zan, 2013). By requiring the declination of value in the paradigm of sustainability in the presentation of the proposal, highlighting the expected impact on the territory, the same public calls seem to be increasingly avoiding this approach. As defined by Catturi (2007), sustainability is the ability of an organization to continuously produce value for all stakeholders over a medium- to long-term horizon. In this study, it is evident that values are at the core of every sustainability project examined. In its many forms, "sustainable" value is cocreated by cultural organizations with visitors/users and the community. In fact, the cultural organization is sustainable if it provides services derived from the management of its collections for the benefit of current and future generations.

If values are developed rationally and responsibly, using management accounting logics and tools, then the community of individuals dedicated to the management of cultural heritage will be able not only to be resilient to external shocks, but to contribute also to the achievement of the objectives set out in the Agenda 2030 (Magliacani, 2022).

For all SGDs, organizational sustainability is a *conditio sine qua non* in light of what UNESCO supports. The shift from organizational sustainability to environmental sustainability requires a capacity-building process in the same direction. The successful practical cases addressed in this study have shown how this is possible only through the community engagement in the various cultural projects and networking; without this participation, they are destined to be modestly or at all legitimized and therefore will generate less value than expected because there will be no acts of cocreation.

It is recommended (Bäckstrand, 2006) to use accounting and accountability tools to ensure continuity of the value cocreation process. As a result, cultural organizations are able to legitimize every social innovation concerning value cocreation (Thomas & Lamm, 2012).

These reflections are brought to the attention of academics involved in the management of cultural heritage. In addition, further investigations on organizational capacity building in cultural contexts other than those investigated in this study are recommended. Moreover, the conceptual models proposed, based on accounting knowledge, provide insights to professionals to understand how accounting can assist cultural organizations in operating their ordinary lives in accordance with sustainable development principles while remaining resilient under exceptional circumstances.

References

Agostino, D., Arnaboldi, M., & Lampis, A. (2020). Italian state museums during the COVID-19 crisis: From onsite closure to online openness. *Museum Management and Curatorship, 35*(4), 362–372.

Bäckstrand, K. (2006). Multi-stakeholder partnerships for sustainable development: Rethinking legitimacy, accountability and effectiveness. *European Environment, 16*(5), 290–306.

Catturi, G. (2007). *La valorialità aziendale: Vol. I, La determinazione e la rilevazione del valore creato: presupposti teorici e metodologici*. CEDAM.

Donato, F., & Lohrasbi, A. (2017). When theory and practice clash: Participatory governance and management in Takht-e Soleyman. *Journal of Cultural Heritage Management and Sustainable Development, 7*, 129–146.
Lusiani, M., & Zan, L. (2013). Planning and heritage. *Journal of Cultural Heritage Management and Sustainable Development, 3*(2), 108–115.
Magliacani, M. (2022). How the sustainable development goals challenge public management. Action research on the cultural heritage of an Italian smart city. *Journal of Management and Governance*, 1–29.
Thomas, T. E., & Lamm, E. (2012). Legitimacy and organizational sustainability. *Journal of Business Ethics, 110*, 191–203.

Index

M. Magliacani, V. Toscano, *Accounting for Cultural Heritage Management*, https://doi.org/10.1007/978-3-031-38257-4